The
Chicago Plan
&
New Deal
Banking
Reform

The
Chicago Plan
&
New Deal
Banking
Reform

Ronnie J. Phillips

**Foreword by
Hyman P. Minsky**

M.E. Sharpe
Armonk, New York
London, England

Library of Congress Cataloging-in-Publication Data

Phillips, Ronnie J., 1951–
The Chicago plan and New Deal banking reform / Ronnie J. Phillips
p.   cm.
Includes bibliographical references and index.
ISBN 1-56324-469-1   —   ISBN 1-56324-470-5
1. Banks and banking—United States—History. 2. Banking law—
United States—History. 3. New Deal, 1933–1939. I. Title.
HG2481.P5   1994
332.1′0973′09043—dc20   94-17713
CIP

Printed in the United States of America

The paper used in this publication meets the minimum requirements of
American National Standard for Information Sciences—
Permanence of Paper for Printed Library Materials,
ANSI Z 39.48-1984.

MV (c)   10   9   8   7   6   5   4   3   2   1
MV (p)   10   9   8   7   6   5   4   3   2   1

To P.D.

Contents

Foreword

More than sixty years have passed, since the U.S. economy degenerated into virtual chaos during the four months from Roosevelt's election in November of 1932 to his inauguration on March 4, 1933. Aspects of this chaotic downward process included an unprecedented wave of bank failures, a collapse of output and asset prices, and an explosion of unemployment. The popular story, that upon being inaugurated President Roosevelt closed the banks, misrepresents what happened. The banks in more than thirty states had been closed by their governors before inauguration day. After his inauguration, which was on a Saturday, the new President was confronted with the news that the New York banks would not be able to open on the following Monday. The closing of the banks was a preemptive strike, aimed to prevent a further cataclysmic explosion of bank and financial institution failures which would be accompanied by a horrendous decline of asset prices.

The closing of the banks moved the solution of the immediate problem of broad insolvency of banks to the legislative sphere of Washington, rather than leaving it to the machinations of the financial community.

The resolution of the bank holiday took the form of a quick examination of the closed banks, which divided banks into three classes: those that could reopen without any aid, those that were deemed so thoroughly bankrupt that they were to remain closed and be liquidated and those that were reopened after an infusion of equity from the Reconstruction Finance Corporation, an agency of the federal government. Some 50 percent of the banks that reopened after the bank holiday received an equity infusion, that is, were at least partially government owned.

The Federal Reserve System, which had been created, in the aftermath of the banking panic of 1907, in the belief that a central bank could contain panics, was unable to prevent the collapse of the financial system from 1929 to 1933. Furthermore, it was not the main player in the reopening of the banks. In 1933 the Federal Reserve System, itself, was a failure.

As a result of this history of bank failures and the inability of the

Federal Reserve to contain the failures, the early 1930s was a period of intense and wide debate in the United States, as well as in the rest of the capitalist world, on what had gone wrong to cause the disaster and what could be done to prevent such disasters in the future. One subject of the debate was the constitution of the financial and banking systems: the reform of the private banking and financial system as well as the Federal Reserve was very much on the agenda.

One proposal, which was actively considered by prominent legislators and members of the administration, became known as the *Chicago Plan for Banking Reform*. This was a proposal to split banks and the banking system into two parts: one would administer the part of the payments system that takes the form of deposits subject to check; and the other would participate in the financing of "the capital development of the economy." The "Chicago Plan" called for deposits subject to check to be offset on the books of the banks with 100 percent reserves. Because they were so reserved, the question of deposit insurance, a popular nostrum of the day, was irrelevant.

The institution comprising the other part of the banking system, that which participates in the short-term financing of business, state, and local governments, as well as households, were to have only conditional, valued liabilities: that is, they were to be like our present money market and other mutual funds. As these institutions could have a variety of liabilities, each specialized as to the assets it owned, the analogy to the present day mutual funds is rather exact.

The idea of 100 percent reserves for checkable deposits—that is for the reserves of banks to be liabilities of the federal government—was a natural extension of the manner in which the National Banking Act had required that the circulating notes of national banks be fully offset, on the books of the issuing banks, by government bonds. Furthermore these circulating notes were fully guaranteed as to their face value by the United States Treasury: that is, they were fully insured.

The 100 percent government-debt reserve currency of the National Banking Act broke down, because there was not enough government debt outstanding to enable the currency supply to be responsive to the needs of an expanding economy.

The original Federal Reserve Act of 1913 demonetized government debt as the offsetting asset for circulating currency. According to the act, currency was to be a liability of the Federal Reserve banks that was to be offset by a combination of gold and eligible bank loans to business that member banks discounted at their district Federal Reserve bank. The 1913 Federal Reserve Act represented a 180 degree turn from the National Banking Act: a currency that was 100 percent offset by government debt was replaced by a currency that was 0 percent offset by government debt. Furthermore there was no Treasury insurance on either the Federal Reserve currency or member bank deposits.

The provisions of the Federal Reserve Act in place in 1933 reflected a belief that the shortage of government debt was a natural state of the economy. In the first years of this century, as well as in the 1930s, an axiom of the conventional blueprints for a banking and financial system was that there would not be enough government debt to support a currency based on government debt, let alone to support a government, debt-based, demand deposit system.

The "radical" 100 percent money schemes required a government debt that was large enough to act as the offset on the books of banks for the transaction balances, in the form of both currency and deposits subject to check, of the economy. Furthermore this government debt was not to be so scarce that it was all used as reserves: some government debt was to be held outside the banking system. A sophisticated view of the significance of government debt as an asset and of government deficits as income-maintaining devices lay behind the 100 percent money schemes.

We now have in place the institutional prerequisites for a successful 100 percent money scheme. These are:

1. A large government debt that can be monetized;
2. A Federal Government fiscal posture which readily can be adapted to keep constant the ratios of payments balances and government debt to the gross national product; and
3. Money market and other mutual funds that provide liquid balances and which have the property of being immediately cashable into deposits subject to check at a price which is determined by asset values. The price of these savings balances is not guaranteed by any agency, public or private, against falling to a discount from face value.

Some of the bank money market funds, as well as finance companies, will hold assets that, like bank loans, are based upon private knowledge rather than upon the public knowledge such as the assets held by conventional money market funds.

The banking and financial system of the United States and the rest of the rich capitalist countries are now undergoing rapid changes as repercussions of technological changes that have annihilated distance and greatly reduced the costs of record keeping, information retrieval, and communication. Banking and financial systems are also undergoing changes, because the barriers that restrict the lines of business and geographical reach of banks and other financial organizations are breaking down. Furthermore throughout the rich capitalist countries, unprecedented losses by banks and other financial institutions have required either direct or indirect government financial intervention to contain the repercussions of such losses. Therefore, it is likely that we are now experiencing another era of serious discourse about the fundamental nature of the banking and financial systems.

Ronnie Phillips in this volume has recovered part of the memory of those exciting days in the 1930s when the best of abstract thought was wedded to the need to resolve pressing crises. We owe him a debt of gratitude for reminding us that the economists and public figures who participated in the discourse of the 1930s were sophisticated thinkers who were alert to the issues which now are to the fore: *the creation of a financial system that is consistent with a full utilization of resources and which provides for the broad based economic well-being that is a prerequisite for a strong and viable democracy.* The economic and political crises of the 1930s made policy oriented economists aware that narrowly defined economic efficiency was not the ultimate policy objective: a performance of the economy that is consistent with the maintenance of a participatory democracy is the greater good. This may require interventions which lead to the real economy deviating from the theoretically pure.

Our current discourse on policy would serve us better if it were grounded in a knowledge of how the existing institutions and usages were born out of the combination of theoretical insights and practical compromise. Ronnie Phillips will serve us well if this book leads us to respect the past even as we try to meet the challenges of today.

Hyman P. Minsky
The Jerome Levy Economics Institute
June 1994

Acknowledgments

This book was completed while I was a resident scholar at The Jerome Levy Economics Institute of Bard College. I would like to thank the Board of Governors of the Institute for their sponsorship of this research project, especially Leon, Jay, and David Levy. Dimitri B. Papadimitriou, executive director, and Hyman P. Minsky, distinguished scholar and director of the Institute's Project on the Reconstitution of the Financial Structure, provided encouragement throughout the entire period that this research was undertaken and an environment conducive to the work at hand. I am very grateful for their help.

I would also like to thank my colleagues at Colorado State University for their willingness to tolerate an extended leave of absence during the writing of this book and for their support during this research project; in particular, James Ronald Stanfield has been a close friend throughout my career.

Additional research funding was provided by The George Edward Durell Foundation and the Professional Development Program of the College of Liberal Arts at Colorado State University.

Though the New Deal began six decades ago, I have been fortunate to be able to rely on a number of individuals who had a firsthand knowledge of the monetary reform proposals and legislation during the early years of the Roosevelt Administration for advice, comments, and discussion. The late Lloyd W. Mints first stimulated my interest in the Chicago Plan for Banking Reform during discussions in his later years in a rest home in Fort Collins, Colorado. The late Lauchlin Currie read and commented on the manuscript and gave me the benefit of his perspective as a Roosevelt administration insider. Albert Gailord Hart of Columbia University, an original signer of the Chicago Plan, also read and commented on the entire manuscript. I have incurred a *real* debt to these three individuals for their help in the writing of this book.

Others who read the entire manuscript and deserve thanks are: Kenneth Spong (Federal Reserve Bank of Kansas City), James R. Barth (Auburn University), Gary Dymski (University of California at Riverside), Frank Steindl (Oklahoma State University), John Hotson (University of Waterloo), Gordon Tullock (University of Arizona), Alex

Pollock (Federal Home Loan Bank of Chicago), Walker Todd (Federal Reserve Bank of Cleveland), Thomas Humphrey (Federal Reserve Bank of Richmond), and Robert Hetzel (Federal Reserve Bank of Richmond).

Those providing comments through letter or conversation include: William R. Allen (UCLA), Milton Friedman (Hoover Institution), Rodney D. Peterson (Florida Department of Development), Robert E. Litan (U.S. Department of Justice), R. Alton Gilbert (Federal Reserve Bank of St. Louis), Philip F. Bartholomew (Office of the Comptroller of the Currency), Gerald A. Vaughn (University of Delaware), William Hixson, Jane D'Arista (Boston University), and Roger Sandilands (National University of Singapore). I have also benefited from discussions and published exchanges with Charles Whalen who provided a copy of the November Chicago memorandum.

Though all of the above have made important contributions to this book, they are absolved from any responsibility for errors of fact, interpretation, or other shortcomings that remain.

No historical work could be done without the assistance of archival librarians. I would like to thank those at the University of Chicago D'Angelo Law Library, Yale University, Princeton University, the National Archives, the Library of Congress, and, especially, the staff of the Franklin D. Roosevelt Library in Hyde Park. The capable research assistance of Shana T. Goldberg and James Cash, and the excellent help of the staff of the Jerome Levy Economics Institute, is greatly appreciated.

Finally, I would like to thank my family and friends for "everything." I will miss the late Ed A. Hewett, teacher and friend from my graduate school days.

Blithewood
Annandale-on-Hudson, New York
June 1994

The
Chicago Plan
&
New Deal
Banking
Reform

—————— Introduction ——————

The Quest for Stable Banking

In 1823 the great economist David Ricardo drafted a "Plan for the Establishment of a National Bank" that was published in February 1824, six months after his death. The document opened with the following statement:

> The Bank of England performs two operations of banking, which are quite distinct, and have no necessary connection with each other: it issues a paper currency as a substitute for a metallic one; and it advances money in the way of loan, to merchants and others. That these two operations of banking have no necessary connection, will appear obvious from this—that they might be carried on by two separate bodies, without the slightest loss of advantage, either to the country, or to the merchants who receive accommodation from such loans. (Ricardo 1951, vol. 4, 276)

The Bank Charter Act of 1844, commonly known as Peel's Act (after Robert Peel), implemented Ricardo's plan. The Bank of England was separated into a lending department and a money issuing department. In 1933 this same proposal was put forward by a group of economists at the University of Chicago as the "Chicago Plan for Banking Reform" (Hart 1951). The plan was presented as an expedient in getting the United States out of the Great Depression, as well as providing a basis for long-term reform of the financial system. Legislation was introduced to implement the Chicago plan by Progressives, including Senator Bronson Cutting of New Mexico, as part of the debate over the Banking Act of 1935. The objective of this book is to document the role of the Chicago plan in the debates over New Deal banking reform and provide an assessment of its impact on the legislation ultimately passed. Advocates of the Chicago plan viewed the New Deal banking legislation as a first step in the evolution of the financial system toward what Henry Simons referred to as the "financial good society" (Simons 1948, 239).

During 1933 and 1934 members of the Roosevelt administration were drafting proposals very similar to the Chicago plan. Within eighteen months of the private circulation of the Chicago plan, a memorandum written for Secretary of the Treasury Henry Morgenthau put forward essentially the same proposal. Support for this restructuring of banking is found in the statements and writings of New Dealers such as Adolf Berle, Rexford Tugwell, Gardiner Means, and Lauchlin Currie. Irving Fisher, who frequently advised Roosevelt, was yet another prominent economist who supported the Chicago plan. Though Roosevelt never stated publicly his support for the plan, his statements revealed an understanding of the basic issues involved, and he was at the very least, quite interested in the solution proposed by the Chicago plan.

In the first of his famous fireside chats, FDR directed his remarks at both "the comparatively few who understand the mechanics of banking" and the "overwhelming majority" who do not necessarily understand the mechanics but "who use banks for the making of deposits and the drawing of checks." Roosevelt believed that the banking crisis of 1933 was in part a result of a failure of the average person to understand how our banking system works.

Though Roosevelt's fireside chats were undoubtedly reassuring to the populace (and this was presumably his main intent), the explanations he presented of how the financial system operated seldom went beyond very superficial notions that would seem like common sense to the public at large. In his first fireside chat, Roosevelt explained that when someone makes a deposit, "the bank does not put the money into a safe deposit vault," but rather "invests your money in many different forms of credit." What banks in fact do is lend on the basis of excess reserves and therefore create additional claims. If there were no excess reserves (i.e., the bank functioned as a warehouse for deposited funds), there would be no lending and no further creation of deposits. Roosevelt implicitly assumed that the uniting of two banking functions (providing a convenient medium of exchange and making loans) was in fact "what banks do."

However, as Roosevelt recognized, the uniting of these two functions requires above all *confidence* in the banking system. The nature of this confidence is that the depositors who have short-term promises from the banker that they can convert their bank money (deposits) into government money (currency) must not exercise this option all at once. The essential dilemma, as Roosevelt stated it, was that "on the spur of the moment it . . . [is] impossible to sell perfectly sound assets of a bank and convert them into cash except at panic prices far below their real value." In making the statement regarding "perfectly sound assets," Roosevelt was repeating what a host of economists, politicians, and the general public had accepted as common wisdom. This doctrine is generally known as the "real bills doctrine" or the "commercial loan theory of credit." Simply stated, it is the belief that as long as banks make short-term, self-liquidating loans for bona fide commercial reasons, then banks can provide both deposit and lending services without any difficulties (Whittlesley 1954, 110). As Lloyd Mints declared in his classic study, *A History of Banking Theory*, the real bills doctrine is "utterly subversive of any rational attack on the problem of monetary policy" (Mints 1945, Preface). This statement by Mints underlies the Chicago plan for banking reform.

As Ricardo observed, banks serve two primary purposes: provide a means of payment (money) and provide for the capital development of the economy (credit). The uniting of these functions in banks is largely an historical accident. A misunderstanding of the respective definitions and roles of money and credit has created much confusion in the legislative history of monetary reform in the United States.

Article I, Section 8 of the U.S. Constitution states: "The Congress shall have power . . . to coin money (and) regulate the value thereof." In the over 200 years of American history since these words were written, this has meant a direct involvement of government in the private credit market as well. The purpose of the Chicago Plan for Banking Reform was to abolish fractional reserve banking and thereby clearly differentiate government's right to create money from its role in regulation of the private credit markets. However, the result over the past 200 years has been a variety of interpretations of the above quoted passage from the Constitution. As one author argued, Congress has been trying to "get money right" from the Continental Congress's issuance of currency, through the First and Second Banks of the United States, the National Bank Act, the Federal Reserve Act, and the legislation of the past decades (Hurst 1973).

One of the most dramatic and well-documented periods is the twenty-eight months from Franklin D. Roosevelt's inauguration in

March 1933 until the passage of the Banking Act of 1935 (Burns 1974; Kennedy 1973). This period saw the enactment of the Emergency Banking Act, the Banking Acts of 1933 and 1935, as well as reforms of the stock market, housing mortgages, and agricultural credit. The strengths, and the weaknesses, of our present financial system can be traced directly to the banking legislation passed in the early years of the New Deal.

Though surviving largely unchanged for nearly five decades, the legislation of the period was not really viewed as a permanent solution to our banking problems. Circumstances at the time allowed the New Deal legislation to become a long-term solution, but there were many both inside and outside the Roosevelt administration who viewed the job of financial reform as unfinished in 1935. It is perhaps a surprising fact to realize today that there was a recognition in some quarters in the thirties that the banking problems had not been definitively solved.

As argued in this book, the ultimate goals of the administration with regard to banking reform were never carried out. The result was a system which, though moving in the direction of greater centralized control, was viewed at the time as incomplete. Roosevelt undoubtedly had the final word on how far the administration was prepared to go with reform. Ultimately, given the political environment, FDR and his advisers were for the most part satisfied with what had been achieved by 1935. However the long-run goal of banking reform, as envisioned by many in the administration, was for a more fundamental and radical restructuring of the financial system over the decades after 1935.

A detailed analysis of the financial history of the United States is beyond the scope of this book, which focuses on the period 1933–35. This period was one of greatest dislocation in the economy, and one which witnessed the collapse of the financial system. The recent savings and loan debacle, as well as the turmoil within the banks, and anticipated problems with other financial institutions (insurance and pension funds), has led to a resurgence of interest in the financial system (Barth 1991). Perhaps not since the Great Depression has there been so much public concern and debate over the structure of our payments and credit allocation system.

The Chicago plan in the 1930s is also of interest in the contemporary debates over financial reform. Milton Friedman, a student of Henry Simons and also a long-time Chicago plan (or 100 percent reserve) advocate, stated to Congress in 1975 that he believed that the

100 percent reserve proposal "emerges naturally whenever banking reform is discussed" (U.S. Congress, House, 1976, 2157). Until recently, there has been little discussion of how to reform the system to avert another crisis in the future. Both in the popular press and in Congress much of the debate and concern has centered on who is to pay for the bailout. Fundamental reform, such as altering the nature of federal deposit insurance, has generally been rejected as politically untenable. It is assumed, and with some evidence, that the public, though leery of the impending tax liability, is not willing to give up a government guarantee. The Chicago plan, by restricting bank assets, would not have saddled the taxpayers with an enormous liability from federal deposit insurance. Recently, proposals have been put forward for "narrow" or "core" banks, which restrict bank assets and embody many of the components of the Chicago plan (Tobin 1985, 1987; Litan 1987; Bryan 1988, 1991).

The Chicago plan is also relevant to the contemporary debates over independence of the Federal Reserve Board, the abolition of the discount window (Schwartz 1992), the revival of the Reconstruction Finance Corporation (Todd 1992) and the postal savings system (Jessup and Bochnak 1992), as well as the proposals to establish a national system of community development banks (Minsky et al. 1993). The Chicago plan also merits consideration because it was supported by some of the preeminent economists of the twentieth century.

A fundamental restructuring of the financial system is by no means a foregone conclusion. As one economist wrote in 1934 regarding the then recently established deposit guaranty program: "the worse it works the more necessary it will be regarded by public opinion" (Emerson 1934, 241). Whether we can change the system fundamentally is an open question.

1

A History of Currency and Banking in the United States

The history of currency and banking in the United States is a long and often complicated story. The basic fact to remember is that the power to print money is the power to appropriate the real resources (or wealth) of an economy. The Constitution gives the federal government the exclusive power to "coin money." The authorization for a fiat currency was expressly forbidden.[1] However, the federal government, usually in times of fiscal difficulties, has been compelled to issue currency with a promise of redemption and then renege on that promise to a greater or lesser extent. As a result, the costs of fighting wars, from the time of the Revolution through the Civil War, were to a large extent paid for through the direct printing of currency—which *promised* redeemability at some point in the future upon the cessation of military conflict.

The political struggle over monetary reform has been between those who advocated a strong, centralized monetary authority and those who were against centralization and the concentration of government power (Wilson 1991). The prevailing understanding of banking, and the role of monetary and fiscal policy, often contributed negatively to the debates. Because the introduction of a medium of exchange was frequently tied to the need of the government to finance fiscal expenditures, or on the basis of a loan, there is understandably a great deal of confusion over the distinction, or lack of, between money and credit. This confusion is found through the entire financial history of the United States (and other countries as well no doubt).

Though it is not possible to give a detailed history of the evolution of currency, banking, and fiscal policy in the United States, an understanding of the basic evolutionary trend is important for this study. That trend is one that moves away from a money redeemable in specie on demand to a fiduciary money, that is, one that represents the dual sides of entry on a financial balance sheet.

The Colonial Experience

As Steven Russell notes, many of the most important features of the American monetary system were based on English models (Russell 1991, 41). The Bank of England was given a monopoly in the issuance of a currency convertible into gold and this principle played an important role in the evolution of the American monetary system. Scholars have generally agreed that the problem in the colonies was a species shortage. Numerous studies have examined the nature and cause of this shortage (Calomiris 1988). During the 1650s, the Massachusetts Bay Colony attempted to allay the shortage by operating its own mint (Russell 1991, 44). The British government viewed this activity as usurping a British government prerogative and forced the closure of the mint.

Though there was a need in the colonies for a more convenient means of payment, evidently the introduction of government paper currency was motivated by the fiscal needs of the colonial government (Russell 1991, 44). This motivation for the creation of a government currency was to be used repeatedly in U.S. history.

By the 1730s bills of credit had become the principle currency of the American colonies. These bills were initially issued in anticipation of future taxes. The value of these bills was directly connected to the fact that they would be redeemed in commodity money (gold or other metal coins) at some point in the future. Such bills of credit were unlikely to be inflationary because of their fiscal backing (Calomiris 1988). However political upheavals and financial incentives for the colonies to violate their commitments led to considerable fluctuations in the value of these bills.

Subsequently some colonies began to issue bills of credit that could be lent to individuals who were able to provide land or other sorts of property as collateral. During the first half of the eighteenth century, these so-called loan office or land bank issues became increasingly popular (Russell 1991, 44).

Not surprisingly, currency depreciation became a significant problem for the colonies. This depreciation was compounded by the fact that the colonies typically gave their bills of credit *legal tender* status. Such laws compelled creditors to accept these bills at face, or par, value (Russell 1991, 44).

The Currency Act of 1751 deprived the New England colonies of the right to issue legal tender bills and virtually eliminated their ability to issue any kind of paper currency. The Act of 1764 extended this prohibition to all of the colonies (Russell 1991, 45). Russell notes that by the time of the Revolutionary War, the colonies appeared to be moving in the direction of a system of nonlegal tender land bank currency (Russell 1991, 45). Continuing to circulate as media of exchange were the coins produced in England, Spain, The Netherlands, Portugal, and France. The "money supply" of the colonies at this time was thus a maze of coins and paper currencies.

The Continental Congress

As the revolutionary war approached, one of the most immediate problems was the question of how to finance wartime expenditures for troops, ammunition, food, and so on. Since there was no federal government, and no powers of taxation, the option utilized was the creation of a fiat currency issued by the Continental Congress. The "Continentals" were issued beginning in May 1775 on the well-known principle of redemption in anticipation of future taxes. Since there was no federal government to provide the taxation backing, the delegates to the Continental Congress pledged joint liability on behalf of the colonies, and each colony was expected to create a good faith sinking fund to redeem the Continentals at their nominal value in specie. This strategy seemed to work until about mid-1776 (Calomiris 1988, 55).

As Charles Calomiris notes, many factors contributed to the fluctuation in the value of the Continentals, including success or failure on the battlefield, the French alliance, and later by changes in the redemption value. Though the Continental Congress experimented with other means of finance, roughly 40 percent of the total cost of the Revolutionary War—about $38 million in specie equivalent—was financed by issuance of Continental currency (Calomiris 1988, 58). By mid-1781 Continentals had ceased to circulate, and Congressional power and credit were at an all-time low (Calomiris 1988, 59).

During the period of time from the end of the Revolutionary War in 1783 to the ratification of the Constitution in 1789, the newly independent states reorganized their finances and several states issued, or seriously considered issuing, bills of credit in anticipation of taxes or on loan (Russell 1991, 46). Calomiris concludes that the experience of the

American Revolution created distrust of government money, which contributed to the prolonged inadequacy of financial institutions in the United States (Calomiris 1988, 64).

The Beginnings of Banking in the United States

The first bank established in the United States was the Bank of North America founded in 1781. Within ten years there were three private state-chartered banks in the country. In the early post-colonial days, these banks were viewed chiefly as beneficial in providing a convenient source of currency and, subsequently, in the taking of deposits (Miller, 1927, 11). The importance of banks in the availability of credit was also later recognized (Miller, 1927, 17–18). A considerable debate about the proper functions of banks ensued and is reviewed in detail by Miller (1927).

Since it was widely recognized that banks serve a dual function—providing money and credit—the debate centered on how to achieve these goals most effectively. The basic dilemma for banking is that achieving this dual function requires that a given dollar in money balances be held by more than one person simultaneously. In the commodity money system, as prevailed at the time, the bank note represented a claim on gold or silver held by the bank. However the bank, at any point in time, did not hold enough gold or silver to redeem its bank notes in full without calling in the loans it had made. This led to a theory of banking which at first impression seems eminently reasonable. In fact, the theory confuses regulation of credit with regulation of the money supply. The theory is known as the "commercial loan theory of credit" or the "real bills doctrine." Lloyd Mints provides a succinct statement of this theory:

> Thus the real-bills doctrine runs to the effect that restriction of bank earning assets to real bills of exchange will automatically limit, in the most desirable manner, the *quantity* of bank liabilities; it will cause them to *vary* in quantity in accordance with the "needs of business," and it will mean that the bank's assets will be of such a nature that they can be turned into cash on short notice and thus place the bank in a position to meet unlooked-for calls for cash. (Mints 1945, 29)

The real bills principle is based on liquidating credit obligations and makes sense in that regard, because it is the idea that credit extended which is then repaid is removed from the balance sheet. Though this is a sensible theory of credit, it is not a principle for providing automatic regulation of the money supply. Mints points out that the fundamental flaw in the real bills doctrine when applied as a regulator of the money supply is the instability that results:

> whereas convertibility into a given *physical amount* of specie (or any other economic good) will limit the quantity of notes that can be issued, although not to any foreseeable extent (and therefore not acceptably), the basing of notes on a given *money's worth* of any form of wealth—be it land or merchant's stocks—presents the possibility of unlimited expansion of loans, provided that the eligible goods are not unduly limited in aggregate value. (Mints 1945, 30)

Expressed another way, a fall in nominal income would lead to both a fall in the demand for money as well as the supply of money, and thus a potentially unstable situation is created (Girton 1974, 57–58).

The real bills doctrine is found in the debates surrounding the creation in 1791 (on Alexander Hamilton's recommendation) of the Bank of the United States (Mints 1945, 63–64). This bank was a national organization with a twenty-year charter that was authorized to accept deposits, issue notes, and make loans. The First Bank of the United States had a special relationship with the federal government because all government revenues were deposited in it, and its currency was accepted in payment for all government disbursements and receipts (Timberlake 1965, 162). Though this bank issued a currency that could be used throughout the country, opposition by the states and the state-chartered banks led to its demise. The bank was generally regarded as serving an important function for the government, but little was understood about its role in the regulation of credit. As Miller noted, the theories of banking in the United States prior to 1820 were "wretchedly primitive" (Miller 1927, 3).

After the demise of the Bank of the United States, a second bank was chartered in 1816, again for twenty years. The structure of the Second Bank was similar to that of the First Bank, and it served the same function for the government. It was under Nicholas Biddle that the Second Bank began to function as a central bank. The bank would regulate the private banks through its actions of holding and presenting private bank notes for redemption (Timberlake 1965, 164). Though reserve requirements varied for private banks (state chartered at this time), credit could be constrained by presenting bank notes for redemption in species. Banks would have to restrict credit in order to maintain their desired level of reserves. According to Richard Timberlake, these central bank activities were well recognized by 1830 (Timberlake 1965, 166).

Following the demise of the Second Bank, the United States entered the period that is referred to as the "Free Banking Era." During this period, much of the money stock was privately issued bank notes. This situation, not surprisingly, created a host of problems.[2] The bank notes were by law redeemable in gold or silver, and there were heavy penalties imposed for the failure to do so. There was no central monetary authority that would attempt to regulate credit as the Second Bank had done under Biddle. Congress passed legislation in 1835–36 to impose reserve requirements on the banks that held the federal government's funds, though after "reconsideration" the bill was tabled (Timberlake 1965, 97). Though Congress failed to impose reserve requirements, a number of states did so. The Louisiana Bank Act of 1842 required that deposits and bank notes be backed one-third by specie and the remaining two-thirds by short-term, high quality assets (Timberlake 1965, 98; Pollock 1992).

In 1846, an independent Treasury of the United States was created by legislation. The original plan for the treasury (in 1834) had proposed that it be completely divorced from the banks and that all treasury dealings be conducted on a specie-treasury note basis only (Timberlake 1965, 168). Establishment of the independent treasury eliminated the risks associated with depositing government funds into private banks. The treasury was able to play a stabilizing role during the free banking era. For example, if domestic private sector funding fell, a favorable balance of trade would create an inflow of specie. If the treasury faced a deficit on its budget, it could be financed by issuing securities or notes. During the time period to 1860, the treasury frequently financed its deficit with non-interest bearing notes (Timberlake 1965, 168–69).

Both sides of the Civil War financed part of their fiscal deficits with the creation of legal tender currency. In 1862, Congress passed its first Legal Tender Act to authorize the issuing of "greenbacks." These were notes issued by the treasury, declared legal tender and redeemable in gold at some unspecified point in the future. The value of the greenbacks fluctuated during the war based on battlefield successes of the Union forces.[3]

One consequence of the Free Banking Era was the confusing plethora of monies available and the possibility of fraud and counterfeiting. By the 1860s the idea was circulating that the government should provide a currency that could circulate in place of gold. The National Currency Act of 1863 established both a uniform currency and a national banking system (Grant 1992).[4]

By this act and the National Banking Act of 1864, banks could obtain a national charter. Thus banks could be chartered either by individual states, and subject to their regulations, or by the Comptroller of the Currency, and therefore subject to national bank regulations. Instead of a single national bank, as had been established in 1791 and again in 1816, a system of national banks was created. The national banks could issue notes, but were required to hold $111.11 in government bonds for each $100 of bank notes issued. The national bank notes, though not legal tender, were convertible into greenbacks (McCallum 1989, 318). As Boris Pesek and Thomas Saving note, these conditions made it virtually impossible for the holder of a national bank note to lose in the event of a national bank failure (Pesek and Saving 1968, 398). National bank notes were effectively guaranteed by the federal government since in the event of a bank failure, the Comptroller of the Currency had the right to sell the bonds held as security—and first lien on any remaining bank assets in the event that the bonds did not fully redeem the notes at par (James 1940, 195).

The creation of the dual banking system was supported by Salmon P. Chase, Lincoln's Secretary of the Treasury, who thought that by providing a model of safety and excellence in services in the national banks, the state banks would naturally follow suit (Pesek and Saving 1968). The act thus intended to enhance the safety of the entire monetary system by providing a government debt backing for a portion of the monetary base. Significantly the original act prohibited national banks from making real estate loans.

Initially banks were slow to turn in their state charters for a national charter. In an attempt to increase conversion and to stop the issuing of bank notes by state banks, Congress imposed a 10 percent tax on any new issue (White 1983, 11). This law led state banks to reduce the issuance of bank notes, and instead expand their offering of checkable deposit accounts, thus circumventing the legislation. The fundamental difference between issuing bank notes and checking accounts is that in the case of bank notes, the denominations are specified, whereas with checking accounts, the denomination is the amount of the check. Since both are fiduciary, bank-created money, it was merely a matter of banks promoting the use of checking accounts instead of bank notes. As a result, by the turn of the century, two-thirds of the banks had state charters (Pesek and Saving 1968, 399). As Cyril James notes, the increasing use of bank checks undermined the National Banking Act for reasons similar to those that had prevented the attainment of the aims of the Currency School under the Bank Charter Act of 1844. Ironically the public began to use bank deposits as a medium of exchange precisely at the time the government had perfected its plan controlling the circulation of bank notes at par value. This was quite similar to what happened to the Bank of England after 1844. The United States, however, did not have a central bank with control over bank deposits (James 1940, 198–99).

The Creation of the Federal Reserve System

Though the history of banking panics and crises may lead one to believe the financial system was continually a drag on the economy, the period after the Civil War was one of high growth. Despite the fact that the panics during this period had some impact on monetary reform movements, it was the 1907 panic that led to the creation of a National Monetary Commission and, in 1913, to the creation of the Federal Reserve System (White 1983, 63).

The aim of the Federal Reserve Act was to reduce correspondent banking and "pool reserves in regional reserve banks where they could be used to make rediscounts to member banks" (White 1983, 64). The function of Federal Reserve notes was to provide a ready convertibility of demand deposits into currency. This function is often called the lender of last resort function. The Federal Reserve Act was an attempt to create a national currency that was not issued by the U.S. Treasury Department, but rather by a private corporation owned by member banks and acting as a national clearinghouse. Federal Reserve notes were redeemable in lawful money: gold or greenbacks. The Federal Reserve System was a compromise between those who wanted a single national bank with credit controlling powers, and those who feared the concentration of such power in the hands of the government. The system was established with twelve independent Federal Reserve Banks, each with responsibility for the appropriate "elasticity of currency" in its region. In theory, the Federal Reserve, in times of monetary crisis, would provide a currency to counteract the contraction of the money supply that occurred when there was a shortage of specie.

The functional need for a central bank is primarily due to the fact that private banks do not hold 100 percent reserves against their liabilities. As banking evolved historically, banks held less than 100 percent reserves (usually in specie, gold, or silver) and loaned out some of the specie. Alternatively, the banks could make a loan through the issue of their notes, which were nominally redeemable in specie. Payment of the loan would then, in the first instance, be made in specie, though other forms of money might be accepted as well. Timberlake explains the fundamental problem of a financial system with fractional reserves and multiple types of money:

> Any monetary system that uses more than one kind of money must make provision for the conversion of one form of money, say bank deposits, into another form, say currency, without allowing undue stress on the total quantity in existence. A system without such a characteristic lacks *form* elasticity. Under fractional reserve banking a demand for additional currency in place of deposits may well result in a decline in the total stock of money. . . . "Elasticity of the money supply" thus implied (1) conversion of one form of money into another without changing the total quantity, (2) alteration in the total quantity of money in order to mitigate seasonal or cyclical monetary demands, or (3) a hybrid of these concepts. (Timberlake 1965, 107–8)

A system of less than 100 percent reserves (or fractional reserve banking) means that the reserves of the banking system (specie) are considerably less than the total amount of bank liabilities (money) issued, which are nominally redeemable in specie. In principle, a central bank regulates money and credit by its willingness to convert other bank notes into its own liabilities. This would presumably provide an alternative in times of crisis to the conversion of outstanding bank notes into specie. Put simply, confidence was to be maintained by conversion of private bank notes that stated they were convertible into gold into government paper money. The willingness of individuals to accept one type of money for another is the fundamental axiom on which central banking rests.

As originally structured, the ability to affect credit was through the Federal Reserves's discount mechanism whereby it rediscounted loaned reserves to the private banks. The Federal Reserve was to play a passive role with respect to money and credit in contrast to the treasury's active role. The only tool available to the Federal Reserve was the setting of the discount rate.

The Federal Reserve was also limited in its creation of Federal Reserve notes. The Federal Reserve Banks were required to hold gold reserves and to make loans on the basis of "eligible assets" that, according to the real bills doctrine, encompassed only bona fide commercial loans. Under today's noncommodity monetary system, the Fed is not constrained by reserve holdings in specie or, in fact, any other asset. Until the New Deal reforms, Federal Reserve notes were redeemable in gold or lawful money and were not acceptable for payment of interest on the national debt or customs duties. When such reserve requirements were placed on the Federal Reserve Banks, this limited their ability to issue Federal Reserve notes. After all, the Federal Reserve must issue additional reserves to the banks only on the basis of a reciprocal acquisition of bank assets. If such were not the case, balance sheets would not balance. The Federal Reserve does not issue its liabilities by just printing money and distributing it as manna from heaven.

What are the assets upon which the Federal Reserve could potentially issue reserves to the commercial banks? The assets of a bank are species (if there is a metallic standard), cash, deposits at the Federal Reserve, security holdings, and loans to the private sector. Thus what becomes crucial in monetary policy is the bank assets against which the Federal Reserve may issue Federal Reserve liabilities.[5]

The operations of a central bank can be most easily understood if the following is kept in mind: The central bank has a printing press, and its paper is accepted in the society as money. In theory a central bank can print an infinite amount, but the nature of balance sheet accounting is that the central bank is limited by the extent of assets held by the commercial banks as a whole.

The real bills restriction inhibited the Federal Reserve's ability to serve as a source of an elastic currency—widely viewed as its legitimating activity. This is where the belief in the so-called real bills doctrine comes into play in determining the ability of the Federal Reserve to react to a currency crisis. The real bills doctrine does not provide for the stabilization of the money supply. The structure of the Federal Reserve was flawed, and those flaws would be exposed in the decade following World War I.

Banking in the 1920s

The period 1921–29 was characterized by historically rapid economic growth without major economic downturns. The banking system underwent important changes in credit operations and in the number of banks during the decade of the twenties. Bank holdings of securities rose to around 40 percent of assets from their 1914 levels of 29 percent. There was an increase in real estate lending prompted in part by the relaxation of restrictions on the real estate lending activities of national banks. The percent of loans classified as commercial by banks dropped from over 50 percent to around 45 percent during the period 1914–29 (Friedman and Schwartz 1963, 244–45). On June 30, 1921, there were 31,076 banks in the United States with assets totaling $49.6 billion; by 1929 there were 25,568 banks with $72.3 billion in assets. According to Friedman and Schwartz, the bank failures during this period had no connection to changes in the quality of bank credit, but rather were a result of increased urbanization and agricultural difficulties (Friedman and Schwartz 1963, 249).

As noted, the Federal Reserve's primary assets during the early years were gold certificates (issued by the Treasury) and discounts and advances to private banks. Government securities accounted for only a small part of the Fed's total assets. In 1923 the Federal Reserve began open market operations in government securities, in part to increase the interest-earning assets of the Fed. Two problems emerged for Federal Reserve policy in the twenties: gold flows and stock market speculation. For the most part, especially during 1921–27, there were gold inflows into the United States (Timberlake 1965, 193–94).

The Federal Reserve had gradually increased its understanding of its role in the economy and under the influence of Benjamin Strong, head of the New York Fed, it took credit for the relatively successful economic climate. The one area of conflict was over the attempt to control stock market speculation (Friedman and Schwartz 1963, 240–41).

Both the Federal Reserve Board and the Federal Reserve Bank of New York believed that stock speculation was a problem; the question was what should be the appropriate response. Using 1926 as a base year (index = 100), stock prices in 1921 were 55.2 and 190.3 in 1929. Public utility stocks showed an even larger increase from 57.8 in 1921 to 234.6 in 1929 (Chandler 1971, 27). These figures by themselves do not mean that stock prices were unreasonably high. By examining price earnings ratios, Chandler argued that the increase clearly became speculative no earlier than mid-1928 (Chandler 1971, 29).

Most troubling for the Federal Reserve Board was the belief that easy credit policies were feeding the stock market speculation. Again the empirical evidence is difficult to evaluate, but there was widespread belief that such was the case. The dispute over stock market speculation was between Strong and the Federal Reserve Board in Washington. To curb speculation in the stock market in 1928–29, the New York Fed raised its discount rate. However the Board argued that other means such as direct pressure should be utilized. The Board's view prevailed until August 1929, when the New York Fed was allowed to raise its discount rate (Friedman and Schwartz 1963, 254–55). This dispute centered on confusion about the impact of purchasing real bills versus government securities. The argument was that the Federal Reserve purchase of real bills would not feed speculation; with the purchase of securities "no one could tell where it (money) might go," according to Federal Reserve Board member Charles Hamlin (Friedman and Schwartz 1963, 266).

The Stock Market Crash

The stock market crashed on October 29, 1929. Standard and Poor's price index of ninety common stocks reached a peak of 254 on September 7, and stood at 162 at the close of trading on October 29. Action by J. P. Morgan and Company to organize a pool of funds to support the market, though not totally effective, and the pumping of reserves into banks by the New York Fed confined the immediate financial impact of the crash to the stock market, without arousing the public's suspicions about the safety of banks (Friedman and Schwartz 1963, 305–6).

The response was great concern from political and economic leaders in light of the crash but no one anticipated the economic decline that lay on the horizon. In fact many thought that the stock market crash was a healthy sign since it was believed that speculation had driven the market to unrealistic levels. It was widely believed that there was no reason to connect the crash of a speculative stock market with a deep depression. President Hoover held conferences in November 1929 with businessmen, farmers, and labor leaders to promote a consensus view on the response to the stock market crash. Apparently it was generally agreed at these conferences that wages should not be cut, employment reductions should be through a shortening of hours and not layoffs, and each industry should undertake efforts to alleviate distress among its employees (Dorfman 1959, v. 5, 608).

In November 1929, the Federal Reserve Bank of New York cut the discount rate from 5 to 4.5 percent and there was a $500 million open market purchase as prices, output, interest rates, and personal income began to decline in late 1929 and into 1930. One result of the worsening economy was the election of a Democratic House and a reduction of the Republican majority in the Senate in the elections of November 1930 (Dorfman 1959, v. 5, 610).

The stock market crash was followed one year later by a banking crisis lasting from October to December 1930. As deposits in failed banks rose, a contagion spread to convert demand and time deposits into currency and, to a lesser extent, postal savings deposits (Friedman and Schwartz 1963, 308). In December the failure of the Bank of the United States, though a private commercial bank, further damaged confidence in the banking system (Friedman and Schwartz 1963, 311). After a brief respite, this was followed by the second banking crisis in March 1931 which peaked in June with $200 million in deposits of suspended banks (Friedman and Schwartz 1963, 314). The banking system was poised for a dramatic collapse.

Conclusion

There are two important points to be recognized from the financial history of the United States that are relevant to the New Deal reforms. The first is that the principle of backing a national currency by federal government debt, or future taxes, became well established in U.S. financial history. The federal government frequently resorted to the issuance of a legal tender fiat currency in times of fiscal stress, especially during wars. The value of Continentals and greenbacks prior to redemption fluctuated with the likelihood of future taxes to redeem them. Secondly, over time the money supply has become largely fiduciary, that is, a balance sheet item. We gradually moved away from a system where gold and silver coins formed the basis of the money supply to one where it was largely bank notes or bank deposits.

Despite some dispute about the record of free banking, it appears that much of the history of the financial system in the United States has evolved around how to reconcile the problems of fractional reserve banking with aversion to federal control of the money supply. The fear of federal control of the money supply comes from the fact that the U.S. government has had the tendency to print money to pay for its purchases of goods and services. The experience of the Continental Congress and the greenbacks reinforced those who opposed letting the expenditure controlling institution of government (the treasury and Congress) also create the money supply. The Federal Reserve was created to accommodate the needs for an elastic currency, but not to allow the treasury to print money to pay for current expenditures.

Once the Federal Reserve was established, we still did not have a true central bank. The control of the money supply and the control of credit were intertwined, and it was impossible to provide an elastic currency and still maintain a credit policy that would aid in the stabilization of the economy. These reforms would have to wait until the Banking Act of 1935.

─── 2 ───

Response to the Banking Crisis: Hoover, Congress, and the Economists

The Federal Reserve, as argued above, was not able to stem the downward spiral of the economy in the aftermath of the stock market crash. However, contrary to popular folklore, Hoover did not sit back and do nothing while the economy collapsed. Though he strongly believed in the free market economy and the preeminent role of businessmen, this did not preclude federal government action when necessitated by emergency conditions. As Herbert Stein has observed:

> Hoover and the country confronted the Depression with a package of attitudes and ideas which even today sound modern. They did not believe that they had or wanted laissez-faire. They accepted the need for social action to prevent or correct unemployment. (Stein 1969, 12)

Hoover and Congress

Senator Carter Glass, a Democrat from Virginia who had fathered the Federal Reserve Act, introduced the Banking Act of 1930 on June 17, 1930. This legislation provided for restrictions on the security operations of national banks, the extension of branch banking, the regulation of security affiliates, the distribution of dividends on Federal Reserve stock, and the removal of the Secretary of the Treasury from the Federal Reserve Board (Burns 1974, 8–9). The bill was not passed and since 1930 was an election year, little else was done in Congress. The banking crisis continued throughout 1930 and 1931, and hearings were held amid increasing demands that the president and Congress take action.

Glass believed that four long-range reforms would eliminate the need for short-term rescue of the banking system: (1) restrictions on the use of money for speculative loans; (2) unified federal supervision of the entire banking system; (3) federal chartering and inspection of securities affiliates of banks; and (4) protection of depositors by establishing a federal corporation to liquidate deposits in closed banks (Kennedy 1973, 51–52).

In early 1931, there was concern about the banks as lenders. Hoover appealed to the bankers to display courage and to transmit a sense of optimism to their customers. In May 1931 Irving Fisher informed Hoover that there was the possibility that the banks were being overrestrictive in their lending. Evidence for this was the fact that banks had maintained their traditional lending rate of 6 percent in the face of the discount rate cuts by the Federal Reserve (Barber 1985, 112). Though Hoover had had differences in the past with the Federal Reserve regarding monetary policy, he felt that the Fed's actions could help prevent panics. However, under the Federal Reserve Act, commercial paper was the primary asset eligible for discount by the Fed. Given the decline in business borrowing in 1931, the amount of eligible paper had decreased to the point that the Fed could not take further actions to help the banks (Barber 1985, 111–12). At the same time bond prices were falling, creating problems for bank liquidity and raising the costs of borrowing.

In August, Hoover wrote to Treasury Secretary Andrew Mellon asking if it did not make sense for firms to buy back their previously issued bonds and then take out bank loans. This would have a twofold effect: stem the decline in bond prices and increase demand for bank loans. Though nothing came of this idea, William Barber notes that it indicates doubts had surfaced about how well the banking system could cope with a situation where nominal interest rates rose and bond prices sagged further (Barber 1985, 114).

In a press statement released on October 6, 1931, Hoover called for cooperative action on the part of government and the nation's bankers in order to restore confidence. If necessary, he stated, the establishment of a government finance corporation would be recommended along the lines of the War Finance Corporation, which had operated during World War I.[1] In response to Hoover's request, the National Credit Corporation (an organization of bankers in New York City), made available $500 million for banks to rediscount, when necessary, the sound assets not legally eligible for rediscount at the Federal Reserve Banks (Burns 1974, 14–15; Barber 1985, 128).

In December 1931, Hoover formally requested that Congress establish a government finance corporation—on January 22, 1932, the Reconstruction Finance Corporation (RFC) came into existence with $2 billion to be loaned to business (Dorfman 1959, v. 5, 612). The RFC could lend against appropriate collateral to a wide range of financial institutions: commercial banks, savings banks, trust companies, savings and loan associations, and insurance companies (Barber 1985, 130). The initial treasury subscription to the capital of the RFC was $500 million. The RFC could issue debt instruments and would also be expected to come to the aid of the railroads (Barber 1985, 130–31). The RFC was independent of Congress, the director of the budget and the public. Managed properly, the RFC could operate indefinitely without further Congressional appropriations (Olson 1988, 15).

In addition to the call for a federal finance corporation in his annual address to Congress on December 8, 1931, Hoover stated "our people have a right to a banking system in which their deposits shall be safeguarded and the flow of credit less subject to storms." He further advocated that the different types of banking be separate and suggested that "Congress should investigate the need for separation between different kinds of banking, an enlargement of branch banking under proper restrictions, and the methods by which enlarged membership in the Federal Reserve system may be brought about" (Dorfman 1959, v. 5, 683).

Hoover also urged amendment of the Federal Bankruptcy Act to alleviate the impact of widespread bankruptcies on the economy. He requested an amendment that would allow bankruptcy to proceed with a majority of support by the creditors, rather than an unanimous agreement. Congress agreed to this proposal for individuals and railways, but did not extend it to corporate reorganizations until 1935 (Dorfman 1959, v. 5, 614).

In January 1932, Hoover asked for a strengthening of the Federal Land Bank System, the creation of Home Loan Discount Banks, an enlargement of the discount privileges of the Federal Reserve Banks, a plan to safeguard depositors, and a swifter means of paying off those who held deposits in closed banks (Kroos 1969, 2670–71). On January 27, Hoover summoned Senator Glass and asked him to introduce legislation for temporary expansion of eligible assets under the Federal Reserve Act. The president hoped that government bonds could become security for currency (Kennedy 1973, 47).

Hoover laid the foundations for his "antihoarding campaign" in early February. He argued that every dollar hoarded meant a destruction of $5 to $10 in credit, and that to hoard dollars was to jeopardize the national interest. Hoover asked people to put money back into circulation for the good of the country. Not surprisingly, the campaign failed miserably after some initial success. The success of the program required not only a call to patriotism on the part of the public, but when the banks received the previously hoarded dollars, they were supposed to loan them out. According to Barber, in Hoover's eyes the behavior of the banks was "outrageously antisocial" (Barber 1985, 141–42).

The RFC was labeled "financial socialism" by some in early 1932 and Congress, under pressure, eliminated direct loans from the version of the banking bill it was considering, but retained a clause calling for full publicity for all RFC loans (Kennedy 1973, 40 and 43). The Glass-Steagall Act, passed on February 27, 1932, allowed the Federal Reserve to hold government securities against Federal Reserve notes and widened the circumstances under which member banks could borrow from the Fed (Friedman and Schwartz 1963, 321). As discussed above, restrictions on the assets backing Federal Reserve notes placed a severe constraint on the Fed's ability to act as the lender of last resort (Barber 1985, 140). The Glass-Steagall Act provided the Federal Reserve with the means to undertake expansive open market operations, and it did so beginning in February 1932. Over the next six months, the Fed increased its holding of government securities by $1.1 billion (Barber 1985, 140). At the same time, a bill was offered by Congressman Wright Patman, Democrat of Texas, to pay the bonus promised to World War I veterans in the form of a new issue of greenbacks (Barber 1985, 155).[2]

The Emergency Relief and Construction Act of July 1932 authorized the Federal Reserve Banks to make direct loans to private enterprise. John N. Garner had wanted these powers for the RFC (Kennedy 1973, 48). In the same month, the Federal Home Loan Bank Act was passed in an attempt to respond to the problems of home mortgage financing institutions. This act allowed the Federal Home Loan Bank to make advances to those institutions on the basis of first mortgages (Friedman and Schwartz 1963, 321–22). One piece of legislation that did not pass was a bill for temporary deposit insurance introduced in May by Congressman Henry Steagall, Democrat of Alabama, which was not reported out of committee in the Senate (Friedman and

Schwartz 1963, 321). A bill sponsored by T. Alan Goldsborough, Democrat of Maryland, required the Federal Reserve System to take all available steps to raise deflated commodity prices to their pre-depression level. However, opposition from Glass killed the measure when it was referred to the Senate Banking and Currency Committee (Burns 1974, 21).

Despite his legislation to help the financial sector and the economy in general, Hoover was, as were many Americans then and now, a strong proponent of a balanced budget. As a result, in late 1931, Hoover had asked Congress for a tax increase to balance the budget. The decision on a tax increase was primarily Hoover's for had he not asked for it, there would have been no demand for it from Congress; once he did request it, however, there was no effective opposition to it. Consequently, the Revenue Act, which raised taxes in the middle of a severe recession, was passed in 1932 (Stein 1969, 32–33).

Monetary Reform Proposals

According to Joseph Reeve, by January 1933 the mood of the populace had shifted toward "an attitude of desperation which threw overboard monetary orthodoxy" (Reeve 1943, 36). Reeve observed that "probably every community larger than a hamlet had at least one self-styled 'expert' on the monetary question who believed that he alone had discovered the one and only way out of the economic dilemma" (Reeve 1943, 129–30). The best known, and perhaps the most effective at arousing public opinion, was Father Charles E. Coughlin, a Canadian born Catholic priest who began buying radio time in 1926 to espouse his views on the world's social, political, and economic problems. Coughlin attacked communism, international bankers, Hoover, and, though initially a supporter of Roosevelt, he frequently attacked FDR on monetary matters (Reeve 1943, 133). In early 1934, *Fortune* estimated that Coughlin had 10 million listeners. Coughlin, however, did not have a coherent, well-thought-out scheme to get out of the depression but vacillated between a number of proposals, including those to take the control of money and credit away from bankers and give it to the government (Reeve 1943, 138–47). In a series of lectures on social justice, Coughlin proclaimed:

> There can be no prosperity forthcoming until the immoral mania of borrowing this nation out of debt with bankers' money is destroyed. There can be no prosperity until Congress recaptures its right to coin and regulate the value of money. There can be no prosperity until our national credit is predicated upon our national wealth. (cited in Reeve 1943, 144)

In early 1933 a group of leading business executives launched the Committee of the Nation to Rebuild Prices and Purchasing Power. In February the committee gave its confidential recommendations to the Senate Finance Committee on measures to meet the bank crisis (Reeve 1943, 40–41). The committee announced on April 6 a five point program that included rapid release of frozen bank deposits, cessation of exchange pegging, ultimate devaluation of the dollar to $36.17 per ounce, and stabilization of the price level at the 1921–30 level by a "federal nonpartisan board." At the committee's request, Representative Goldsborough introduced a bill containing most of these recommendations (Reeve 1943, 41).

In April 1933, the Economic Policy Commission of the American Bankers' Association, headed by Colonel Leonard P. Ayres, proposed significant changes in the banking system to grant greater powers over the credit situation to the Federal Reserve System. The Commission recommended compulsory membership of all banks in the Federal Reserve System and centralization under one bank. Three measures had direct monetary implications: establishment of a permanent right to borrow "in exceptional circumstances" by any member bank on pledge of "any acceptable asset"; provisions granting the Federal Reserve Board the right to increase and decrease member bank reserve requirements in emergencies; and modification of the reserve bank reserve requirements to provide for reserves behind the combined total of reserve notes and member bank deposits, in order to obviate the dangers arising from currency hoarding (Reeve 1943, 47–48). The provision for reserve requirement changes was later inserted into the Thomas Amendment to the Agricultural Adjustment Act.

As Reeve (1943) documents, there was no shortage of monetary reform proposals, though many were crank schemes submitted by the public. However banking reform proposals that were not crank schemes were also popular among economists (Reeve 1943, 305). The most ardent advocates of banking reform among economists were: Irving Fisher, Lauchlin Currie, Sumner Slichter, Paul Douglas, Albert

Hart, Henry Simons, and Jacob Viner, among others (Reeve 1943, 305). Congressional advocates included Senator Elmer Thomas, Senator William Borah, and Representatives Alan Goldsborough, William Lemke, Wright Patman, James Strong, and Jerry Voorhis (Reeve 1943, 305–6). Others supporting bank reform included Henry Wallace, Rexford Tugwell, Gardiner Means, and Adolf Berle.

The Economists Respond

Though belief in Say's Law and the tendency toward full employment were pillars of economic doctrine at the time of the depression, economists were not oblivious to the growing depression with its consequent social and economic costs.[3] As economists recognized that the economic downturn was more severe than previous ones, they began to look for explanations and to formulate policy recommendations. Discussion of the causes and remedies for the recession were a focus of the annual meetings of the American Economic Association in December 1929. At those meetings, F. C. Mills of Columbia emphasized that while much of current economic theory was of assistance in understanding the process of change in a modern industrial economy, "classical and mathematical theory were inadequate to provide a rational program and a technique for the study of the economy as a whole" (Dorfman 1959, v. 5, 659).

The economics profession, led in large part by its older and better known members, began to organize into united group action to advise on public policy. In part a response to the widespread feeling that economists never agreed, a unified front was attempted on issues of policy to confront the depression (Dorfman 1959, v. 5, 673). The practice of organizing economists to go on record on controversial issues of the moment had built up steam in the late spring of 1930 when more than 1,000 members of the profession petitioned Capitol Hill and the White House in opposition to the Smoot-Hawley Tariff Bill (Dorfman 1959, v. 5, 674; Barber 1985, 146). In January 1931, the Emergency Committee of Federal Public Works released a statement signed by ninety leading economists of different social philosophies calling for a billion dollar federal public-works program (Dorfman 1959, v. 5, 675). In April 1931, thirteen economists sent a telegram to the Federal Reserve Board urging the immediate easing of the Federal Reserve's credit policy. They also called for a long-range program of planned credit expansion to match the secular growth of production and trade (Dorfman 1959, v. 5, 675).

In November 1931, the Executive Committee of the National Grange began to study a proposal for a Federal Depository System, which would require all commercial banks to hold depositors' funds in trust and to lend out only their own capital resources. Lending funds could also come from funds secured by rediscounting the notes of customers with a newly created Federal Depository Bureau of the Treasury Department (Reeve 1943, 317).

James Harvey Rogers published a book titled *America Weighs Her Gold* in 1931 that argued that rigid adherence to the gold standard was a primary factor in the depression, and the Federal Reserve should engage in "controlled inflation." The book became a bestseller in September 1931, shortly after England left the gold standard and was praised in reviews by Jacob Viner and Rexford Tugwell (Dorfman 1959, v. 5, 689). Rogers later helped draft the Glass-Steagall Act, which allowed the use of government securities to back Federal Reserve notes (Dorfman 1959, v. 5, 690).

In *The Abolition of Unemployment*, Frank D. Graham of Princeton presented a monetary scheme that sought to provide a supplementary monetary unit as an emergency means of stimulating the economy. An Emergency Employment Corporation would make contracts with existing firms for the production of consumer goods and issue consumption certificates out of which the firms could pay their labor. The value of the certificates would be determined by measures of the total dollar value of output. Again, however, though the plan was intriguing, the difficulty of implementation and acceptance of the certificates on a widespread basis hindered its feasibility (Dorfman 1959, v. 5, 721).

In January 1932, a group of twenty-four economists participating in a conference at the University of Chicago sent a telegram to Hoover urging that the Federal Reserve be authorized to use government securities as collateral for the note issue, that open market operations be pursued more aggressively, that the Reconstruction Finance Corporation proceed vigorously in aiding the banks, and that the government continue its public works programs. Significantly, half of the group were faculty at the University of Chicago, including Jacob Viner, Frank Knight, Henry Simons, and Lloyd Mints (Barber 1985, 147). During the same month, another statement from this group calling for further expansion of credit was given much publicity in the press. This statement also urged the creation of the Reconstruction Finance Corporation, "proper economy" in the budgets of all government agencies, and increased taxation. According to the statement, the program recommended was the "least common denominator . . . upon which fairly general agreement appears possible" (Dorfman 1959, v. 5, 676).

In April 1932, in response to a request by Congressman Samuel B. Pettengill (Republican of Indiana), the Chicago economists drafted a lengthy statement which argued for prices being raised through government spending and financed without resort to taxes, generous bonus legislation for the war veterans, the printing of greenbacks to directly infuse purchasing power, and abandonment of the gold standard (Barber 1985, 156). As Barber notes, the policies advocated in the statement were extraordinary since they came from a group who had "been schooled in an analytic tradition which held that occasional downturns in economic activity were inevitable but that they were also self-correcting" (Barber 1985, 157).

One group hurt severely by the depression were the farmers who, in the face of falling farm prices and revenues, held debts whose value in real terms had actually increased. A Committee on Stabilization of the Unit of Value set up by the American Farm Bureau Federation, which included John R. Commons and Henry A. Wallace, urged credit expansion through liberal open market operations (Dorfman 1959, v. 5, 680).

Irving Fisher was the best-known advocate of easy money and credit policies as a cure for the depression. He coined the term *reflation* to describe the desirable increase in the price level to a level at which it could then be stabilized (Dorfman 1959, v. 5, 685). In 1932, Irving Fisher was working on his debt-deflation theory of the Great Depression, which was contained in his book *Booms and Depressions* (1932) and summarized in his 1933 *Econometrica* article. Fisher provided extensive statistical data to support his theory as an explanation for the Great Depression.[4]

To remedy the situation, Fisher supported temporary federal deposit insurance to help restore confidence in the banks. He also advocated a "stamped money" plan that had been advocated in predepression days by Silvio Gesell. Under this scheme, the government would distribute as a "gift" to all citizens a special currency in, for example, a $100 denomination, but would require the purchase of a $1 stamp from the government in order to actually spend the $100 bill. In effect, the gift would be a loan without interest with each $1 stamp representing a 1 percent amortization of the principal. In this example, the principal would be repaid after 100 months. In order to increase the velocity of circulation, any stamp money that had not been spent for a month would lose its entire value. Other versions of the scheme had the money only being distributed to the unemployed. Though ingenious and attracting attention, there were considerable obstacles to its implementation. The fundamental problem was that it still did not prevent hoarding of regular currency (Dorfman 1959, v. 5, 686–87).

Fisher was also associated with the Committee of the Nation to Rebuild Prices and Purchasing Power, headed by James H. Rand, Jr., a business associate of Fisher's in Remington-Rand Corporation. The committee advanced the monetary scheme of George F. Warren and Frank A. Pearson of Cornell, who had predicted a collapse in prices. The Warren-Pearson scheme argued that prices were a ratio between the quantity of goods and gold. Hence by making gold cheap compared to other commodities, general prices could be raised (Dorfman 1959, v. 5, 687–88).

There were many proposals put forward by economists to help end the depression. Some were rather elaborate monetary schemes, but none caught the public fancy, despite gaining at least some exposure in the popular media. What was widespread, however, was the belief that the financial system was not functioning properly and, despite its enormous productive capacity, the economy was stagnant. As Jacob Viner warned in 1932, there was no natural bottom to the economic decline below which the economy could not sink "if the moratorium on the deliberate exercise of intelligence persists" (Dorfman 1959, v. 5, 697).

Conclusion

Herbert Hoover did not rigidly adhere to some dogma of free enterprise. In the midst of the Great Depression, he and his advisers recognized that the government must do something. During the last year of Hoover's administration, two crucial steps were taken: the creation of the Reconstruction Finance Corporation, which was in a position to allocate government credit; and the expansion of the eligible assets for which the Federal Reserve could extend aid to banks. The assets that the Federal Reserve could hold was extended to government securities. This is crucial because it monetizes part of the government debt—in other words, money is printed to finance government expenditures. There was also considerable sentiment in Congress to have a creation of government fiat currency to provide an increase in purchasing power.

There were numerous proposals to end the depression and to implement monetary reform presented during this time. These proposals came from the public as well as professional economists. However the crisis had not yet reached a head, and nothing was done to adequately address the plethora of economic and monetary problems. Action by the government would await a change in administrations.

3

Roosevelt's Election and the Banking Crisis of 1933

As discussed in the previous chapter, the economic collapse brought forth a myriad of proposals to restore the health of the economy. Many believed that the central flaw in the economy was the financial system and that any attempts to counter the trend toward deflation and rising unemployment would require radical transformation of the banking system. In order to understand the dynamics of financial reform in 1933, three facts are crucial: (1) the economy was on a downward spiral over the period 1929–33, and there was no reason to believe— outside of faith alone—there was a bottom in the foreseeable future; (2) the policies of Herbert Hoover were not effectively fighting the depression, and (3) FDR and his advisers had no comprehensive, well-thought-out plan for recovery upon taking office. Government efforts over the period 1929–33 were not enough to halt the economy's tail-spin.

As will be seen, in 1933 the financial system was saved by the government's willingness to issue currency against any assets of the banks and the extension of government credit. This is what led many to conclude that the long-term solution to the ills of the financial system, and therefore the economy and unemployment, lay in government playing a larger, and perhaps exclusive, role in money and credit.

The Brain Trust

In March 1932, Roosevelt formed the so-called "Brains Trust" or the "Brain Trust" as it became known. This group of advisers formulated strategies, agendas, and programs for Roosevelt during his campaign for the presidency. The original group included Raymond Moley, a

Columbia University law professor; Rexford G. Tugwell, economics professor at the Teacher's College of Columbia University and an authority on agriculture; and Adolf Berle, who was also in the Columbia law school and whose study of the modern corporation (coauthored with Gardiner Means) was published in the summer of 1932 (Berle and Means 1932). A fourth member, Basil O'Connor, was FDR's law partner and played only a minor role in the Brain Trust.

After FDR took office, his advisers continued to be referred to as the "Brain Trust" despite a change in personnel from the original group. Though it is difficult to identify a unifying perspective for the Brain Trust, both Berle and Tugwell were influenced by Thorstein Veblen, John R. Commons, and the institutionalist school of economics. In general, the view was that technology had so radically altered the American economic fabric that any attempt to return to a period of atomistic competition and laissez faire would be futile and lead to a complete collapse in the economy, and perhaps social upheaval and revolution. Instead, a union between government, business, and labor was advocated to better plan the allocation of resources in order to promote the full utilization of resources.

According to Elliot Rosen, the New Deal emerged as the creation of the Brain Trust: Moley, Tugwell, and Berle in collaboration with Roosevelt (Rosen 1977, 115). Moley, raised in rural Ohio, was hostile toward international bankers and "fat cat" Republicans on Wall Street. His basic perspective was in the Populist/Progressive tradition (Rosen 1977, 123). Roosevelt's famous "forgotten man" speech in April 1932 reflected both Roosevelt's and Moley's conviction that the root cause of the Great Depression lay in the agricultural collapse of the twenties (Rosen 1977, 131). In regard to financial reform, Moley believed that the malfunctioning of the securities market necessitated a separation of investment and commercial banking. The former, Moley believed, should be treated as a public utility requiring federal and state regulation. Moley also advocated the expansion of the resources of the Reconstruction Finance Corporation to stave off further railroad bankruptcies (Rosen 1977, 143).

Tugwell's views on the economy were well known from his numerous publications. He was an outspoken advocate of government economic planning. In Tugwell's view, technological change made planning imperative. Tugwell's analysis of the depression lay in the proposition that a large decline in the purchasing power of the agricultural population triggered the economic decline. The solution lay in relieving the debt burden of farmers and increasing their purchasing power (Rosen 1977, 159–60). Later, Tugwell and Henry A. Wallace would be the framers of the Agricultural Adjustment Act, which sought to accomplish this goal.

The final member of the Brain Trust was Adolf Berle. He was brought into the group by Moley who sought an expert on the credit collapse. Moley was conscious of creditor/debtor tensions in a deflationary period especially, and felt the need for technical expertise to recommend policies to counter the shrinkage of credit that had occurred during the years of the depression (Rosen 1977, 195). Berle was a recognized expert on finance and a brilliant individual who had graduated from Harvard College at age 18, and received a law degree at age 21 (Rosen 1977, 196–97). Berle shared Tugwell's view that large corporations were now a fact of life and should be controlled rather than broken up in a misguided attempt to resurrect atomistic capitalism. At the request of Moley, Berle together with Louis Faulkner prepared a memorandum in May 1932 on the financial collapse and possible avenues for recovery. According to their memo, the causes of the depression were the sterilization of money and credit through hoarding of cash and insufficient demand for goods. Consumers, bankers, and corporations feared for the safety of their investments and the result was economic stagnation. The memorandum advocated federal insurance of savings accounts and an expansion of the role of the Reconstruction Finance Corporation (Rosen 1977, 207).

The Brain Trust, as noted, utilized a view of the economy associated with the institutionalist school (Rosen 1977, 206). This perspective implied an activist role for the government in the economy both in the short run and, quite likely, in the long run as well. However, this was not the platform that FDR ran on in 1932, and many later found the presidential campaign somewhat embarrassing. Roosevelt ran on a budget balancing platform and attacked the spending programs of Hoover. At the same time, Roosevelt made speeches in which he attacked bankers and business leaders whose actions were detrimental to the "forgotten man" at the bottom of the economic pyramid. As Marriner Eccles later observed about the campaign of 1932, "the speeches often read like a giant misprint, in which Roosevelt and Hoover speak each other's lines" (Eccles 1951, 95).

The Banking Crisis and Roosevelt's Inauguration

After the November 1932 elections, Hoover called Congress into session to deal with the banking problems. On December 6, Hoover made a final plea for banking reform legislation, "Widespread banking reforms are a national necessity and are the first requisites for further recovery" (Burns 1974, 24). Despite his efforts, Hoover did not really press for any fundamental changes in banking, nor did he endorse others' efforts to secure reform (Kennedy 1973, 25). The Hoover administration had failed in its efforts to work through the Federal Reserve Banks by establishing banking and industrial committees to "promote recovery by normal capitalistic processes of reviving private capital investment through regular banking channels" (Kennedy 1973, 49). Hoover had called Congress into session in order to pass legislation to deal with the crisis; however, since it was a lame duck session, there was little if any incentive to tackle the problems.

Prior to his inauguration, Roosevelt had refused to say anything definite about his plans for banking, even in private letters (Kennedy 1973, 59). The Glass bill had been reintroduced on January 5, 1933, and this version called for nationwide branch banking, divorce of security affiliates from national banks within five years, Federal Reserve controls over speculative credit, Federal Reserve removal of officers and directors of member banks who persisted in unsound practices, and establishment of a liquidating corporation to protect bank deposits (Kennedy 1973, 73). Following a filibuster by Huey Long of Louisiana, the Glass bill passed the Senate in late January 1933 and was sent to the House. Long was against the branch banking provisions, arguing that they would harm local communities and concentrate power in the hands of a few institutions (Burns 1974, 25). The hearings on speculation in the stock market, chaired by Senator Ferdinand Pecora, began at the same time (Kennedy 1973, 106).

Hoover tried to generate cooperation with the incoming administration, but his efforts there failed. The Glass banking bill did not go far enough for Roosevelt who wanted greater protection from fraud in securities, segregation of savings and commercial deposits, revisions of the liquidation law to permit a quick reopening of closed banks, and limited branch banking (Kennedy 1973, 73). Without an indication of support from Roosevelt, there was no chance that Congress would pass any banking legislation. In a note sent February 18, Hoover urged Roosevelt to provide prompt assurance that there will be no tampering or inflation of the currency; that the budget will be unquestionably balanced even if further taxation is necessary; that the government credit will be maintained by refusal to exhaust it in issue of securities. (Kennedy 1973, 137; Moley 1966, 142)

Bank failures continued into 1933 and as the currency deposit ratio rose, the money supply fell dramatically after January. By March 3, there were bank holidays declared in about half the states. The pressure intensified on the New York banks and on March 4, a banking holiday was declared in New York state (Friedman and Schwartz 1963, 324–27).

When Franklin Roosevelt took office in March 1933, the banking system in the United States teetered on the edge of total collapse. William Leuchtenburg wrote that there seemed to be a loss of confidence in the president, the Congress, the banks, and the American dream in general. The American way of life was definitely at stake and most, whether reluctantly or not, believed that Roosevelt was the last hope (Leuchtenburg 1963, 28–31).

In his inaugural speech, FDR attacked the bankers' role in the depression, but provided no coherent philosophy of banking reform. The underlying theme of his address seemed to be an attack on greed and especially that of the "money changers." FDR stated:

> Plenty is at our doorstep, but a generous use of it languishes in the very sight of the supply. Primarily this is because rulers of the exchange of mankind's good have failed through their own stubbornness and their own incompetence, have admitted their failure, and have abdicated. Practices of the unscrupulous money changers stand indicted in the court of public opinion, rejected by the hearts and minds of men.... The money changers have fled from their high seats in the temple of our civilization. We may now restore that temple to the ancient truths. The measure of the restoration lies in the extent to which we apply social values more noble than mere monetary profit. (Roosevelt, 1938, p. 11)

The task was to unite government, at all levels, with the private sector in order to put people back to work. To do so, however, would require a restructuring of the financial system:

> Finally, in our progress toward a resumption of work we require two safeguards against a return of the evils of the old order: there must be a

strict supervision of all banking and credits and investments, so that there will be an end to speculation with other people's money; and there must be provision for an adequate but sound currency. (Roosevelt, 1938, p. 11)

Despite the eloquent rhetoric against bankers, Helen Burns observed, Roosevelt never definitively set forth his own views on banking (Burns 1974, 183). During his first press conference he was asked to comment on federal deposit insurance and he did so, but asked that his remarks be kept off the record. Roosevelt said of federal deposit insurance:

> The general underlying thought behind the use of the word "guarantee" with respect to bank deposits is that you guarantee bad banks as well as good banks. The minute the Government starts to do that the Government runs into a probable loss. . . . We do not wish to make the United States Government liable for the mistakes and errors of individual banks, and put a premium on unsound banking in the future. (*Public Papers* 1939, 37)

Roosevelt's concern over the plight of debtors, especially farmers, was also evident. Writing a few months later to his Secretary of Treasury William Woodin, Roosevelt blasted the bankers and economists for their neglect of the problem:

> I wish our banking and economists friends would realize the seriousness of the situation from the point of view of the debtor classes–i.e., 90 per cent of the human beings in this country—and think less from the point of view of the 10 per cent who constitute the creditor classes. (Roosevelt to Woodin, September 30, 1933, *President's Official File 230*)

By March 4, with the information that New York banks would not open on the following Monday, Roosevelt was confronted with an immediate crisis. On Sunday, March 5, the day after his inauguration, Roosevelt began a series of meetings to formulate a strategy for resolving the immediate banking crisis. On the same day, he issued two proclamations: one closing all banking institutions, including the Federal Reserve Banks (from March 6–9), and the other calling Congress into special session on March 9. For authority to close the banks, Roosevelt invoked a hitherto unused section of the Trading with the

Enemy Act of 1917 which gave the president such authority in times of national emergency (Moley 1966, 156–58). This proclamation was prepared by Ogden Mills, Secretary of the Treasury under Hoover, and his undersecretary, Arthur Ballantine. The use of the 1917 law had been known and discussed for at least a year prior to its use (Moley 1966, 158–60).

Once the banks were closed, a plan had to be formulated for their reopening. On Monday, there was a meeting to discuss the bank holiday and steps that should be taken to reopen the banks. Present at the meeting were Moley; Mills; Ballantine; James H. Douglas, Jr., assistant secretary of the treasury; Dr. Emanuel A. Goldenweiser of the Federal Reserve Board; and Parker Gilbert, a Morgan partner and a former assistant secretary of the treasury. Because of his connection with the "House of Morgan," Gilbert was excluded from further meetings. Others who participated were incoming members of the Roosevelt administration: Adolf Berle, Walter Wyatt, Francis G. Awalt, and William Woodin. Numerous proposals were discussed at these meetings, including the issuance of scrip and Federal Reserve notes, the nationalization of the banks, and the conversion of several Federal Reserve Banks into government owned deposit banks (Moley 1966, 169; Burns 1974, 45). FDR rejected any kind of deposit guarantee in the legislation (Kennedy 1973, 169).

During the period of the banking holiday, Roosevelt proposed to his advisers a plan for converting all government bonds ($21 billion at the time) directly into cash at par. His advisers thought it would be a disaster, but Roosevelt told them to come up with an alternative (Kennedy 1973, 173–74). George Harrison's alternative to FDR's plan was to make cash available to holders of government bonds but with controls against inflation. Federal Reserve banks would be authorized to make loans to individuals, firms, or corporations on their own ninety day notes backed by pledge of government securities; the Reserve Banks could fight inflation by raising the discount rate (Kennedy 1973, 174).

The memorandum used in drafting the Emergency Banking bill was written by Mills (Moley 1966, 166). It is for this reason that Leuchtenburg (1963, 43) argues that the passage of the Emergency Banking bill represented Roosevelt's stamp of approval for decisions made by Hoover's fiscal advisers. When the final draft was ready, it was presented to Roosevelt by Moley, Woodin, Ballantine, and George W.

Davison, president of the Hanover Bank in New York (Moley 1966, 172). The actual legislation was drafted by Walter Wyatt, then on the staff of the Federal Reserve Board (Moley 1966, 174–75).

Despite Schlesinger's mention of Tugwell's plan to use the postal savings system (Schlesinger 1958, 5), Moley said he never heard of such a proposal, and Roosevelt never mentioned it (Moley 1966, 1789). Nevertheless, memorandums by Tugwell exist in which he mentions the plans, and it is included as an agenda item for the meetings during the period March 4–9 (see *President's Personal File 431*). Moley also acknowledged that during February 1933, while working on the inaugural draft, he and Roosevelt discussed the possibility of using the postal savings system (Moley 1966, 113).

The postal savings system had been established in 1910 during Taft's Republican administration for the benefit of small savers in wake of the panic of 1907 in which public confidence in the banking system was severely eroded (O'Hara and Easley 1979, 742). During the early depression years, postal savings accounts grew from $164 million in 1929 to $1.2 billion, a ninefold increase. At the same time, deposits in savings and loans fell. Because they operated as mutuals at the time and could refuse to redeem their shares, withdrawals from savings and loans are underestimated. Interest rates payable on postal savings accounts were limited to 2 percent, and the funds could only be invested in government securities or placed in "solvent" national banks (O'Hara and Easley 1979, 744). As a result of the limits placed on the postal savings accounts prior to the depression, funds went from savings and loans—and to a lesser extent banks—into postal accounts, thus reducing credit available from banks.

Use of the postal savings system was also urged by Progressives in the Senate and by Supreme Court Justice Louis D. Brandeis. In a letter to Roosevelt on March 9, Senators Robert LaFollette (R-Wisconsin) and Edward Costigan (D-Colorado) argued that drastic measures were necessary to restore confidence in the banking system, and that the use of clearing-house certificates as in the crisis of 1907 would not be adequate. LaFollette and Costigan urged that the federal government issue and control all emergency money, that government aid and government control go hand in hand, and that public credit must be conserved for the necessary program of reconstruction and permanent economic recovery. To accomplish this goal, the Federal Reserve Banks would be allowed to accept deposits from individuals and to issue loans subject to the general rules of banking. The postal savings banks would be designated to act as agents of Federal Reserve Banks for the duration of the emergency period (LaFollette to Roosevelt, March 9, 1933, *President's Official File 230*).

Others also supported the use of the postal savings system during the bank crisis. In a letter to Felix Frankfurter the day before Roosevelt's inauguration, Supreme Court Justice Louis Brandeis said:

> What it (the Government) should have done was to open wide the Postal Savings & take itself the risk of lending to worthy banks—making them, in effect, its agents to lend to worthy businesses. Then there would have been little hoarding. (Lash 1988, 107)

Clearly the use of the postal savings system to meet the banking crisis was a widely recognized and supported proposal. It was an alternative that could have effectively dampened the crisis, but one that would have eliminated the commercial banks. Because banks opposed the plan and FDR did not want radical change to lead to a perception of greater crisis, he did not institute such a proposal.

The Emergency Banking Act

In its five Titles, the Emergency Banking Act validated the president's actions of March 6–9, provided a plan for reopening the banks, authorized national banks to issue preferred stock for sale to the public or the RFC in order to rehabilitate their capital structure, provided Federal Reserve advances on any acceptable assets, and appropriated $2 million for carrying out the act. Under this act, federal government debt become eligible as collateral for Federal Reserve discounts. Many other bonds, bills, drafts, and acceptances were also made temporarily eligible. Moreover the Reserve Banks could make similar advances to any individual, partnership, or corporation on its promissory note secured by U.S. bonds (Kennedy 1973, 177). Banks were authorized to create special trust accounts for receipt of new deposits, though banks were opposed to this on the grounds that those who had funds were the ones who hoarded it before bank closings (Kennedy 1973, 165).

In permitting the establishment of the trust accounts, the Emergency Banking Act drew upon the principle employed in the National Banking Act. The acts of 1863 and 1864 had backed bank notes with government debt, and the Emergency Banking Act permitted banks to offer deposit accounts backed with government debt or other secure assets.* The relevant section stated:

> The Secretary of the Treasury . . . is authorized and empowered . . . (c) to authorize and direct the creation in banking institutions of special trust accounts for the receipt of new deposits which shall be subject to withdrawal on demand without any restriction or limitation and shall be kept separately in cash or on deposit in Federal Reserve Banks or invested in obligations of the United States.

The Emergency Banking Act was passed in less than an hour with little debate. In the House, only Congressman Steagall had a copy. In the Senate, the only opposition came from progressive Republicans who thought that the president had not moved far enough in providing government control over banking. The act did not provide any permanent solutions to the problem, it only gave the Congress and the president a breathing spell in which to formulate a plan. During his first fireside chat, Roosevelt explained his reasons for closing the banks and announced their reopening. It is a tribute to Roosevelt's charisma that when the banks reopened on Monday, March 13, the runs had virtually ended. Walter Lippmann remarked that "In one week, the nation, which had lost confidence in everything and everybody, has regained confidence in the government and in itself" (Schlesinger 1958, 13). Raymond Moley wrote, "Capitalism was saved in eight days" (Moley 1939, 155).

According to the emergency plan, the banks were divided into three classes, in declining class of solvency: A's were solvent, B's were marginal, and C's must be closed. Where no Class A banks would be available in a particular city, and the B status of existing institutions remained questionable, Mills suggested that the secretary of the treasury offer to establish a new bank where the government would buy preferred stock to furnish capital, and the new institution could take over assets of the old banks in return for assumption of a percentage of their deposit liabilities (Kennedy 1973, 171). Thus one-half of the

---

*I am grateful to Alex Pollock for bringing this to my attention. Pollock calls the principle employed in the National Banking Acts and the Emergency Banking Act of backing money with "safe" assets, "collateralized money."

banks, with 90 percent of deposits, were open by March 15, 45 percent were under conservators, and 5 percent were closed permanently (Kennedy 1973, 187).

In the decision to close the banks and then reformulate the financial system, FDR listened not to the radicals in the Brain Trust and Congress (Tugwell and the Progressives in the Senate), but rather to bankers and more conservative advisers who urged less dramatic reforms. According to Raymond Moley, the plan was conservative, but implemented boldly:

> The necessity, therefore, was for swift and decisive and well-publicized action by Roosevelt and Congress. Since the great majority of people were accustomed to orthodox banking procedures, this, too, was essential to gaining their confidence. Therefore, we were determined to exclude from the group of major participants—who were known to the press, the bankers, and the public—all the reputedly radical and visionary individuals who were hovering in the background with novel, even revolutionary, ideas (which, we were to learn later, went so far as nationalizing the banking structure). There was nothing revolutionary in our plans. The only unusual feature was the boldness and swiftness of their application. (Moley 1966, 171)

According to Susan Kennedy, President Roosevelt never considered nationalization seriously, though he clearly considered a broad array of plans. In the end, FDR listened to conservative advisers such as Raymond Moley, and chose to avoid radical solutions, seeing no reason to embrace socialization when a more conventional approach would serve as well. Roosevelt had no plan of his own for opening the banks, but "in calling on this particular set of advisers, he apparently took an orthodox solution for granted, believing that the financial system could be made to grind on with only minor corrections to avoid another general breakdown" (Kennedy 1973, 168).

Conclusion

There were two aspects of the banking crisis: the failure of the payments system and the reluctance, for whatever reasons, of the banks to extend credit. Both Hoover and Roosevelt sought to deal with these issues. Roosevelt's first action was to close the banks. It is important to remember that the banks were reopened without federal deposit insurance, but the government was standing behind the banks in a way that previously it had been reluctant to do. The federal government stood ready to aid the capital structure of banks through the RFC, and it stood ready to issue Federal Reserve notes against any assets of the bank in order to enable a bank to withstand a run. Banks were also permitted to offer accounts backed by government liabilities (cash, government securities) or by Federal Reserve liabilities. Bank runs ceased after the reopening, and this lesson was impressed upon many: When confidence in private institutions vanished, it was still possible to save the financial system as long as confidence remained in government. The idea that government backing for deposits promoted confidence in the banking system was established. This was the critical and monumental accomplishment of Roosevelt and the members of his administration during the first week in office.

Roosevelt's actions presented the government with time to prepare a banking reform agenda. However, the measures would have to come quickly. It is not at all clear how long confidence in the banks would have remained without quick and decisive action on the part of the administration and Congress. The opening of the banks on March 13 coincided with the beginning of the 100 days that saw numerous and sweeping legislation introduced by the administration. It also set off a period of public discussion on banking reform. In this context, economists at the University of Chicago prepared a plan for banking reform that they believed would not only solve the immediate problems, but provide a permanent remedy to the ills of the American financial structure. This proposal, prepared and presented to Roosevelt within two and one-half weeks of his inauguration, was destined to play a prominent role in the debates over banking legislation during the New Deal years.

4

The March 1933 Chicago Memorandum

The idea that government backing of the currency was fundamental to its acceptance at par value in exchange was a well accepted principle in American monetary history. In the wake of the collapse in the early 1930s, it is not surprising that the principle would be recommended as a remedy. In 1926 Frederick Soddy had made a proposal to back bank liabilities with government cash. Others, including prominent economists, supported this idea.

As discussed earlier, economists at the University of Chicago prepared policy recommendations in 1932 that they distributed to government officials, and others. Most of the signers of those documents strongly advocated policies to promote competition in the market economy. Four members of the faculty—Frank Knight, Henry Simons, Jacob Viner, and Lloyd Mints—were later to be known as the founders of the Chicago School of Economics.[1] Though they were strong proponents of laissez faire in industry, there is no indication in their writings (at this time, 1933–34) that they questioned the right of the federal government to have an exclusive monopoly on money production. In his review of Alvin Hansen's *Economic Stabilization in an Unbalanced World*, in the April 1933 issue of the *American Economic Review*, Frank Knight criticized Hansen for accepting commercial banking as currently structured as an inevitable feature of capitalist society. He stated:

> No violation of the basic principles of extreme laissez faire theory would be involved in separating the monetary system from the vicissitudes of speculative private business. (Knight 1933b, 244)

Seven years earlier, in a roundtable published in the *American Economic Review*, Proceedings, Knight had already expressed questions about fractional reserve banking—referring to their "alleged service of

economizing gold and increasing the supply of exchange-medium"
(Knight 1926, 121).[2] In his review of Frederick Soddy's book (Soddy
1926), which proposed 100 percent reserves for transactions deposits,
Knight said:

> The practical thesis of the book is distinctly unorthodox, but is in our
> opinion both highly significant and theoretically correct. In the abstract,
> it is absurd and monstrous for society to pay the commercial banking
> system "interest" for multiplying several fold the quantity of medium of
> exchange when (a) a public agency could do it at negligible cost, (b)
> there is no sense in having it done at all, since the effect is simply to
> raise the price level, and (c) important evils result, notably the frightful
> instability of the whole economic system and its periodical collapse in
> crises, which are in large measure bound up with the variability and
> uncertainty of the credit structure if not directly the effect of it. (Knight
> 1927, 732)

Knight agreed with Soddy that the fractional reserve banking system
raised the price level and created a potentially unstable situation. The
ideas of the Chicago economists on banking reform were influenced by
Soddy, and his ideas require further examination.[3]

Frederick Soddy's Theory of Money and Banking

In 1933 Soddy, who won the Nobel prize in chemistry in 1921 and was
a professor at Oxford, published a summary of his theories in the
Economic Forum (Soddy 1933a). His basic argument was that technology had created an age of plenty, and that only the structure of the
banking system prevented the full realization of this abundance and the
elimination of poverty (Soddy 1933a, 291–92). The crucial problem
was between *true* wealth—that created by using raw materials—and
virtual wealth—that represented by claims on real wealth. These
claims were represented by money in the modern economy since
money was debt, at least the largest part, which was backed only
fractionally by metals such as gold. All economic problems emanated
from the fluctuations surrounding the production of the stock of real
wealth and the production of virtual wealth. Soddy argued that these
fluctuations could be minimized if the government alone had the
power to create money and created it in order to maintain a stable price

level. In order to achieve a government monopoly on the creation of money, it would be necessary to eliminate the money created by banks in the process of making loans. This could be effected by requiring that banks hold dollar for dollar in government money against their checkable accounts (Soddy 1933a, 300). This proposal, originally stated in Soddy's 1926 book, is the proposal with which Frank Knight agreed in his book review. Hence Frank Knight, acknowledged as one of the greatest economic minds of the twentieth century, embraced the heretical proposal of a noneconomist to transform radically the banking system. The growing bank failures of the early thirties, and the eagerness of economists to make policy proposals in a time of crisis, provided Knight and others at Chicago with the opportunity to restate and refine the Soddy proposal.[4]

The Chicago Response to the March Crisis

In the face of the widespread banking holidays and a new administration in Washington, the Chicago economists prepared a statement on banking reform. The six-page memorandum on banking reform was given limited and confidential distribution to about forty individuals on March 16, 1933 (Knight 1933).* A copy of the memorandum was sent to Henry A. Wallace, then Secretary of Agriculture, with a cover letter signed by Frank Knight. The letter listed the following supporters of the plan: F. H. Knight, L. W. Mints, Henry Schultz, H. C. Simons, G. V. Cox, Aaron Director, Paul Douglas, and A. G. Hart.[5] Though the proposals were presented at a time of crisis in the financial system and were intended to alleviate the problems of the moment, they were also intended to provide a long-term solution to the banking problem. The Chicago economists stated that their proposals would "meet the immediate emergency, provide a permanent solution of the banking problem, and bring about marked improvement in production and employment" (Knight 1933a, 6). They wrote to Wallace: "most of us suspect that measures at least as drastic and 'dangerous' as those described in our statement can hardly be avoided, except temporarily, in any event" (Knight to Wallace, March 16, 1933, *President's Official File 230*). The authors anticipated skepticism about their plan as evi-

---

*This memorandum along with the letter to Secretary Wallace is reproduced in the Appendix.

denced by a typed postscript in the letter to Wallace that stated: "We hope you are one of the forty odd who get this who will not think we are quite loony, I think Viner really agrees but doesn't believe it good politics."

The proposal opened with the statement, "It is evident that drastic measures must soon be taken with reference to banking, currency, and federal fiscal policy." The general recommendations were that any federal guarantee of deposits only be taken as part of a drastic program of banking reform that will certainly and permanently prevent any possible recurrence of the present banking crisis; and that the administration announce and pursue a policy of bringing about, and maintaining, a moderate increase in the level of wholesale prices not to exceed 15 percent (Knight 1933a, 1).

The detailed suggestions advocated outright ownership of the Federal Reserve Banks; banks operating with a federal guarantee of deposits would be subject to full Federal Reserve supervisory control over the management of the banks. Federal Reserve notes, which should be declared legal tender, should be issued in any amounts that may be necessary to meet demands for payment by depositors.

In order to prevent a recurrence of bank runs, the Federal Reserve Banks should liquidate the assets of all member banks, pay off liabilities, and dissolve all existing banks. New institutions should be created that accepted only demand deposits subject to a 100 percent reserve requirement in lawful money and/or deposits with the Reserve's Banks. Saving deposits would be handled through the incorporation of investment trusts. Present banking institutions would continue deposit and lending functions under Federal Reserve supervision until the new institutions could be put into place. The government should then undertake to raise the price level by 15 percent by fiscal and currency means but prevent further inflation (beyond 15 percent).

Finally there should be suspension of free coinage of gold, an embargo upon gold import, prohibition of private export of gold, exchange for Federal Reserve notes for all gold coins, suspension of the gold clause in all debt contracts, and substantial government sale and export of gold abroad (Knight 1933a).

The Proposal Goes to FDR and Others

Henry Wallace, the Secretary of Agriculture, gave the Chicago plan to Roosevelt less than a week after it was distributed. Wallace hoped

FDR would give the plan serious consideration, though the plan was a radical break with the past.[6] Wallace wrote to Roosevelt:

> The memorandum from the Chicago economists which I gave you at (the) Cabinet meeting Tuesday, is really awfully good and I hope that you or Secretary Woodin will have the time and energy to study it. Of course the plan outlined is quite a complete break with our present banking history. It would be an even more decisive break than the founding of the Federal Reserve System. (Wallace to Roosevelt, March 23, 1933, *President's Official File 230*)

Wallace added that there was a failure to recognize the crucial role that open market operations played in monetary policy. He wrote FDR:

> I still have the feeling that practically no one in the Government real- izes how tremendously important is the centralized control of the open market policy of the Federal Reserve System. When Benjamin Strong was Governor of the Federal Reserve Bank some rather constructive things were done with this open market policy, but in recent times this tremendous power has been exercised in a rather hap-hazard [sic] fash- ion by men from the twelve regional banks who did not have the train- ing to fit them to deal with the matter of a central banking policy. I hope these open market operations can be taken completely out of the hands of these representatives from the regional banks and placed in the hands of men who have the viewpoint that central bankers must have. This phi- losophy is the same as that of Bagehot, the English banking historian. (Wallace to Roosevelt, March 23, 1933, *President's Official File 230*)[7]

The Chicago memorandum prompted numerous replies, including one from Irving Fisher who responded with an eight page letter ad- dressing each point. Fisher agreed with the deposit guarantee as an immediate expedient if there were permanent reform. Fisher disagreed that 15 percent inflation was adequate. According to his statistical work, based on a scale where the 1926 price level was 100, and the present level 56, he would raise it to about 80. This would be about a 60 percent increase. Based on his work on the debt-deflation theory of booms and depressions, Fisher's inflation recommendation was ori- ented toward reducing the real burden of debt. As to the proposal to establish 100 percent reserve banks, Fisher was very interested, but it was not a total, immediate embracing of the idea. Fisher stated:

I realize that you offer this as an academic rather than a practical proposition but I am extremely glad that you are doing so. If it can be made
practical I would, I think, favor it and I have been thinking along those
lines myself. At any rate, and this is the main point I suppose, deposits
must in the future in some way be made certain instead of uncertain.
(Fisher to Simons, March 19, 1933, Simons Papers)

Though unsure of the practicality of the 100 percent reserve plan,
Fisher believed its basic thrust was correct. He wrote:

Even if so extreme a proposition as this is impractical, as I feel sure it
is, at any rate at this time, I think it ought to be practical to at least
divorce the demand deposit business from investment business. Behind
quick liabilities there should only be quick assets. A certain amount of
divorce is accomplished, of course, by getting rid of the bank affiliates
but even with the bank itself it is important that there should be a
further separation of functions and that the banks which have slow
assets or even so-called quick assets consisting of long time securities
should not have demand deposits against them. This suggestion of making two types of banking is emphasized by Frank Vanderlip of the
Committee for the Nation, and, I think, is an excellent one and probably
could be made practical in the not distant future. It goes much further
than the Glass banking bill. I think it would also help in demand deposits if there were a clause permitting the banks to require, say, ten days'
notice when and if desired whether of an individual or of all concerned.
This sort of a clause for savings banks solved the problem of runs in
New Haven a couple of years ago. (Fisher to Chicago group, March 19,
1933, Simons Papers)

Simons replied to Fisher, "We appreciate especially your sympathetic comments on the purely banking features of our scheme. The
proposals may perhaps further be explained in terms of two objectives:
(1) abolition of private credit as an element in the circulating media—
concentration of complete and direct control over the quantity of media
in the hands of the central monetary authority; and (2) attainment of
substantial homogeneity in the exchange medium. . . . we are proposing a monetary authority substantially without discretionary power"
(Simons to Fisher, March 24, 1933, Simons Papers).

Though both Fisher and the Chicago economists wished to reduce
the role of gold, their thinking on how to accomplish this was curiously
reversed. The Chicago proposal was to lower the mint price of gold,

which would imply a revaluation upward of the dollar with respect to gold. Fisher stated in his letter, "you doubtless, when you said lowering, meant raising the price of gold." Fisher's reasoning was that you would devalue the gold-backed dollar, but gradually replace it with non–gold-backed Federal Reserve notes, eventually going off the gold standard. Simons replied that they advocated lowering the dollar price of gold for precisely the same reasons, but imposing a loss on gold holders, rather than a gain (Simons to Fisher, March 24, 1933, Simons Papers).

With respect to long-run currency management, Simons acknowledged that the problem was not adequately addressed in the memorandum, but the authors would oppose any type of "managed currency" system whereby the monetary authority had broad discretionary powers. As Simons viewed their differences with Fisher, the only serious one was the degree of inflation necessary. Though admitting that their 15 percent figure was arbitrary, Simons did not agree with Fisher's use of the debtor-creditor relationship as a criterion for reflation. The reason for rejecting this criterion was, Simons argued, that no inflation could be brought about without inducing "all the unhealthy developments of a furious boom." Further, there was little reason to believe that inequities in contracts that had continued for many years could be adequately addressed by inflation. Simons reiterated that they favored only the inflation necessary to bring about reasonably full employment. Despite some critical remarks, Simons closed the letter by saying: "Looking back, I find that my remarks about our sentiments with reference to your letter sound sadly perfunctory—like merely the customary ritual of polite correspondence. I wish I could indicate clearly how warm those sentiments really are" (Simons to Fisher, March 24, 1933, Simons Papers).

Though Fisher's comments were among the longest and most detailed, numerous others wrote as well. There was even a brief note from John Maynard Keynes that read, "Much interested by the memorandum which you kindly send me" (J. M. Keynes to Simons, March 31, 1933, Simons Papers). Henry Hazlett wrote that he was only in partial agreement. He was against a government guarantee of deposits, in favor of reducing real estate loans by banks (as were the Chicago economists), and in favor of a 50 percent devaluation of the dollar, which he said, "other things equal, should lead to a 100 percent increase in wholesale prices." Hazlett stated that the devaluation was the only way to secure a price rise that was controllable. He noted, "I am not an adherent of the quantity theory of money as expounded by

Irving Fisher and others and do not believe that an increase in circulating media would [affect] prices in the way that the memorandum assumes" (Hazlett to Simons, March 20, 1933, Simons Papers).

By early April, Simons had revised the last three pages of the memorandum dealing with short-run and long-run currency management. The revisions under point 11 appear to be in direct response to Fisher's comments. The revised page 5 opened with:

> The objective of monetary policy should now be conceived, we insist, in terms of the volume of employment, with only incidental regard for the circumstances of debtors and creditors. In others words, currency measures should aim to correct, and to avoid over-correcting, the general maladjustment between product-prices and operating costs. Our recommendation of a fifteen percent increase in wholesale prices has little or no statistical foundation; the figure represents merely our guess of what would be necessary. (Simons 1933a, 5)

The revision also warned of any attempts by the monetary authorities to establish justice between debtors and creditors because such actions could not likely be undertaken without the "unhealthy developments of a furious boom."

The long-run objective would be substantial homogeneity in our circulating medium and "toward a situation where the central monetary authority will exercise complete and direct control over the total quantity of effective media."

The revised memo concluded with the argument that though there was a need for a strong monetary authority, it should be one without discretionary powers. The memo stated:

> We feel that any body like the Reserve Board should only be entrusted with a largely technical and strictly administrative function of applying some explicit rule of currency-management—the rule being chosen by Congress and incorporated in legislation under circumstances designed to minimize the possibility of frequent or drastic change. (Simons 1933a, 7)

Conclusion

The March proposal was distributed immediately after the Emergency Banking Act, at the time when deliberations were beginning on bank reform legislation. The Chicago economists presented their plan as an alternative to nationalization of banking, which they considered to be a real possibility. FDR learned of the plan from Wallace and had an opportunity to weigh its recommendations. Though Roosevelt's views on the Chicago plan are unknown, the plan addressed deposit safety, the separation of investment and commercial banking, and reflation. It also provided an alternative to those who advocated branch banking, which Roosevelt was very much against because he thought it would mean the domination of the small banks by the larger banks. As the 100 days began, the idea embodied in the Chicago plan—that government backing of bank money would be necessary—was firmly established. This idea had a long tradition and already had been utilized in legislation to meet the banking crisis. The proposals to expand the postal savings system were similar to the Chicago plan for checking accounts. The safety of the payments system was to be addressed by the Banking Act of 1933, but the Chicago proposals relating to credit and monetary policy would wait until the debates over the Banking Act of 1935.

─────── 5 ───────

The 100 Days Legislation and
the Banking Act of 1933

During the first 100 days of the Roosevelt administration, numerous measures were passed to deal with the economic situation, especially the crisis of the banking system and agriculture. Though Roosevelt at first hesitated to move on comprehensive banking reform, he sensed that the political climate was ripe for such an opportunity. Congress had already considered deposit insurance legislation, and the Pecora hearings on stock market practices continued throughout the spring.

On March 11, 1933, Senator Carter Glass reintroduced his banking reform bill. On March 14, Senator Thomas P. Gore, Democrat of Oklahoma, introduced a joint resolution calling for a constitutional amendment to give Congress control over all banking in the United States (Burns 1973, 79). In mid-March, there was a conference at the White House and an subsequent announcement that banking legislation would be introduced along the lines of the Glass bill. It was stressed that the immediate aim of the administration would be to revive quickly the banking system with the long-run objective "to get a permanently united and coherent banking system" through a "restructuring of the Federal Reserve system" (Burns 1974, 80). However, the Economy Act, passed on March 20, was the first legislation specifically originating with Roosevelt and fulfilled a campaign pledge to reduce government. The measure, which cut government employment and spending, was more deflationary than anything Hoover had advocated.

The Thomas Amendment and the
Emergency Farm Mortgage Act

One of Roosevelt's major concerns was the debt situation of farmers, and when he took office he appointed Henry Morgenthau as Chairman of the Federal Farm Board. On March 27, he issued an Executive Order to become effective May 27 (unless rescinded by Congress) to create the Farm Credit Administration (FCA) with Morgenthau as head. The FCA consolidated within one agency all functions, powers, and funds of existing federal agencies dealing with agricultural credit. Specifically, the FCA took over the functions of the federal land banks, the National Farm Loan Association, the Federal Intermediate Credit Banks, Crop Production and Seed Loan Offices, and so on (Hoag 1976, 233–34).

The farm bill consisted of Title I: the Agricultural Adjustment Act; Title II: the Emergency Farm Mortgage Act; and Title III: Monetary issues and the Thomas amendment. The latter was introduced by Elmer Thomas, Democrat of Oklahoma. The amendment was subtitled "Financing and Exercising Power Conferred by Section 8 of Article I of the Constitution: To Coin Money and to Regulate the Value Thereof." Whenever the president deemed that "an economic emergency requires an expansion of credit," he was authorized to permit the Federal Reserve to engage in open market operations in U.S. government securities, or in obligations of any corporation in which the government is the majority stockholder. Further, the Federal Reserve Board, with the approval of the Secretary of the Treasury, may require the Federal Reserve Banks to take such action deemed necessary to "prevent undue credit expansion." If the president were unable to secure the assistance of the Federal Reserve in these actions, he would be authorized to issue legal tender U.S. notes (greenbacks) to monetize gold and silver, and to allow the Federal Reserve Banks to acquire directly from the treasury, and to hold up to $3 billion of government securities in addition to those already in their portfolios (Kroos 1969, 2719–20). Though FDR never used these powers, they existed, and prompted increased holdings of government securities by the Federal Reserve. The passage of the amendment was also indicative of the state of the Congress at the time where the demand for reflation was strong (Schlesinger 1958, 199–200; Chandler 1971, 273).

The Emergency Farm Mortgage Act was passed in May and provided for the refinancing of farm mortgages. The Federal Farm Loan system, begun in 1916 under Woodrow Wilson, was re-established along the lines of the Federal Reserve System with a supervisory agency, a board, twelve federal land banks, and a private system of joint-stock land banks (Hamilton 1991, 150). Despite Hoover's attempts, by 1932 the Federal Farm Loan System was a failure at meeting the needs for credit (Hamilton 1991, 168).

In June the passage of the Farm Credit Act gave the FCA the power to refinance farm mortgages and to establish a system of regional banks to make mortgage, production, and marketing loans and to provide credits to cooperatives. In its first seven months of operation, it loaned $100 million—nearly four times the amount loaned in 1932. The FCA played a significant role in restructuring the farm debt problem (Schlesinger 1958, 45).

The month of June also saw the passage of the Home Owner's Loan Act, providing for the refinancing of home mortgages and charters for federal savings and loans and the National Industrial Recovery Act, which included a public works program (Barth 1991, 16). There was also a joint resolution by Congress to suspend the gold standard and abrogate the gold clause; and perhaps most importantly, the Banking Act of 1933, which separated investment and commercial banking, established temporary federal deposit insurance, and made the previously informal Federal Open Market Committee an official body.

The Banking Act of 1933

Though Roosevelt had opposed deposit insurance, there was strong support for it within Congress and the general public. Federal deposit insurance was neither requested nor supported by the Roosevelt administration (Golembe 1960). The Chicago economists had supported it only as a temporary expedient to more fundamental reform.

Deposit insurance was purely a creation of Congress where, for nearly fifty years, there had been attempts to introduce it. Its adoption in 1933 was, according to Carter Golembe, due to a uniting of two groups: those who wished to end the destruction of circulating medium due to bank failures and those who sought to preserve the existing bank structure (Golembe 1960, 182). In the temporary plan, deposits up to $2,500 were insured 100 percent; up to $5,000, insured 75 percent; and over $10,000, insured 50 percent. The temporary plan went into effective on January 1, 1934, to be followed by a permanent plan scheduled to go into effect July 1.[1] According to a survey by the Comptroller of the Currency in May 1933, the $2,500 ceiling would fully cover 96.5 percent of depositors and 23.7 percent of total deposits in member banks (Flood 1992, 62). Institutions becoming members of the FDIC were also required to subscribe to stock in the FDIC in an amount equal to half of 1 percent of their total deposit liabilities (Barth 1991, 101–2).

There was also widespread support for the separation of commercial and investment banking because it was believed that bankers had speculated with depositor's funds in the stock market, and when the stock market speculation spree ended, many banks became insolvent. The separation of investment and commercial banking was supported by prominent bankers such as Winthrop Aldrich (Leuchtenburg 1963, 60). In summary:

> The final legislation was a two-stage compromise between Senator Glass's push for unification and the Steagall-Long coalition's desire to preserve the dual banking system. In the first stage, Glass agreed to support a deposit guaranty in exchange for provisions for significantly expanded Federal Reserve authority. . . . In the second stage, the dual banking supporters obtained several concessions, most notably immediate insurance coverage for non-member banks under the temporary plan, and grand-fathering of small state banks under the new minimum capital standards for Fed membership. (Flood 1992, 71)

The two proposals, for federal insurance and separation of commercial and investment banking, were linked in the Banking Act of 1933. The linking of these two reforms is vital in the understanding of the subsequent evolution of the debates and reforms. Though they became identified as administration measures, the crisis nature of 1933 and the support of a new administration merely facilitated their passage. Deposit insurance made banks "safe" not by direct restrictions on their assets, but rather by the promise that the government would guarantee a percentage of the deposits in *all* banks, both good and bad.[2]

The separation of commercial and investment banking removed some abuses resulting from the use of depositors' funds in stock market speculations, but it did not address directly the issue of financing for the capital development of the economy. On passage of the act, J. P. Morgan predicted that the separation would have dire effects on his firm's ability to supply capital "for the development of the country" (Schlesinger 1958, 443). William O. Douglas observed that the act was a nineteenth century piece of legislation that ignored the problem of capital structure and the need to manage investment (Schlesinger 1958, 445). While it is true that the RFC had undertaken the role of providing capital funds for industry, the banking legislation attempted to restore credit availability by restoring confidence in the medium of exchange, and therefore encourage a flow of deposits back into banks. The Banking Act of 1933 was intended to enhance the safety of depositor's funds and thus restore confidence in the banking system. Though it succeeded in stopping bank runs, it did not adequately address the second primary functions of banks—namely, to provide funds for the capital development of the economy. From 1933 on, bankers' pessimism about the economy and their fear of failure hindered lending. Coupled with a lack of power on the part of the Federal Reserve Board, this effectively undermined the ability of the financial system to supply adequate investment funds. In 1929 the ratio of loans to total assets for all commercial banks was 58 percent. By 1934 that ratio had fallen to 38 percent, as total bank assets began increasing after falling steadily from 1929 to 1933. This was also in spite of the fact that total bank failures went from 4,000 in 1933 to 61 in 1934. Though total bank assets were increasing, bank loans remained at about the same level from 1933 to 1936.

Adolf Berle and the Future of American Banking

The Banking Act of 1933 was an attempt to reconcile the views of Democrats Carter Glass and Henry Steagall. The act was a product of a period of crisis, though the immediate bank runs had ceased. No one, including the bankers, was satisfied with the act, and none viewed it as the last word on banking reform (Burns 1974, 93). The debates continued within the administration, Congress, and in the banking community. One who strongly believed that further legislation was necessary was Adolf Berle.

Though Berle had been part of the Brain Trust and a participant in the discussions on emergency banking legislation, he did not join FDR's administration in a prominent position. FDR had wanted to appoint Berle as a Federal Trade commissioner, but Berle declined (Schlesinger 1957, 473). In April 1933, he did become a special assistant to Jesse Jones at the Reconstruction Finance Corporation.

Shortly after the passage of the Banking Act of 1933, Berle gave a speech to the New York State Bankers Association entitled "The Future of American Banking" (Berle 1933a). First, Berle discussed the immediate outlook for banking. The first serious problem was that the

1933 act, together with the Securities Act, gave little recognition of the problem of underwriting. While prohibiting banks from the activity, which was all to the good according to Berle, new institutions to pool money for investment had not yet emerged in the immediate future. There could be severe problems during the transition prior to the charting of a new course for investment banking. By itself, the 1933 legislation was not a long-term solution to the banking problems. Berle stated:

> As to the Glass-Steagall Act itself, I think I am safe in saying that most students of it agree that it is in a transitory phase. We have to regard it as a bridge or a transition rather than as a permanent solution for the situation. (Berle 1933a, 6)

The fundamental problem, as Berle saw it, was that competition among banks in lending activities invariably led to a reduction in the quality of the loans. Berle believed that "Competition between the two banks can only end in weakening one at the expense of the other, to the advantage of neither" (Berle 1933a, 8). What can be done about a banking system in which "bank deposits are largely made by credit"?

Federal deposit guaranties were a faulty solution to the problem, Berle argued, but it did recognize the demand by the public for a safe medium of exchange (Berle 1933a, 9–10). The long-run solution, according to Berle, was to end bank competition with regard to either deposits or credit because "it is not good banking, it is not sound economics, it is not common sense" (Berle 1933a, 10–11).

Though Berle was uncertain about the solution to the problem, he did have recommendations. Since the public had great faith in the mutualized savings banks and insurance companies, Berle suggested that all national and state banks should move toward mutualization (Berle 1933a, 12). Second, and Berle thought the bankers would find this highly disagreeable, is the suggestion that "bankers must be exclusively bankers." What Berle meant was that the banker could not be actively seeking his own self-interest, while at the same time being a "disinterested administrator of the credit and currency machinery of the country" (Berle 1933a, 14). The reforms of the early New Deal had tackled the problems, but Berle believed that the main issue had not been addressed, which was

> to find a means by which we can weld the entire scheme into a single unit—a system where the strength of one is the strength of all, instead

of a system where the weakness of one is the weakness of all; where the central control is at all times in thoroughly responsible hands; where local interests are nevertheless preserved, but under which a national policy is possible, presumably through the agency of our already developed Federal Reserve System. *And under it the banker must be always and only a banker, a trustee for the community.* (Berle 1933a, 16, emphasis added)

In a memorandum on a proposed speech in October 1933 to the American Bankers Association in Chicago, Berle further developed his arguments about the current state and future of banking (Berle 1933b). Since Roosevelt ultimately gave the speech to the ABA, it may be presumed that the speech Berle drafted was intended for Roosevelt's presentation. The long-run solution to the financial problems lay in separating the various functions of banks:

A large part of our banking difficulties arise from the haphazard growth of our banking system. At no time has there been any attempt to delimit the functions, and to provide that in each department of banking there shall be orderly functioning, no department being at the risk of any other department. A start has been made towards this end in the Glass-Steagall Act and in certain restricted legislation but it has not dealt with the major problem. (Berle 1933b)

According to Berle, banks have five distinct activities: (1) savings banks that invest in long-term securities; (2) personal checking accounts that are convenience deposits for money; (3) true mercantile banking that receives deposits from merchants; (4) *Banque d'affaires* that receive deposits but handle securities and lend on nonliquid collateral; and (5) the trust business, both corporate and personal. Berle thought that these functions should be kept separate and distinct at all times. This delimitation should be maintained, even given a system of small local banks which may increase difficulties in equating supply and demand in local markets for the various functions Berle wrote:

However, assuming that these banks were properly limited as to their functions—that is, that they could receive deposits only at extremely low rates of interest (if any); handle checking accounts and mercantile accounts only and *invest their funds only in Government securities, rediscountable paper and mercantile notes*, we could have a system of complete safety in each one of these banks. (Berle 1933b, emphasis added)

The *Banque d'affaires* could be organized to pay a rate of interest but announcing that they were not intended to be liquid—"the depositor in such a bank really investing his money in a pool"— Berle acknowledged that these functions, provided they were kept separate, could be carried on under one institution. Berle questioned, however, whether the *Banques d'affaires* could ever be operated under the same roof as the commercial bank with the segregated savings bank deposit.

A final feature of the system would be one where the government, if it wished, could augment or diminish the flow of funds through government borrowing. In conclusion Berle placed his proposed reforms in the current context:

> This has to be so phrased as to be in substance a mere carrying forward of the principles of the Glass-Steagall Act. For example, the prohibitions on national banks contained in that act are really an attempt to segregate these various functions, though I doubt if the authors of the Act realized it. My thought is that the Act could be so amended that the temporary insurance fund, with or without guaranty, could be a bridge towards the ultimate reorganization of the system. (Berle 1933b)

Clearly, Berle felt that much more was necessary in order to achieve a well-functioning financial system (see Berle 1933c).

Conclusion

The banking legislation passed in 1933 is crucial to the subsequent evolution of the banking system. The legislation restored confidence in the payments system. Though the banking system had been saved in March without deposit insurance, there was a public demand perceived by members of the House of Representatives for federal deposit insurance. There was also a popular sentiment, shared by Roosevelt and Carter Glass, that the separation of commercial and investment banking was necessary. Roosevelt was against branch banking, as was Steagall, but Glass had included it in his original banking bill. The Banking Act of 1933 was thus a union of congressional and executive views of what each believed the public wanted. By uniting these two proposals into legislation, Congress created two potential problems for the future: There was no provision to further help the private sector provide for the capital development of the economy once investment and commercial banking were separated, and the establishment of a government guaranty created a potential situation that could promote bad banking and failures in the future.[3]

Since both the payments system and the provision for financing the capital development of the economy were longer-run problems, and the legislation was really intended to be a short-run solution to immediate problems, it was a foregone conclusion that Congress would have to return to the problems of credit and the payments system at some point in the future. It was to be the credit problem that became paramount over the period 1933–35, while the deposit insurance problem would be postponed for nearly five decades.

6

The November
Chicago Memorandum

The passage of the Banking Act of 1933 was not the end of FDR's concern about economic recovery and the state of the financial system. In his fourth fireside chat in October 1933, Roosevelt stated that the policy of his administration was first to restore the price level, and then seek to establish and maintain a dollar that "would not change its purchasing and debt-paying power during the succeeding generation" (Kroos 1969, 2780). He announced that the government would begin buying gold at a price to be determined in consultation with the Secretary of the Treasury. According to Arthur Schlesinger, the gold purchase program set the financial community in an uproar and the result was a national debate over monetary policy that had not been seen since the William Jennings Bryan campaign of 1896 (Schlesinger 1958, 244–45). With the Seventy-third Congress meeting for a second session, it was clear that 1934 was to be a decisive year for debate on monetary reform.

Though much had been accomplished by November 1933, the central problem that remained was the Federal Reserve's inability to use all means available to it to affect monetary aggregates. In order to rectify this situation, changes would have to be made to the Federal Reserve Act that would restrict the power of individual Reserve Banks, especially New York, while strengthening the power of the Federal Reserve Board in Washington. This was the focus of the November Chicago memorandum, and it was to become the crucial issue in the Banking Act of 1935. The November memorandum advocated greater centralization of monetary authority in the hands of the Federal Reserve Board and open market operations as the primary tool of monetary policy implementation.

The Revised Proposal

During the period March to November, the Chicago economists received comments from a number of individuals on their proposal and in November 1933 another memorandum was prepared. The memorandum was expanded to thirteen pages with a supplementary memorandum on "Long-time Objectives of Monetary Management" (seven pages) and an appendix titled "Banking and Business Cycles" (six pages). Though signed by the same group of economists, this document was evidently written by Henry Simons.[1] The proposal began by noting that government had failed in its primary function of controlling currency by allowing banks to usurp this power. Such "free banking" in deposit creation "gives us an unreliable and unhomogeneous medium; and it gives us a regulation or manipulation of currency which is totally perverse." What was necessary was a "complete reorientation of our thinking" and "a redefinition of the objectives of reform" (Simons 1933b, 1).

With regard to solving long-term financial problems, the Chicago economists argued that "no effective solution is to be found by seeking to realize more fully the objectives contemplated by sponsors of the Federal Reserve Act" (Simons 1933b, 1). Branch banking, another proposed solution to financial difficulties in the economy, implied "an intolerable concentration of power in private hands." Though branch banking offered safety for depositors, this was only because *"the government could never afford to let private institutions like this kind fail."* If this were the alternative, the memorandum stated that a "good case could be made for outright socialization of the banking system (Simons 1933b, 2). The better solution was the "outright abolition of deposit banking on the fractional-reserve principle" (Simons 1933b, 2).

The instability of the banking system is a direct consequence of the fact that the money supply is backed by private sector debt. Whenever the system of loans collapses, the money supply collapses, thus aggravating an economic downturn. In the memorandum's appendix, Simons outlined the relationship between banking and business cycles. According to Simons,

> In a private-bank-credit economy, the quantity of effective money, as well as its velocity, responds markedly to changes of business earnings. When profits rise, customers are more anxious to borrow and banks are more willing to lend. Bank loans increase, and new money (deposits) are created; these changes bring still larger earnings, which in turn

induce further expansion of loans. . . . Once a crisis has developed, and once earnings have begun to decline, the process is even more chaotic. Each bank seeks to contract its loans; . . . Every reduction in bank loans means reduction in the community's effective money; and this in turn means lower prices, smaller volumes of business, and still lower earnings. (Simons 1933b, Appendix 2, p. 5; also see Whalen 1988)

The proposal included many of the items in the March memorandum: (1) federal ownership of the Federal Reserve Banks; (2) exclusive Congressional powers to grant charters for deposit banking; (3) suspension of all powers of existing corporations to engage in deposit banking within two years; (4) creation of a new type of deposit bank with 100 percent reserves in the form of notes and deposits at the Federal Reserve Banks; (5) abolition of reserve requirements for Federal Reserve Banks; (6) replacement of private bank credit with Federal Reserve Bank credit over a two-year transition period, and restricting currency to only Federal Reserve notes. However, they went on to add (7) enacting a simple rule of monetary policy; (8) and achievement of a price level specified by Congress. There is no mention of federal deposit insurance, which had already been passed in June and scheduled to go into effect on January 1, 1934. There is also no provision for a Federal Reserve discount window.

As before, the plan would displace existing commercial banks by two types of institutions: deposit banks and investment trusts. If private companies failed to provide new deposits, then government through the extension of a postal savings system could offer such deposits (Simons 1933b, 6). Investment trust banks would acquire funds exclusively by sale of their own securities, thereby limiting their lending capacity to the funds so obtained. Investment trust banks would provide a service by bringing borrowers and lenders together, and could therefore charge for this service (Simons 1933b, 7). The memorandum also evaluated a return to the gold standard, which it found to be inferior to a fiat system because of the waste of resources in gold production. It recommended the gold standard be rejected outright unless it was a 100 percent gold standard (Simons 1933b, 8–11).

In carrying out a monetary policy rule, the present fractional reserve system had a serious flaw:

any rule which contemplates continuous increase in the volume of effective money has a critical defect if carried out under the existing banking system. . . . In a real sense (such a policy) means continuous taxation of the community by the banks . . . any scheme which contemplates continuous dilution of the circulating media *by private institutions* cannot evade the charge of being preposterous on that score. (Simons 1933b, 11)

The proposal noted that a monetary rule that set money supply growth could be carried out by conversion of interest-bearing federal debt into non-interest-bearing debt, open market operations by the Reserve Banks, an increase in federal expenditures, or a reduction in federal taxes (Simons 1933b, 12). In summary, in regard to policy the memorandum advocated (1) temporary adoption of a rule of monetary policy expressed in terms of a precisely specified price-level objective; (2) commitment to any permanent rule of monetary policy should be postponed until a full examination of the issue; and (3) Congress should provide within two years its recommendations for permanent monetary arrangements (Simons 1933b, 13).

The supplementary memorandum on long-term objectives of monetary management evaluated the proposed rule of maintaining a fixed quantity of circulating medium (either the money supply, money times velocity, or some per capita measure). Though they recognized the difficulty of both determining the appropriate rule and assuring that the monetary authority stuck to the rule, they viewed the rule as superior to alternatives such as price-level stabilization, which they noted was made more complex because of price rigidities (Simons 1933b, Supplement, pp. 6–7). The memorandum stated that the Federal Reserve Act had faulty objectives because commercial paper offered no real liquidity, and that the answer lay in the abolition of fractional reserve banking so that a reconstituted Federal Reserve would have precise power over the money supply. However, monetary management was not to be discretionary, but subject to definite rules laid down by Congress.

Fritz Machlup responded to the November memorandum by noting his general agreement with the reasoning on the supplementary memorandum on "Longtime Objectives of Monetary Management" and the arguments in the appendix on "Banking and Business Cycles," which he noted closely paralleled his own published analysis (in German). He also agreed with the underlying idea of the banking reform. As he expressed it, "If inflationary or deflationary effects are to be avoided, demand-deposits should be covered by a 100 percent reserve and savings-deposits by a zero reserve." The only point of disagreement was the means suggested for achieving the separation of the two functions of banks.

Machlup thought that concentration of power was not a sound argument against branch banking. Further he felt that even 15 percent inflation was dangerous and that raising the price level was not a good substitute for adjusting relative prices. On the other hand, he thought that stabilizing exchange rates was much more important than the Chicago memorandum implied. Machlup remarked "Would you wish to have 'domestic currencies' in the 48 states of this country or do you acknowledge the advantage of a stable exchange rate between Seattle and New York?" (Machlup to Chicago Group, n.d., Simons Papers). As to the rules of long-term monetary management, Machlup was not optimistic about the government's role. If the gold standard could be circumvented, other rules could as well. In monetary matters, government invariably did worse than the private sector. Machlup stated, "The dangers of an uncontrolled system of private banking are multiplied in a system of complete governmental control of currency" (Machlup to Chicago Group, n.d., Simons Papers).

Fisher received a copy of the November 1933 memorandum from the Chicago group. In a letter to Beardsley Ruml, Fisher commented extensively on the memo (Fisher to Ruml, December, 27 1933, Simons Papers). Ruml in turn passed the letter on to Henry Simons who replied to Fisher on January 19, 1934. At one point Simons notes:

> Your remark about the Bank of England reminds me that I got started toward this scheme of ours about ten years ago, by trying to figure out the possibilities of applying the principle of the English Act of 1844 to the deposits as well as to the notes of private banks. This Act would have been an almost perfect solution of the banking problem, if bank issue could have been confined to notes. (Simons to Fisher, January 19, 1934, Simons Papers)

Indeed, a comparison of David Ricardo's "Plan for the Establishment of a National Bank," which served as a guide for the 1844 legislation, with the November 1933 Chicago memorandum indicates a striking similarity on several key points. Ricardo suggested that five commissioners be appointed to the National Bank and be given "full power of issuing all the paper money of the country," and all other bank notes should be removed from circulation. Unlike the Chicago plan, however, Ricardo would have the money issuing department of the National Bank hold 100 percent in gold reserves (Ricardo 1951, vol. 4, 276–300).

Simons was troubled by what he saw as a serious omission in the November memorandum: "We have said nothing about the problem of preventing a transformation of deposit banking which might render our drastic reform quite empty, nominal, and unsubstantial" (Simons to Fisher, January 19, 1934, Simons Papers). Simons attached a tentative addendum of about five pages. Simons reiterated his concern in a later letter to Fisher:

> The problem of just what to do about such things as savings accounts, time deposits, and brokers' accounts still bothers me; but (constitutional difficulties apart) I think I have now some notion of what the minimum requisite measures should be. (This whole problem, by the way, is common to all schemes for really significant banking reform.) (Simons to Fisher, March 29, 1934, Simons Papers)

Despite Simons's reservations, the November memorandum stimulated discussion within the New Deal administration in addition to the various private responses Simons received. In late 1933 and early 1934, the administration debate over the Chicago plan was centered within the Department of Agriculture. This is not surprising given the concern over the debt situation of farmers. Henry Morgenthau was the head of the Farm Credit System, and Rexford Tugwell was Assistant Secretary of Agriculture; both had a strong interest in reform of the financial system.

The Agriculture Department Response

As noted, Tugwell favored government taking over the deposit function of banks. In a memorandum written for Roosevelt on November 14, 1933, he argued:

> The banking situation makes an excellent argument for the separation of various banking functions, such as loans and deposits. We might have one kind of institution which kept our funds for us and charged for it. The post-offices do this now for savings and their services could be

expanded to include checking accounts—with the funds invested in government bonds and therefore wholly liquid and as good as the government itself. The loaning of funds might be done by loan companies in which many individuals with funds to spare took stock. A stock buyer does not expect his money on call and he knows the investment is only as good as the concerns to which credit is extended. (Tugwell Papers, Roosevelt Library; also see Sternsher, p. 314)

Working as Tugwell's assistant was Gardiner Means who prepared two memorandums on banking reform shortly after his memorandum on the November version of the Chicago plan. The earliest draft "Proposals for Banking and Currency Reform," is an eight page document that refers to the Chicago "groop [sic]." The second document is a well organized final version of ten pages, and is titled "Reorganization of the Banking System." This memorandum contains Means's fully developed proposal in light of his review of the Chicago proposals on "Banking and Currency Reform."[2]

Means provided a succinct statement of the basic problem in the reorganization of the banking system:

> How (to) get the banking centralization demanded by our modern economy yet avoid on the one hand the dangers of political lending implicit in government ownership and on the other hand the dangers of irresponsible power implicit in the creation of a few great private banks? (Means 1933d, 1)

The solution proposed, Means argued, would introduce a new principle into banking and defuse the bank branching controversy since his plan would "allow both centralization and decentralization with the advantages of both" (Means 1933a, 5). The basic elements in the fundamental problem were two, according to Means: " 'Taking care' of deposits requires *relatively little judgment* and *can be easily routinized* and administered centrally." Secondly, in direct contrast to the deposit function, "the making of loans requires *very great judgment* and *cannot be easily routinized* or centrally administered." He notes, "It is in the making of loans that political favoritism or irresponsible judgment could play havoc in a banking system." The solution to this dilemma could be achieved through the separation of the depository and lending banking functions (Means 1933d, 2). The lending function should ideally be "performed by local organization completely in the hands of local people, with the local bodies assuming the major risk of loss through poor judgment in making loans" (Means 1933a, 5).

Means proposed a layered structure to achieve the separation of the functions but to provide safety for deposits and depoliticalization of loans. First, there would be a United States Deposit Bank that held only U.S. government securities, which would take over the deposits of all existing banks. Second, there would be local credit banks, which would be private and operated strictly on a profit basis (equity based, no deposits). There would also exist intermediate credit banks, which would be a partnership between government and local banks and not run for profit, much like Federal Reserve Banks. These intermediate credit banks could obtain loans from the United States Deposit Bank, but the private ownership aspect presumably would reduce the political influence on loan making. Using figures for 1933, Means presented the balance sheets (in billions) for this system. The U.S. Deposit Bank, whose liabilities would be the basic money supply, would have $47.4 billion in deposits and national bank notes:

U.S. Deposit Bank

Assets		Liabilities	
		Monetary Medium of U.S.	
Gold	$ 7.8	Deposits	$43.7
Government Securities	$12.0	Bank Notes	$ 3.7
Loans to Intermediate		Capital Stock	$ 3.0
Credit Banks	$28.9		
Other Assets	$ 1.7		

The U.S. Deposit Bank would then extend credit to the intermediate credit banks in the amount of $28.9 billion. The intermediate credit banks could then extend credit to local private credit banks in the amount of $18.7 billion, and the consolidated balance sheet would be as follows:

Local Private Credit Banks

Assets		Liabilities	
Loans	$22.3	Debt to Intermediate Credit Banks	$18.7
Deposits with U.S. Deposit Bank	$ 3.9	Capital and Surplus	$ 7.5
Total Assets	$26.2	Total Liabilities + Capital	$26.2

Means discussed other minor details and possible variations in the balance sheets of each of the institutions. He then discussed the effect of the reorganization on banks, depositors, borrowers, the monetary system, and the government. Banks' total assets and liabilities would decline by transferring government bonds and other securities to the central part of the system. They would be handling deposits in the name of the U.S. Deposit Bank, for which they would be paid. The loaning activities of the banks would be reduced to loans to local individuals and businesses—greatly simplified by separation from the deposit function. The earnings on their capital would probably increase, Means thought, and would turn much more on the quality of judgment they exercised in making loans—earnings would, of course, drop for inefficient banks. Deposit insurance, with its problems, could be eliminated as irrelevant and bank runs would be a thing of the past. Overall the effects would be positive for small and intermediate banks.

The effect for large banks would be quite different, Means believed, because his proposal would reduce their power, particularly over "out-of-town" banks and industry. To reduce their resistance to the proposal, all banks over a given size could be allowed to continue to purchase securities, since they presumably could afford the staff necessary to manage portfolios. Ultimately they would have to be convinced of "the social danger of too great power in the hands of private bankers" (Means 1933d, 8).

For small and intermediate borrowers, the reforms would likely result in lower interest rates since there would be increased competition in lending. For the large borrowers, interest rates might increase, but the likelihood of their coming under the dominance of big bankers would be reduced. Means believed that in general the large industrialists who were independent of the big banks would favor the proposal, and those who were aligned with the big banks would resist the plan (Means 1933d, 8–9).

According to Means, the effects on the monetary system would be significant and totally desirable. We would have a homogeneous monetary medium, it would be safe, deposits would be simplified, and the monetary authorities would have greater control over the money supply and discount policy. Further, it would dissipate lending power and enable, if desired, greater government controls over loanable funds.

For the government, the plan would reduce outstanding debt as it would be taken over by the U.S. Deposit Bank. Means estimated that the reduction could be from $5 to $7 billion since "it would be transferring to the *banking system* debt that belongs there and clearing the Government debt from those items which are essentially business loans and which will not have to be met out of taxes." Other benefits would be to reduce economic power via banking, to increase facility for essential data, and finally, to "allow the Federal Government to perform that basic function given to it by the Constitution—namely, 'to coin (create?) money and regulate the value thereof' " (Means 1933d, 10).[3]

With the onset of severe erosion problems in a number of western states in 1934, Agriculture Department attention focused on the immediate concerns of conservation. As output fell, prices of agricultural products rose, thus further easing financial pressures on farmers. Between 1932 and 1936, gross farm income increased 50 percent, and cash receipts from marketing, including government payments, nearly doubled. The relative price of agricultural products rose as farm debt decreased dramatically. At a time when the economy was still experiencing high unemployment, agriculture was beginning to recover (Schlesinger 1958, 71).

Congressional Interest in the Chicago Plan

By 1930 there was a block of progressive Republicans in the Senate who were urging Hoover to take action to combat the economic conditions. There were twelve members of this group including William Edgar Borah of Idaho, George W. Norris of Nebraska, Robert M. LaFollette, Jr., of Wisconsin, Gerald P. Nye of North Dakota, and Bronson Cutting of New Mexico (Schlesinger 1960, 134–35). They had little success in 1931 and charged that Hoover was callously indifferent to the plight of the unemployed (Feinman 1981, 19–21). At the end of November 1931, Norris called a conference of Senate Progressives to develop legislative proposals for unemployment insurance, public works, and an anti-injunction bill (Feinman 1981, 29). Norris, LaFollette, and Cutting, along with Democrats Burton K. Wheeler of Montana and Edward P. Costigan of Colorado, held a Progressive Conference in March 1932 in order to formulate a Progressive program. On the second day of the conference, Norris called for "another Roosevelt" in the White House. This was widely interpreted to be an endorsement of Franklin Roosevelt as a candidate and an indication that the Progressives would bolt the Republican party and support a liberal Democrat (Feinman 1981, 23–25). The Progressives continued their attack on Hoover and speculation rose about a union of progressive Republicans and Roosevelt. Though the progressive Republicans failed in their legislative agenda in 1932, they did succeed in bringing the issues to the forefront of debate and set the stage for the 1932 presidential campaign (Feinman 1981, 32).

During September 1932, Roosevelt actively sought the support of the Senate Republican progressives. During a swing through the West he visited California (Hiram Johnson), New Mexico (Bronson Cutting), and Nebraska (George Norris). Bronson Cutting was born on Long Island, and his father was a New York City lawyer and reformer. Cutting was a descendant of prominent American public figures dating back to the American Revolution (Feinman 1981, 15). In his speech in New Mexico, Roosevelt declared that his family had been friends with Cutting's for generations. Though Cutting had recently resigned his chairmanship of the Republican National Committee, he had not yet endorsed Roosevelt for President (Feinman 1981, 39–40).

Cutting finally endorsed Roosevelt in October, though he believed that Norman Thomas, the Socialist Party candidate, would be the best president. In a statement issued on October 21, Cutting urged a vote for Roosevelt, asserting that FDR was an average American who had sought to improve the living conditions of the masses and that he was "an idealist who has sought to put his ideals into practice" (Feinman 1981, 43).

Despite FDR's landslide victory, Cutting remained unsure of Roosevelt's commitment to liberal programs. He thought that the Senate progressive Republicans had an important task in keeping FDR on the Progressive path. Despite his concerns about Roosevelt, he was invited to join the cabinet as Interior secretary. He rejected the offer, telling a colleague that he could not "somehow, trust Franklin" (Feinman 1981, 50).

Robert M. Hutchins, the President of the University of Chicago, mailed a copy of the November Chicago plan to Senator Cutting in December 1933. As Schlesinger has noted, Cutting's emphasis on planning and the role of government was very much in line with New Dealers such as Tugwell, Means, Berle, and others (Schlesinger 1960, 389–91). Cutting was quite interested in the Chicago proposal and largely in agreement. He replied to Hutchins:

I may say at once that I agree decidedly with most of the views expressed by the members of your faculty. I wonder if any of them has considered the idea of drafting a bill embodying their views? I suspect that Bob LaFollette would be as much interested in this matter as I am, and if we could get a draft in tangible shape, it would at least give us something to shoot at. (Cutting to Hutchins, December 15, 1933, Cutting Papers)

Hutchins replied, "We'll set to work drafting a bill" (Hutchins to Cutting, December 22, 1933, Cutting Papers).

In January 1934, Roosevelt sent a message to Congress asking for legislation to organize a sound and adequate currency system. Roosevelt requested that Congress enact legislation to vest in the United States government sole title to all American owned monetary gold and "other monetary matters (which) would add to the convenience of handling current problems in this field." FDR furthered indicated that the secretary of the treasury was prepared to submit information concerning changes to the appropriate committees of the Congress (Kroos 1969, 2791). It was soon after FDR's address to Congress that there was direct involvement by the Chicago group in the drafting of legislation to enact the Chicago plan for banking reform.

Conclusion

The November memorandum was written after the passage of the Banking Act of 1933. Unlike the six-page March memorandum, the November version provided a theoretical underpinning for the policy recommendations. The later memorandum was also more widely distributed for critical comment, both from academic economists and economists in the Roosevelt administration. The passage of the Banking Act of 1933 was, as Berle had noted, a step in the right direction toward the segregation of the various banking functions. However both Berle and the Chicago economists agreed that it did not go far enough in this separation. The November memorandum represented a shift of emphasis from the previous urgency in March to restore the payments system to a focus on monetary policy in the long run. The failure to mention the federal guarantee of deposits in the November memorandum probably reflects a belief of the Chicago economists that it would become a permanent feature of the financial system. The provisions of the temporary plan were not necessarily cause for alarm, despite the record of state operated deposit programs. Safeguards had presumably been incorporated into the legislation, such as limits on coverage, and less than 100 percent of any large deposit holder's account was guaranteed.

The concern now was a monetary policy to promote restoration of economic growth and stability. The conclusion of the memorandum was that the Federal Reserve must become more centralized, and the primary tool for implementing monetary policy was to be open market operations. In the following chapters, it will be seen that this view was in line with those of Congress and the administration. It was generally agreed that greater centralization of money and credit was a desirable feature of a reformed financial system.

It is also significant that, in late 1933, support for the Chicago plan was found in the Department of Agriculture as evidenced by Gardiner Means's numerous memos. Also by the end of 1933, the progressive Republicans, who were always on their guard about Roosevelt's progressiveness, became interested in the plan. A base of support for the plan was established at precisely the time that debate over further banking reforms was on the agenda. As 1934 began and the recovery did not appear, FDR became convinced of the need for further changes in the financial system. This set the stage for the Banking Act of 1935.

7

The Banking Reform Agenda:
A Federal Monetary Authority
and Credit Allocation

At the end of 1933, New Deal policies had stopped bank runs through the creation of federal deposit insurance and legislation to separate investment and commercial banking. Despite an easing of the banking situation, the fiscal policies of the Roosevelt administration were not expansionary in 1933, and the economy continued to falter. Gross National Product was 30 percent below its 1929 level, and nearly one quarter of the work force remained unemployed.

Roosevelt had discovered that it was much easier to get depositors to put money back in the banks than to get the bankers to make commercial loans. Because economic growth remained slow, and the real burden of debt high, there were demands in Congress to generate inflation by a government induced monetary expansion. In his January 15, 1934, message to Congress, Roosevelt called on Congress to "improve our financial and monetary system." He argued that because the issuance and control of the medium of exchange was a "high prerogative" of government, the circulation of gold coins was unnecessary, gold was only needed to settle international trade balances, and therefore should be held only by government. He asked Congress to vest in the government title to all gold and that the gold certificates "will be, as now, secured at all times dollar for dollar by gold in the Treasury— gold for each dollar of such weight and fineness as may be established from time to time." This implied that the government could periodically devalue the dollar (Kroos 1969, 2792).

Roosevelt, in a bow to the silverites in Congress, also stressed the monetary importance of silver, though he refrained from making a specific recommendation with respect to its use. In concluding he stressed two principles: a sound currency and government ownership of gold reserves. On January 30, Congress passed the Gold Reserve Act that gave Roosevelt what he asked for with respect to gold, but also included the purchase of silver and the issuance of silver certificates (Kroos 1969, 2793–802). On January 31, Roosevelt devalued the dollar from 25.8 grains of gold nine-tenths fine to 15.24 grains nine-tenths fine. The price of gold went from about $20 per ounce to $35 per ounce thereby imposing a loss on dollar holders, but a huge gain for the treasury's gold holdings.

The debates in Congress often confused money and credit. Whereas the Chicago economists had stressed the control of the money supply through a centralization of the monetary authority of the Federal Reserve, others argued for an expansion of credit by the Federal Reserve. The Chicago plan had advocated a rule of monetary policy to enhance financial stability, while the bills in Congress often viewed the problem as the need to create more credit. Because of the fractional reserve system, a creation of credit by the Federal Reserve or credit allocation through the RFC did not necessarily imply an increase in bank lending. This was demonstrated clearly to FDR in late 1933, as bank lending failed to respond in the way he thought warranted by the bank recovery.

The Demand for a Federal Monetary Authority

Two issues dominated Congressional debate during the period 1933–34: government credit allocation and the creation of a Federal Monetary Authority. As Joseph Reeve noted, the damage inflicted upon the financial system by the 1933 crisis remained long after the cessation of bank failures. Complaints were heard that bank examiners were being too harsh, and as a consequence, small business—whose working capital had been depleted—often could not qualify for bank credit. This led to demands for government credit allocation (Reeve 1943, 71).

In 1934 there were numerous proposals in Congress to extend RFC loans to a wide variety of borrowers with the greatest attention given to direct loans for business firms and closed banks (Reeve 1943, 71–72). A proposal emanating from the Federal Reserve Board and the Treasury at the time suggested the creation of a completely new agency for industrial loans and the creation of a special system of twelve intermediate credit banks (Reeve 1943, 72). The new banking system would parallel the Federal Reserve System, but would make five-year loans to business firms and participate with commercial banks and other financial institutions in similar loans up to 80 percent of the total lent (Reeve 1943, 72). At the same time, Jesse Jones submitted a similar proposal to expand the lending powers of the RFC.

According to Reeve, a more modest proposal was adopted under pressure from Senator Carter Glass of Virginia, which in its final form authorized $280 million in Federal Reserve Bank loans and $300 million for RFC loans (Reeve 1943, 72). In addition, Representative C. J. McLeod introduced a bill in February 1934 to use RFC loans to pay off depositors in all closed banks (Reeve 1943, 72). It was defeated by a skillful parliamentary move that succeeded in preventing full Congressional consideration of the bill (Reeve 1943, 73). The administration also made attempts to ease credit conditions through standardizing and relaxing the severity of bank examinations in order to encourage longer-term bank loans (Reeve 1943, 85–86).[1]

During 1933–34, there were persistent rumors that a central bank would be established with sweeping authority over money and credit. Some thought that centralization of monetary policy was the same as socialization of credit. The Chicago plan had been offered as an alternative to socialization of credit.[2] Again the misunderstanding was due to a failure on the part of many to clearly distinguish between money and credit.

Congressman T. Alan Goldsborough, Democrat of Maryland, introduced a bill (H.R. 7157) to create a Federal Monetary Authority (FMA) on January 20, 1934. Goldsborough chaired hearings of the Subcommittee of the Banking and Currency Committee of the House of Representatives held from January 30 through March 8, and the revised bill was resubmitted as H.R. 8780.

The bill provided for the establishment of a government agency to be called a "Federal Monetary Authority," which would have an independent status similar to the Supreme Court (Fisher 1934, 206–7). The seven directors of the FMA would be appointed by the president and subject to removal by the president or by Congress. The directors would be drawn from industry, agriculture, and banking. The FMA would have the sole right to issue legal tender and national bank notes would no longer be issued. The FMA would own the monetary gold and silver and would be able to rediscount commercial paper for the Federal Reserve Banks and to buy and sell government securities, commercial paper, and foreign exchange. The policy to be carried out by the FMA was:

> To restore as promptly as possible and maintain the normal purchasing power of the dollar, which shall, for the purposes of this Act, be the average purchasing power of the dollar for all commodities during the year 1926. (Fisher 1934a, 206–7)

As amended, the bill provided for five directors of the FMA who would be chosen for their fitness for the position, and not merely as representatives of business. In order to lessen political influence, they were to be subject to removal only by impeachment.

Most of the discussion in the hearings on the FMA centered on the gold and silver provisions and the creation of a central currency issuing body. Goldsborough repeatedly raised the question of whether it would not be possible to divorce the currency system from the debt structure of the economy. As Fisher reported on the hearings:

> Many people have thought that there should be a divorce between the loan function and the monetary function, that it ought to be possible to loan and liquidate loans *without affecting the volume of the circulating medium*. Of this problem no witness offered a solution. (Fisher 1934a, 208)

In his testimony, Secretary Morgenthau urged that Congress wait for nine months to a year before making changes in the financial system. He stated this would give the administration time to put forward its proposals (Fisher 1934a, 208). The Monetary Authority bill was unanimously given a favorable report by the subcommittee, but further action was not taken.

The Cutting Bill

The problems of 1933 and 1934 convinced Cutting and other Progressives that FDR had made a mistake when he failed to nationalize the banking system in 1933. University of Chicago President Robert M. Hutchins had promised a draft of a bill and in March 1934, Cutting wired Hutchins inquiring as to its status (Cutting to Hutchins, March 7, 1934, Cutting Papers). Henry Simons traveled to Washington and met with Cutting on March 16 to discuss the essential features of a bill (Simons to Cutting, March 10, 1934; Cutting to Simons, March 14,

1934, Cutting Papers). Simons did not feel that he was qualified to draft an entire bill since he would not be familiar with many of its technical features. His outline for a bill was given to Cutting and Senator Robert LaFollette, Jr. The actual bill was written by Robert H. Hemphill, a writer for the Hearst newspapers.[3]

To kick off the campaign for his bill, Cutting published an article in the March 31, 1934, issue of *Liberty* magazine entitled "Is Private Banking Doomed?" Cutting's answer, of course, was that it was doomed by the New Deal because government should control money and credit without the interference of private banks. Cutting was quite direct in his intentions: "Control of credit is a government power that does not belong in private hands. . . . Private control of credit must be abolished" (Cutting 1934, 7). Cutting thought that bankers were responsible for the severity of the depression. He wrote:

> During the Hoover administration government credit was poured out generously through the Federal Reserve and the Reconstruction Finance Corporation in the hope that this credit would "sift" down to those needing it. But the credit never got any farther than the private banker. He was the dam where it gathered in a large pool.
>
> The banker was so in control of the nation's finances that even the government was powerless to get its credit to those needing it to lift us out of the depression. How fully he exercises this power is shown by the fact that there was little or no credit available in the United States in 1932 save through the government. (Cutting 1934, 10)

Cutting remarked that unless the administration introduced such legislation to deprive private bankers of this power, he would introduce such a measure (Cutting 1934, 10).

Banks could remain, in Cutting's view, if they held 100 percent reserves against deposits, but they would not be allowed to create credit. Cutting expected a battle against the bankers would not be easy, and lamented FDR's failure to nationalize the banks in March 1933. Cutting wrote:

> The fight against the abolition of the credit power of private banks will be a savage one, for their power as a unit is without equal in the country. Knowing this is why I think back to the events of March 4, 1933, with a sick heart. For then, with even the bankers thinking the

whole economic system had crashed to ruin, the nationalization of banks by President Roosevelt could have been accomplished without a word of protest. It was President Roosevelt's great mistake. Now the bankers will make a mighty struggle. (Cutting 1934, 12)

On May 19, 1934, Senator Cutting gave a speech to the People's Lobby in which he announced his intention to introduce a bill to create a national bank that would have a monopoly of credit and consequently prohibit private bankers from making profits through lending activities. Cutting was quoted as saying:

The bankers are collecting tribute from the community on the community's credit. . . . Commercial banking and issuing of credit should be exclusively a government function. Private financiers are not entitled to any profit on credit. (*New York Times*, May 20, 1934, 32)

Business Week, noting that radical ideas for banking reform were receiving wide support, wrote in reference to Cutting's remarks:

The fact that the more radical opinions are so widespread as to be reflected in the House indicates that the banks have not resold themselves to the public. . . . But unless the banks convince the people the present system is best or unless business picks up markedly by the start of 1935, Congress may go beyond the small changes of the deposits insurance bill and alter the whole banking setup—despite the anguished wails of established banks. (*Business Week*, June 2, 1934, 27)

The bill (S. 3744), developed from Simons's outline, was introduced by Cutting and Congressman Wright Patman of Texas (H.R. 9855) on June 6, 1934. Its stated objective was to "provide an adequate and stable monetary system; to prevent bank failures; to prevent uncontrolled inflation; to prevent depressions; to provide a system to control the price of commodities and the purchasing power of money; to restore normal prosperity and assure its continuance." To achieve these goals, the bill proposed to (1) segregate demand from savings deposits; (2) require the banks to keep 100 percent reserves against their demand deposits; (3) require them to keep 5 percent reserves against their savings deposits; (4) set up a Federal Monetary Authority with full control over the supply of currency, the buying and selling of government securities, and the gold price of the dollar; (5) have the FMA take over enough of the bonds of the banks to provide 100 percent reserve against their demand deposits; and (6) have the FMA raise the price level to its 1926 position and keep it there by buying and selling government bonds. As a consequence of this bill, the only money that would exist would be either in currency issued by the Federal Monetary Authority, or in demand deposits backed 100 percent by lawful money (gold) or government securities. The bill would retain squarely within the federal government the power given to it in the Constitution to create money and maintain its value. This bill would also achieve the other long-run New Deal objectives of raising the price level and strengthening government's influence on economic activity, in this case through monetary policy. The bill even prompted a favorable response in Canada (Abramson 1934).

The bill would grant to the FMA "all of the rights, duties, and powers conferred by law upon the Federal Reserve Board and the Secretary of the Treasury." Though there was no provision for a permanent FMA discount window, the agency would be able to rediscount assets of banks in order to achieve the 100 percent reserve level against demand deposits. The FMA was authorized to expand the currency until there existed bank deposits equal to $250 per capita of the total population, but the rate of increase could not exceed 4 percent per annum. The Cutting bill therefore envisioned a merging of monetary and fiscal policy, but subject to a rule laid down by legislation—similar to what the Chicago economists had proposed. After its introduction, Cutting received hundreds of letters of support for his bill from the general public.

Cutting, who shared Roosevelt's background as a graduate of Groton and Harvard, should have been a natural political ally for FDR. However, Cutting had alienated Roosevelt over the issue of payment of the veterans' pensions. Cutting had worked hard against Roosevelt's attempt to reduce veterans' pensions (Schlesinger 1960, 140). Whether warranted or not, Roosevelt personally disliked Cutting, who was the only Progressive that Roosevelt failed to endorse for reelection in 1934. There is little doubt that the animosity between Roosevelt and Cutting would mean little likelihood of administration support for Cutting's bill.

It is also clear that Cutting did not view the measure as one that would be politically acceptable at the time, but it would help set the agenda. He wrote:

The bill which I introduced is merely tentative, and there is no intention of pressing it at the present session, when, you will understand, passage would be impossible. I introduced it largely as a target for criticisms and suggestions, such as yours. (Cutting to E. W. Mason, June 16, 1934, Cutting Papers)

Robert Hemphill, who drafted the bill, was convinced that the 100 percent reserve plan was the only real solution. In an article in the November 1934 *Magazine of Wall Street*, he stated that he knew of no valid argument against the Cutting bill's reforms and, in fact, believed that they were inevitable (Hemphill 1934, 109).

Hemphill was optimistic that the bill he had drafted for Cutting would play an important role in the debates on banking reform and intended to garner wide support for the plan. He wrote of its importance to Cutting:

I have a hunch this bill is going to inaugurate a prolonged battle which you will finally win, and I regard this legislation as the most important that has been offered in a century . . . I am going to use every effort and every avenue, and believe we can assemble a very powerful and influential group behind this legislation. I am going to cable Mr. Hearst, and am sure he will get right in behind the movement, and am also going to keep closely in touch with the Treasury and the study they propose to make of this question this summer. (Hemphill to Cutting, June 7, 1934, Cutting Papers)

Hemphill's reference to the forthcoming Treasury study undoubtedly reflected his view that the 100 percent reserve plan would be given serious consideration. The studies undertaken during the summer and fall of 1934 by the Treasury formed the backbone research for the administration's version of the Banking Act of 1935. The studies were undertaken in a context that sweeping reform of the system, especially the Federal Reserve, was necessary and politically possible for the next Congressional session. The November election results were very favorable to the New Deal, and FDR was in a strong position to continue overhauling the banking system.

Cutting's bill served to put the Roosevelt administration on notice that there were those in Congress prepared to take drastic and extreme measures if the administration's reforms did not go far enough toward complete government control of money and credit. The goal of the bill was to correct the shortcomings of the Banking Act of 1933. That act had not addressed the problem of the availability of credit, nor had it dealt with the issue of the Federal Reserve's control over the money supply. The Cutting bill sought to make both the money supply and credit availability subject to government control.

In his book *Stable Money*, Fisher stated his support of the Cutting bill and noted that he was currently at work on a book about the 100 percent reserve system. He said:

> As soon as politically feasible, I would go even further, along the lines of Senator Cutting's bill. I would have the Government practically take away from the banks the entire function of creating or destroying circulating medium but leaving to the banks the strictly banking functions such as lending money. (Fisher 1934a, 397)

The Silver and Inflation Lobby in Congress

There had long been demands to remonetize silver, and 1934 provided a new impetus to do so. The silver lobby in Congress pushed legislation to increase the role of silver in the monetary system. The call for the remonetization of silver coincided with the demands for inflation, or reflation, of the economy. The strategy was to stimulate the economy by getting government silver certificates into circulation. Though Roosevelt had previously been given the power to issue silver certificates both in the Thomas amendment to the Agricultural Adjustment Act (AAA), and in the Gold Reserve Act, he did not exercise his power. Congress now wished to force his hand into buying silver (Everest 1950, 37).

One group that was strongly in favor of inflation was the Committee for the Nation, whose chief economists were Irving Fisher and George Warren (the architect of the gold buying scheme of late 1933). Also pushing silver was the radio priest, Father Charles Coughlin. Congressmen from the West, and especially the Progressives, were the strongest advocates for silver monetization. An amendment to the Gold Reserve Act, offered by Senator Burton Wheeler of Montana, to require that the government purchase 50 million ounces of silver monthly until 1 billion ounces had been purchased was defeated only by a 45 to 43 vote (Everest 1950, 37).

The administration fight against the silver lobby was led by Secretary of the Treasury Henry Morgenthau. The Treasury also undertook an investigation of silver speculation and subsequently published the names of the individuals involved. This was clearly an attempt to embarrass silverites by implying that they were strictly acting in their own self interest. A poll of members of the American Economic Association in February revealed that more than 85 percent opposed the increased monetary use of silver. This had no effect on the silver lobby, and more than forty bills relating to silver were introduced in the spring.

Despite its best efforts, the administration was forced to accept a mandatory bill on the purchase of silver. The Silver Purchase Act, passed in June, reflected some compromise between the administration and Congress. The act required the purchase of silver until it represented one-fourth of the monetary reserves of the U.S. government. The treasury was directed to issue silver certificates backed 100 percent by silver holdings.

The Credit Problem and the
Reconstruction Finance Corporation

Through the National Industrial Recovery Act and the Agricultural Adjustment Act, the Roosevelt administration sought to restore the viability of both industry and agriculture. However this required the availability of sufficient credit to enable production to go forward. Unless the commercial banks were willing to make working capital loans to business, the National Recovery administration had little chance of success (Olson 1988, 84). Roosevelt's Brain Trust had worried about the credit crisis throughout 1932 and 1933 (Olson 1988, 87).

Roosevelt had saved the banks, but the continuing problem was the reluctance of banks to loan. The two competing policy options were to expand the role of the RFC and to restructure the Federal Reserve system. Though deposits fell throughout the early years of the depression, bank loans fell by even more. Between 1929 and 1933, deposits fell by 28 percent, while loans fell by 47 percent. In 1934 bank loans were about one-half of the 1929 levels, in nominal terms, falling from $42 billion to $21 billion. At the same time, holdings of government securities more than doubled from $5.5 billion to over $11 billion (*Federal Reserve System* 1959, Table A–1).

How could the economy be stimulated? At this time, the Federal Reserve and its policies were still greatly under the influence of the individual bank governors, especially George Harrison at the New York Fed. The administration viewed the central problem to be the unwillingness of banks to return to loaning for bona fide commercial enterprises. The response to this was the demand that the government get directly involved in the lending business. This is where Jesse Jones and the newly revived Reconstruction Finance Corporation came into play.

Reviving the RFC

The RFC came into existence in the final year of the Hoover administration. It was a direct descendant of the War Finance Corporation, which had functioned during World War I. The WFC made direct loans, mostly to public utilities, banks, and building and loan associations. After the war, the WFC became an important tool in promoting U.S. exports (Olson 1988, 13). The structure of the RFC was very similar to the WFC and had the same purpose: temporary state capitalism in hopes of reviving the private money markets with injections of government money (Olson 1988, 15).

Established in January 1932, by July the RFC had loaned more than $1 billion to banks, railroads, credit unions, and mortgage loan companies. The efforts of the RFC did not provide a stimulus for the banks to begin loaning again as bank failures continued and the accumulation of excess reserves intensified. Hoover was convinced that the credit crisis was prolonging the depression and tried to increase commercial loans, but was not successful (Olson 1988, 17). RFC and Federal Reserve loans to banks were being used to increase the liquidity position of the banks, and not necessarily resulting in more loans (Olson 1988, 26). Despite nearly $2 billion in loans in just over a year to financial institutions, railroads, farmers, and others, the financial system had ground to a halt by Roosevelt's inauguration (Olson 1988, 29).

The Emergency Banking Act had given the RFC the power to purchase preferred stock in banks. This act was largely the work of Hoover's advisers, and most of its features had been discussed and developed within the Hoover administration over the past year. In effect, the first action taken by Roosevelt was to implement a policy that Hoover's staff had developed (Olson 1988, 39–40). As Olson notes, the first major achievement of the New Deal was also the last major proposal of the Hoover administration (Olson 1988, 41).

Roosevelt also appointed Texas banker Jesse Jones as the new head of the RFC. Jones brought to the RFC not only a suspicion of Wall Street and big business, but also an honest and businesslike manner of operation. Unlike other figures in the New Deal, Jones was not concerned with planning the economy, but rather that government money be spent wisely to save capitalism. He was a very conservative businessman and the policies of the RFC reflected that (Olson 1988, 42–45). The RFC was the capital bank for the New Deal (Olson 1988, 44); by the mid-1930s, the RFC was making loans to banks, savings banks, building and loan associations, credit unions, railroads, industrial banks, farmers, commercial businesses, federal land banks, production credit associations, farm cooperatives, mortgage loan companies, insurance companies, school districts, joint stock land banks, and livestock credit corporations (Olson 1988, 43–44). Jones's appointment was also viewed favorably by the progressive Republicans in Congress who had viewed the RFC as a captive of big business. Jones was a smart politician and was successful in building the power and prestige of the RFC among the political spectrum in Washington (Olson 1988, 53). The only dark cloud on the political horizon for Jones and the RFC was Secretary of the Treasury Henry Morgenthau. Jones's problems with Morgenthau were philosophical and personal. Morgenthau was a budget balancer and favored cuts in government spending as a means of stimulating the economy. Morgenthau (or, as called by FDR, "Henry the Morgue") was as far from a Texas "good old boy" as one could be (Olson 1988, 56–57). FDR viewed Jones with respect because he knew he needed the support of the Texas Congressional delegation, but he was also suspicious of Jones's loyalty and disliked his independence (Olson 1988, 61).

Though the task of the RFC during 1933–34 could be stated simply—to expand bank credit—the achievement of that goal would be elusive. Just as Hoover found, Roosevelt realized that increasing the liquidity of banks did not guarantee an increase in commercial loans. Increasingly the banks were holding government securities rather than making new loans (Olson 1988, 82). Under Hoover, the RFC had made only short-term loans, but the RFC was to evolve into extensive federal support of the credit structure during FDR's administration (Olson 1988, 88).

The reform of credit also involved changes in the bankruptcy laws. On June 7, 1933, Roosevelt had signed legislation that permitted an insolvent corporation to reorganize if 25 percent of its creditors in each class of claims and 10 percent of its total creditors agreed (Olson 1988, 89). The Frazier-Lemke Act of 1934 permitted the scaling down of farm debts to a value in line with the appraised value of the farm property (Olson 1988, 91).

In the summer and fall of 1933, the Roosevelt administration pushed the view that banks should sell preferred stock to the RFC in order to enable the banks to give "the credit necessary for the recovery program" (Olson 1988, 77). On October 23, Roosevelt said that he hoped all banks would take advantage of the RFC capital purchase program to put themselves in a position to aid the recovery. By September 1934, the RFC owned stock in one-half of the nation's banks (Olson 1988, 81). By the end of the capital purchase program in June 1935, the RFC owned more than one-third of all the outstanding capital in the entire banking system (Olson 1988, 82).

In the operation of the revived RFC program, there was the belief that the way out of the depression was an increase in bank credit. Both Hoover and later Roosevelt were convinced that what was stifling the economy was the refusal of banks to make loans for bona fide, legitimate concerns. The empirical evidence mounted into 1934 that the RFC program was having little impact in getting banks to loan. There was indeed something to the argument that loan demand was weak, and it was not because bankers were somehow conspiring to restrict credit. Roosevelt was expecting a revival of loan activity in the wake of the recent devastation of the banking system. Banks, it would appear, were not quite ready to return to their pre-1929 balance sheets.

The attack on the RFC came from Morgenthau at the Treasury. The most important study was put together by Jacob Viner and C. O. Hardy on credit conditions in Chicago. The basic question was whether or not conditions were making it difficult for businesses to obtain credit. The conclusion of the study was that indeed there was unsatisfied loan demand, but that the actions of the RFC were having little effect on rectifying the situation (Olson 1988, 166–69). Though the integrity of the study could not be questioned, it did serve the interests of Morgenthau who disliked Jones and was also interested in reform of the Federal Reserve System. By providing evidence that the RFC program was not helping dramatically, Roosevelt would be more open to arguments that the central problem to be addressed was a complete over-haul of the Federal Reserve System.

Adolf Berle wanted the RFC to go further than Jones, who saw the RFC in a short-term role of rebuilding the capital structure of banks. Berle viewed the RFC as a key institution in the financial restructuring of the economy and its role as being one of supplying long-term capital for the development of the economy. Berle also proposed to revitalize small business by establishing "capital credit" banks throughout the country, which would actively seek and finance new investment possi-bilities. In March Roosevelt recommended the establishment of just such credit banks "for the small or medium-sized industrialist" (Schlesinger 1958, 432).

Jones and others, especially Roosevelt's conservative economic ad-visers such as Raymond Moley, were against a long-term role for the RFC. As a result of this opposition, and because other advisers were assuring Roosevelt that a revamped Federal Reserve could adequately address the credit issue, the focal point for financial reform moved to the treasury—especially to the group headed by Jacob Viner, who was a special assistant to Morgenthau.

Simons Reevaluates the Chicago Plan

While the Chicago plan was generating some interest in Congress, Henry Simons was reflecting further on the plan in light of debate and discussions with others. The omission in the original plan, Simons now believed, was the total absence of any discussion of "preventing a transformation of deposit banking which might render our drastic re-form quite empty, nominal, and unsubstantial" (Simons to Fisher, Jan-uary 19, 1934, Simons Papers). This concern about the development of near monies was the most troubling aspect of the 100 percent reserve plan for Simons. In a letter to Paul Douglas, Simons added the post-script:

> Have been a little upset lately about the banking scheme—trying to figure out how to keep deposit banking from growing up extensively outside the special banks with the 100% reserves. Just what should be done, for example, to prevent savings banks (a) from acquiring funds which the depositors would regard as liquid cash reserves or (b) from providing through drafts a fair substitute for checking facilities? After

all, it is important that the reform which we propose should be more than nominal! The problem can be dealt with, of course; but just what is the best combination of expedients? Perhaps you will have some suggestions to pass on. (Simons to Douglas, January 25, 1934, Simons Papers)

Continuing concern is also emphasized in a letter to Fisher in which he wrote:

Much is gained by our coming to regard demand deposits as virtual equivalents of cash; but the main point is likely to be lost if we fail to recognize that savings-deposits, treasury certificates, and even commercial paper are almost as close to demand deposits as are demand deposits to legal-tender currency. The whole problem which we now associate with commercial banking might easily reappear in other forms of financial arrangements. There can be no adequate stability under any system which permits lenders to force financial institutions into effort at wholesale liquidation, and thus to compel industry to disinvest rapidly—for orderly disinvestment on a large scale is simply impossible under modern conditions. Little would be gained by putting demand deposit banking on a 100% basis, if that change were accompanied by increasing disposition to hold, and increasing facilities for holding, liquid "cash" reserves in the form of time-deposits. The fact that such deposits cannot serve as circulating medium is not decisively important; for they are an effective substitute medium for purposes of cash balances. The expansion of demand deposits, releasing circulating medium from "hoards," might be just as inflationary as expansion of demand deposits—and their contraction just as deflationary; and the problem of runs would still be with us. (Simons to Fisher, July 4, 1934, Simons Papers)

When he drafted the monetary section of his pamphlet on *A Positive Program for Laissez Faire* (published in late 1934), Simons included in a footnote what he believed to be the essential problem of our financial system. In that footnote he made three important points: (a) "Our financial structure has been built largely on the illusion that funds can at the same time be both available and invested . . . (b) A major source of instability is also to be found in the widespread practice of borrowing at short term. (c) Effective administration, through a monetary authority, of any sound rule of monetary policy would be impossible apart from the closest cooperation, on the part of the Treasury and Congress, with respect to fiscal practices" (Simons 1948, 320–21).

In responding to Simons's pamphlet, F. A. Hayek, though expressing great sympathy for the general spirit, felt that "in my opinion many of your concrete suggestions will not stand criticism." Hayek thought this applied particularly to the 100 percent reserve plan. Hayek said:

> If it is not possible—and it clearly is not—to regulate the quantity of all media of exchange including even the very liquid resources which will occasionally be used in lieu of cash balances, then it is also impossible to regulate any arbitrarily selected part of the total quantity of money according to any "simple rule or principle of monetary policy." (Hayek to Simons, December 1, 1934, Simons Papers)

Simons wrote back in agreement with Hayek's point:

> I agree enthusiastically with your comments on the 100% plan, and am happy to say (pardonably, I trust) that they are no longer applicable to my position. I have completely repudiated the position taken in the Addendum to the mimeographed memorandum (and taken only tentatively there) as to the merits of fixing the supply of *circulating media*. (Simons to Hayek, December 18, 1934, Simons Papers)

Simons added that he had been unable to explain the problem of near monies to Fisher:

> Incidentally, I'd give a lot to be able to make clear your point (and mine) to several over-hasty and overly enthusiastic converts—above all, to Irving Fisher, with whom I've spent hours and hours without making him see what you have expressed so clearly. If I were to try now to organize all I understand about money, I'd start with the (b) part of the footnote. (Simons to Hayek, December 18, 1934, Simons Papers)

Hayek discussed the 100 percent reserve plan briefly in his book *Monetary Nationalism and International Stability* published in 1937. Though again stating that he felt the 100 percent plan was not a solution, he believed it accurately stated the nature of the problem:

> within the field of instruments which are undoubtedly generally used as

money, there are unnecessary and purely institutional distinctions of liquidity which are the sources of serious disturbances and which should as far as possible be eliminated. (Hayek [1937] 1989, 83)

In a letter to Simons, Fisher replied to Simons's concerns about the development of close substitutes for demand deposits, especially savings banks:

As I see it, savings deposits turn over very slowly and are dislodged in any large volume only by some big force. Even during the depression many people kept on their systematic savings deposits. It seems to me quite preposterous to consider savings deposits as on all fours, or very similar to, deposits subject to check. I feel sure that a statistical study will convince you of this if you will take the trouble to make it. The statistical fact is that anything held for interest does not circulate as fast as what bears no interest. . . . When I see you we can iron this out further perhaps but I have not seen anything in any of your statements so far which would seem to me to justify your fears in regard to savings accounts. (Fisher to Simons, December 14, 1934, Fisher Papers)

Not surprisingly, Fisher provided an empirically based answer to Simons's theoretical concerns.

Conclusion

During 1933 and 1934, Roosevelt and Congress continued to face the problem of slow growth in the economy. Though the payments system function had recovered somewhat, banks were still not lending. According to the Chicago economists, this was directly attributable to the fractional reserve nature of the banking system and could not be rectified without abolishing such a system. The solutions offered by Congress and the administration during 1933 and the first half of 1934 were to create greater centralization of monetary policy through establishing a Federal Monetary Authority and to expand the credit allocation ability of the Reconstruction Finance Corporation.

For personal and political reasons, there was opposition to a further use of the Reconstruction Finance Corporation beyond what previously had been authorized. There were also those in the administration who believed that only a reformed Federal Reserve System could adequately deal with the problem of bank lending. The various bills to create a Federal Monetary Authority failed in large part because they required strong administration support—which meant convincing Roosevelt that such reforms were necessary. This task was to fall to others, particularly Marriner Eccles and Lauchlin Currie, beginning in the fall of 1934. By the end of 1934, reform of the Federal Reserve System moved to the head of the administration's agenda. The Banking Act of 1933 was concerned with depositors; the banking agenda for 1934 was to restore the confidence of lenders.

At this time, the ideas embodied in the Chicago plan continued to be in line with prevailing views found in Congress and the administration. The Chicago plan continued to be debated, but Simons and others reduced active involvement in Washington. This undoubtedly reflected concerns about the possibilities for reasonable reform in Congress, but also the fact that others, both in the administration and economists such as Irving Fisher, began to play a more prominent role in the legislative debates. The ideas of the Chicago plan continued to play an important role even though Simons had concerns about its ultimate effectiveness.

8

Currie, Eccles, and
the Ideal Conditions
for Monetary Control

Though important steps had been taken in revitalizing the financial system in 1934, both Congress and the Roosevelt administration recognized that further measures were necessary to improve the conduct of monetary policy. While Congress continued its debates, the administration turned its attention to the question of further monetary reform. The locus of the research began in the Department of the Treasury, and later shifted to the Federal Reserve System with the appointment of Marriner Eccles to the Federal Reserve Board.

The Freshman Brain Trust

William Woodin was Roosevelt's first Secretary of the Treasury. When he resigned for health reasons in November 1933, Roosevelt nominated an old friend, Henry Morgenthau, to take his place. The appointment was confirmed in January 1934, and soon afterward Morgenthau suggested to Jacob Viner, who was a special assistant to the secretary, that he assemble a group of the best minds he could find in monetary matters, banking, and public finance, to see what they could come up with.[1] This group was referred to as the Freshman Brain Trust (Sandilands 1990, 56–57). In May, Viner sent a proposal to Morgenthau entitled "Plan for Currency and Banking Inquiry." Viner stated:

> The scope of the research should be limited to an inquiry into the general principles which should govern the organization and functioning of our currency and banking system. Its report should be along the lines of a typical British Royal Commission Report, and the detail and drafting of the measures necessary for putting such principles into effect

should be postponed until after there has been opportunity for discussion and criticism of the report. (Viner to Morgenthau, May 10, 1934, Morgenthau Papers)

The group would include Viner, four senior staff, four junior research staff, and clerical and secretarial staff. On June 27, 1934, Secretary Morgenthau announced that the Treasury was undertaking a number of studies in preparation for next year's legislative program in the areas of currency and banking and taxation and revenue (Treasury Department 1934). Those temporarily employed by the treasury to work on the Monetary and Banking Survey studies were Lauchlin Currie, Harry D. White, Albert G. Hart, Benjamin Caplan, Virginius F. Coe, and Edward C. Simmons.[2] It is important to note that two of this group, Currie and Hart, were already known advocates of the 100 percent reserve plan, while Viner appears to have been at least sympathetic.

Richard Lester, a Princeton professor and also a member of the Freshman Brain Trust, published an article in August 1934 entitled "Are Small Depositors Over-Charged?" He noted:

There is a movement on foot in this country to do away with private commercial banking as we have known it since the Civil [W]ar. Certain groups have pointed to the disadvantages in the private manufacture of bank credit or "bank money." To the small depositor who seldom borrows from a bank, such a step should prove advantageous. At present his bankers do not share with him the profits arising from the creation of bank credit; yet, through bank failures or the expenses of deposit insurance, he is forced to pay for the higher risk involved in the process of credit expansion by our commercial banks. (*Bankers Magazine*, August 1934, 163)

In September, the *New York Times* reported that

Another report expected shortly will be that of a committee of experts, headed by Dr. Viner, studying a wide range of economic conditions and data including taxes, banking, monetary policy and many others. The experts are said to be considering the idea of a central bank or modification of the Federal Reserve System as an alternative, the idea in either case being a centralization of credit. (*New York Times*, September 19, 1934, 27)

In the November 30, 1934, issue of *American Banker* it was reported that former Senator Robert L. Owen backed 100 percent reserves. Owen stated that the Treasury had been studying the problems for a year and was about ready to present its reports on the importance of controlling the money supply. The leading figure, after Viner, in this research at the Treasury was Lauchlin Currie.

Lauchlin Currie's Monetary Theory

Currie was a Canadian by birth who became a naturalized U.S. citizen in 1934. He received his Ph.D. from Harvard University under the direction of Allyn Young, and was on the faculty there until he joined the Department of the U.S. Treasury. He was considered an expert in monetary theory and had published several articles on the problems of monetary control.[3]

His book, *The Supply and Control of Money in the United States,* which included material from his articles, was published in 1934. In this book, Currie presented a model of the money supply mechanism in which the major source of variation in the money supply was the level of excess reserves, while the Federal Reserve's primary means of control of the money supply was the level of required reserves (Steindl 1992, 452–53). At the time Currie wrote, the Federal Reserve did not have the power to change reserve requirements. The Federal Reserve actions were firmly grounded in the "real bills doctrine." The Fed was allowed to discount only real bills, and thus its monetary policy was pro-cyclical. Currie saw this as a major limiting factor in effective monetary control. Currie then went on to discuss the "ideal conditions" for monetary control which, he argued, could be achieved with 100 percent reserve requirements on demand deposits.[4]

According to Currie, if it was desired to precisely control the money supply, this could be achieved by direct government issue of all money, both notes and deposits subject to check (Currie [1934] 1968, 151). This could be achieved by a nationwide system of government agencies, which would purchase government securities to expand deposits, and sell securities to contract them. This did not amount to a nationalizing of the banking system, however. The underlying theme in Currie's book was that the confusion between money and credit had compounded monetary reform proposals. Thus those who called for nationalization were thinking of the control of credit by the government. Currie believed that his proposal was superior to nationalization since:

> The merit of the proposal here set forth lies, in the writer's view, in the fact that it divorces the supply of money from the loaning of money. We have noted, at various places throughout the book, the unfortunate consequences of the association of these two functions. Logically they are quite distinct. Their association in modern monetary systems is purely an historical accident. (Currie [1934] 1968, 152)

Currie went on to discuss various difficulties in the transition to such a system, such as the problem of service charges, and the availability of government debt, and he noted additional benefits in that eventually government interest-bearing debt could be replaced by non–interest-bearing liabilities in the form of notes and deposits.

The most serious objection to the direct government issuance of money is not economic, Currie believed, but rather political. The remedy to this would be to establish an independent body, perhaps a revamped Federal Reserve System, which would regulate the supply of money independent of political considerations (Currie [1934] 1968, 155). This concern, as previously discussed, led the Chicago economists to advocate a monetary growth rule to eliminate the possibility of the discretionary use of monetary policy.[5]

Currie clearly recognized that his "ideal" system was not presently politically acceptable. However, he addressed the question of what measures could be taken to move in the direction of greater control over the money supply. The problem in the past, Currie said, was the criterion of monetary control had not played a role in previous financial reform legislation. The use of an ideal goal could be a guide to legislation, he argued:

> While doubtless little can be done to influence the ever changing body of legislators in the problem of control yet if the reserve administration (Federal Reserve Board) had an ideal or objective in mind it could do much to guide legislation and prevent laws being enacted which would tend to work against effective control of money. Before this can happen, however, a radical change is necessary in the whole attitude toward banking at present held by the reserve administration. (Currie [1934] 1968, 157)

Currie believed that the attitudes and the banking theories of the central bank administrators were more important than the relative degree of effectiveness of the instruments of control. This view influenced greatly his actions in regard to the Banking Act of 1935 as will be seen. What was important was not that the reserve requirements be immediately raised to 100 percent on demand deposits, but rather, that the control of the money supply be divorced from the control of credit in the actual decision making of the Federal Reserve Board. This separation was vital because, Currie wrote, "It is, for example, useless to increase the administration's control over money if what it is really trying to do is to control the quality of bank assets" (Currie [1934] 1968, 157).

Currie's Memorandum on Monetary Reform

In September 1934, Currie submitted a comprehensive proposal for monetary reform to the Secretary of the Treasury, Henry Morgenthau. Currie left little doubt that he viewed the present banking system as the worst case scenario. He opened his memorandum with the statement:

> Most monetary writers would agree, I think, that at the moment America possesses one of the poorest, if not the poorest, monetary system of any great country. Instead of operating as a maladjustment-compensating factor it has, for the most part, operated as a maladjustment-intensifying factor. Certainly the severity of the depression must in large part be attributed to the faulty operation of the monetary system. (Currie [1934] 1968, 197)

The memorandum is an elaboration on the "suggested improvements in the existing system," which Currie discussed in his book. Currie did not provide an elaborate theoretical rationale for the proposal (it was contained in the book). The Chicago economists had given their theoretical rationale, which was similar in the main to Currie's, in their appendix on "Banking and Business Cycles." Currie noted that the monetary system had been acting as a "maladjustment-intensifying factor" due to the "unsatisfactory nature of the compromise of private creation of money with government control" (Currie [1934] 1968, 197).

Currie proposed that the reserve ratio for checkable deposits be 100 percent; for noncheckable deposits, 0 percent; and an end to interbank deposits unless subject to 100 percent reserves. During the transition to the new system, Currie sought to insure that banks would not see a loss of income with the increase in the reserve requirements. When the new policy was announced, banks would initially meet the 100 percent requirement with a non-interest-bearing note from the Reserve banks. This note might be left outstanding indefinitely, or only retired upon suspension or merging of the bank. Alternatively, the debt might be retired over a period of time from five to twenty years by the member banks turning over government bonds to the Reserve Banks (Currie [1934] 1968, 200–201). Any excess reserves held at the time of the imposition of 100 percent reserves may be loaned out, but there will be no multiplier effect because of the 100 percent reserve requirement (Currie [1934] 1968, 202). Assuming the reserve ratio was initially 15 percent, once the 100 percent reserve policy goes into effect, a typical balance sheet might look as follows:

Assets		Liabilities	
Required Reserves	100	Checkable Deposits	100
Excess Reserves	0	Note Payable to Fed	85
Loans	85		

There would be no impact on the current earning capacity of the bank, nor would there be a significant increase in expenses, since the note payable to the Fed would be non–interest-bearing and with negligible transactions costs. However if banks experienced an increase in deposits, say in the amount of 10, then under 100 percent reserves they could not acquire any earning assets. Currie proposed that under these circumstances banks be paid interest on that portion of the addition to reserves that could have been loaned out under the fractional reserve system. Thus for example, if deposits increased by 10, Currie would propose that interest be paid to the banks by the Reserve Banks on 8.5 of the addition to reserves. The interest rate paid would be that on specified government bonds (Currie [1934] 1968, 202). Of course, if deposits declined, then the process would be reversed and banks would pay the Reserve Banks a comparable amount.

If it was decided that banks must repay the Fed loans made at the time of the implementation of the 100 percent reserve system, the interest earned on those bonds would be paid to the commercial banks. Again there would be no impact on the current income/expense situation of the bank. However once those initial loans were repaid, banks could no longer acquire earning assets by selling checkable deposits. As a final policy recommendation, Currie proposed that banks be allowed to make service charges for their checkable accounts to avoid incurring a loss (Currie [1934] 1968, 204).

Currie's plan would also create a Federal Monetary Authority (FMA). The FMA would be composed of five individuals, appointed by the president and approved by Congress, who had given evidence by means of publications, or otherwise, of more than a superficial knowledge of the interrelationships of economic and particularly of monetary phenomena (Currie [1934] 1968, 210). All existing note issues would be replaced by Federal Reserve notes and a further extension of branch banking would be permitted (Currie [1934] 1968, 219). In the event that the implementation of the 100 percent reserve plan created a shortage of loanable funds in a particular area, then the Reconstruction Finance Corporation (RFC) would be empowered to subscribe to the capital of local loaning agencies, to make secured loans, or to establish loaning agencies (Currie [1934] 1968, 219).

The FMA would have had only one tool for affecting the money supply after the establishment of 100 percent reserve banking: open market operations. The discount window would be abolished, and with it the possibility of a politically motivated bailout of banks on the part of the central bank. Congress would be directly responsible and accountable for monetary policy.

One difficult problem, Currie noted, was whether the FMA was to be an autonomous monetary authority or responsible to the administration. After reviewing the arguments pro and con, Currie concluded that the arguments in favor of the latter "appear to be the more weighty" (Currie [1934] 1968, 209). The reasoning came from the fact that the populace tended to hold the party in power responsible for economic conditions and for monetary policy. In order to combat the inflationary tendency of such an arrangement, Currie suggested, as had the Chicago economists, that Congress lay down fairly specific monetary objectives (Currie [1934] 1968, 209). As Currie pointed out in stating the argument against an independent monetary authority, democracy should apply to monetary policy as well:

> Majorities may and do abuse their power, but it is worth remembering that as long as we remain a democracy, the will of the majority is

expected to prevail in a monetary as well as in other matters. It is argued that our system of political representation, faulty as it may be, constitutes a better guarantee that the general interest is more adequately represented than it would be by a group of individuals chosen, let us say, by bankers. The same argument appl(ies) to a board appointed by the President for a long term of years. While originally its members may have adequately represented and interpreted the dominant point of view, in time they may become out of sympathy with the changing will of the majority. (Currie [1934] 1968, 207)

Federal deposit insurance would continue for deposits not subject to check up to $5,000. The office of the Comptroller of the Currency would be abolished and his duties assumed by the head of the FDIC (Currie [1934] 1968, 220). Currie stated that his plan was a model of simplicity and its chief merit was "not that it provides for a perfect instrument of control over the volume of money but that it enhances the probability of better monetary management in the future" (Currie [1934] 1968, 225).

Around this same time, Roosevelt had requested that Irving Fisher provide comments on current economic policies. Fisher suggested, among other things, that FDR "read chapter I, left with you, of my proposed 100 per cent system of money and banking" (Fisher to Roosevelt, September 6, 1934, *President's Personal File 431*). FDR forwarded Fisher's memorandum on the 100 percent plan to Secretary of the Treasury Morgenthau and in a memo dated September 15, 1934, said: "This is the memorandum made out by Professor Irving Fisher, and *I honestly think it is worth your looking over*" (Roosevelt to Morgenthau, September 15, 1934, *President's Personal File 431*, emphasis added). Thus during the same month that Morgenthau was receiving a report from Currie on the 100 percent reserve plan, he was being urged by Roosevelt to give consideration to Fisher's 100 percent reserve plan.

Marriner Eccles and the Reform of the Federal Reserve

Currie's views are important because he was soon to become intimately involved with drafting the administration version of the Banking Act of 1935. The key figure in the administration's strategy for banking reform in 1935 was Marriner Eccles, a Mormon banker who had impressed Tugwell and Morgenthau, and had been brought to Washington in early 1934 to work in the Department of the Treasury. It was Morgenthau who suggested to Roosevelt that Eccles would be the perfect choice as the head of a restructured Federal Reserve System.

Eccles agreed to take the job if certain changes were made to enhance the power of the Federal Reserve Board and therefore reduce the power of the regional banks. Eccles told FDR:

> Mr. President, if *you* will help bring about by *law* the necessary legal changes in the Federal Reserve System, then I would welcome any consideration you might give to my personal fitness to serve as governor of the Federal Reserve Board. (Hyman 1976, 155)

Following the Democratic gains in the elections of 1934, it was widely recognized by New Dealers that there was an opportunity to pass new legislation going beyond those previously discussed. In this climate, Roosevelt was very interested in Eccles's thoughts on reform and requested that Eccles prepare a statement of his proposed reforms. On November 4, Eccles brought to his meeting with FDR a memorandum he and Lauchlin Currie had prepared with their desirable reforms in the Federal Reserve system (Eccles 1951, 166). Eccles welcomed Currie's refinements "on points of detail' (Hyman 1976, 155). The central concern of the memorandum was the Federal Reserve's ability to control monetary aggregates, precisely the problems Currie had addressed in his book. Eccles shared Currie's view that the real bills constraint on the Federal Reserve undermined any attempt to undertake an appropriate monetary policy.

The memorandum was titled "Desirable Changes in the Administration of the Federal Reserve System." The memorandum first outlined the history and fundamental problems with the Federal Reserve System as currently structured. It noted that the present structure gave power to each Federal Reserve Bank and its president, who was selected by local bankers. The Federal Advisory Committee, composed of the regional bank officials, met with the Federal Reserve Board to advise on policy, but the Board did not have the power to implement policy. Open market operations and an Open Market Committee, which were not a part of the original 1913 act, were authorized by the Banking Act of 1933. The flaw in the 1933 revisions was that each regional bank could refuse to participate in decisions by the Open Market Committee. The problem was that

> The Federal Reserve Board, which was ultimately held responsible for policy, could not initiate open-market operations; it could only ratify or veto the policies initiated by the Open Market Committee. That committee could initiate policy but could not execute it. The board of directors of the individual Reserve banks, who took no part in forming policy, had the power to obstruct it. A more effective way to fragment responsibility, and to encourage inertia and indecision, could hardly have been devised. (Hyman 1976, 157)

The memorandum was drafted by Currie and generally reflected his views on the problems of controlling the money supply. These were the major points in the memorandum: money is important in business fluctuations; short-term support for emergency financing is necessary, but the avoidance of subsequent inflation and depression is essential; the Federal Reserve Board should take responsibility for monetary policy and the conduct of open market operations; and the reforms were necessary in order to create a true central bank (Hyman 1976, 157–58).

Sandilands notes that Eccles added one point that he considered important, but Currie was less interested in. Eccles thought that an extension of bank assets available for rediscount by the Fed was vital. The Federal Reserve Act restricted discounting to short-term commercial loans and investments. This point boiled down to the substitution of "sound assets" for the Federal Reserve Act's "eligible paper." The significance of this is that it would allow banks to continue making long-term loans, but at the same time provide some incentive to assure the quality of those loans—since such loans could potentially be available for rediscount in the event of a run on the bank (Eccles 1951, 173; Sandilands 1990, 63).

In summary, Eccles and Currie believed that two important changes necessary in the Federal Reserve System were:

1. Complete control over the timing, character, and volume of open market purchases and sales of bills and securities by the Reserve Banks should be conferred upon the Federal Reserve Board.

2. The Governors* of the individual Federal Reserve Banks should be appointed annually by their Board of Directors subject to the approval of the Federal Reserve Board (Burns 1974, 145).

Conclusion

In 1934 the United States did not have a true central bank, but rather a clearing-house with some federal government support that remained tied to the real bills doctrine. In light of the slow economic recovery and the reluctance of banks to loan, Roosevelt and Congress expanded the powers of the RFC. Roosevelt was convinced by Eccles and others that what was really needed was a restructuring of the Federal Reserve System and lent his support to Eccles's efforts. The two key figures in the administration's banking legislation agenda for 1935 were Eccles and Currie. Together, they drafted the bill which they felt would be politically feasible, but would establish a true central bank with the power to control the supply of money.

The Currie plan was essentially identical to the Chicago plan, save for its suggestion that branch banking might be extended. Even there, Currie believed that the 100 percent reserve system would provide a better institutional framework for the evolving financial system than reforms such as branch banking. Currie emphasized monetary control as a primary reason for his plan. This was in line with the November version of the Chicago plan. As a member of the administration, Currie was in an important position to influence subsequent legislation.

There were others who became actively involved in the 100 percent reserve scheme.[6] The most important was Irving Fisher who, after studying the Chicago plan, became a strong champion of the proposal and sought to influence the legislative agenda as well.

---

*The 1935 legislation changed this to president.

————— 9 —————

100% Money:
Fisher's Version of
the Chicago Plan

Following the stock market crash and the loss of a substantial fortune accumulated for over three decades, Irving Fisher became preoccupied with the explanation of booms and depressions and their cure. William Allen wrote of Fisher's activities during these years:

> after the fateful autumn of 1929, the fortune was soon gone. And Fisher's professional activity entered a period—lasting until his death, at age 80, in 1947—that saw him in persistent, almost frenetic effort to refine explanations of "booms and depressions," to devise effective and acceptable policies of recovery and stabilization, and to persuade those holding political power—including the president—to adopt in time such measures of immediate correction and long-term reform. He labored not only with perseverance and intensity, but with imagination, with a sense of pragmatism (even if with zeal which some deemed excessive), and with gallantry. He labored, also, with only diluted effect and modest appreciation. (Allen 1993, 703)

Though he became a very active proponent of the Chicago plan, or 100% Money, as Fisher referred to his version, he had a somewhat different view of both the purpose and impact of the reform.[1] The Chicago economists and Fisher were both concerned about monetary control and the safety of the payments system. However, the Chicago economists were more concerned than Fisher about a resurgence of inflation. The essential difference boiled down to a difference of opin-

---

This chapter has benefited from the excellent scholarly work of William R. Allen on Fisher's efforts to influence Roosevelt during the New Deal (Allen 1977, 1993).

ion on the extent of the reflation that was necessary during the economic recovery. Though both the Chicago economists and Fisher believed that fractional reserve banking was inherently unstable, Fisher emphasized the role of debt-deflation. Simons, for one, explicitly rejected the use of monetary policy to alter debtor-creditor relations.

Fisher on Booms and Depressions

In his book *Booms and Depressions,* and later in an article published in *Econometrica,* Fisher set forth his "Debt-Deflation Theory of Great Depressions" (Fisher 1933a).[2] Though various explanations had been offered for business cycles—overproduction, underconsumption, overcapacity, and so on—Fisher believed that in all great booms and depressions of the past, the predominant factors were overindebtedness and deflation.[3] Though he was open to evidence to the contrary, he had a strong conviction that the "debt-disease" and the "dollar-disease" are more important than all other causes of booms and depressions put together (Fisher [1935] 1945, 121). The chain of events, according to Fisher, proceeded as follows: (1) debt liquidation and distress selling; (2) contraction of checkbook money; (3) a fall in the level of prices; (4) a still greater fall in the net worth of business; (5) a fall in profits; (6) a reduction in output, in trade, and in employment; (7) pessimism and loss of confidence; (8) hoarding and slowing down still more the velocity of circulation; and (9) complicated disturbances of the rate of interest (a fall in nominal rates but a rise in the real rate). Though this is a representative chain of events, there are interrelationships among them that may cause variations, but the principle of debt-deflation remains the same (Fisher [1935] 1945, 122–23).

Fisher argued that it was difficult to determine an exact measure of overindebtedness because it could not be measured simply by the dollars owed, as it was relative to national wealth and income. Psychological factors came into play in determining the extent of overindebtedness. According to Fisher's estimates, between late 1929 and March 1933, real debt had increased by 140 percent (Fisher [1935] 1945, 127). What measures would correct a debt-deflation? Fisher stated:

> If the foregoing analysis is correct, it is almost always economically possible to stop or prevent such a depression, simply by substantially

restoring the volume of money which has been destroyed, which means reflating to substantially the proper price level, and then maintaining that level unchanged. The creation of more money increases buying, which includes buying labor, i.e., re-employment, raises prices, increases profits and so, again increases employment. (Fisher [1935] 1945, 128).

Though Fisher developed his theory of debt-deflation before he embraced the 100 percent reserve plan, he believed that the plan offered the surest, quickest, and easiest means for curing and preventing debt-deflations.[4]

100% Money

Fisher, well known for his monetary schemes, had previously proposed a compensated dollar and a script money scheme to help during the depression. Though learning of the plan in March 1933, Fisher did not immediately embrace the 100 percent scheme as the solution to the present ills of the economy. In a meeting with FDR in August 1933, Fisher did not bring up the 100 percent reserve plan (Allen 1993, 706). However, by the end of 1933, Fisher was an active advocate of the plan and sought to spread awareness of the proposal, giving due credit to the Chicago authors (Allen 1993, 707).[5] Whereas the Chicago economists had provided a theoretical rationale and Currie had given a proposal for policy implementation, Irving Fisher picked up the cause of banking reform and actively sought to promote legislation and educate the public.

Evidently as early as January 1934, Fisher was preparing a bill incorporating the 100 percent reserve proposal for Representative T. Alan Goldsborough. Fisher and Robert H. Hemphill met with Secretary of the Treasury Morgenthau in mid-January, but not with FDR. At this time, Hemphill had already agreed to write the foreword to Fisher's *100% Money* book (Hemphill to Fisher, January 14, 1934, Fisher Papers).

In March, Fisher wrote to Simons of the need to bring Cutting and Goldsborough together in order to get anything accomplished with regard to legislation (Fisher to Simons, March 26, 1934, Fisher Papers). In July, Fisher mailed a copy of the manuscript for *100% Money* to Senator Cutting, among others (Fisher to Cutting, July 16, 1934,

Cutting Papers). Cutting replied that he would study the book with utmost interest, and he hoped that "we can fix something up by next session of Congress which may be satisfactory to all (Cutting to Fisher, August 1, 1934, Cutting Papers). At least four times in late 1934, Fisher urged FDR to consider the proposal and talk about it with him. Fisher wrote later to his son that, though "Congress is ready" to accept the 100 percent reserve idea, "the President is afraid of the bankers" (Fisher to I. N. Fisher, February 24, 1934, Fisher Papers, cited by Allen 1993, 710).

There is some indication in Simons's correspondence that he thought that Fisher was perhaps a little overenthusiastic about the possibilities for banking reform. Simons was leery of popularization of ideas that should be subjected to serious scholarly debate. He thus wrote to Fisher: "I would question seriously the wisdom of publishing the material which you have prepared, unless it were accompanied by a special section for special students in which the problems were dealt with more broadly and with less (or no) regard for popularization" (Simons to Fisher, March 29, 1934, Simons Papers).

Fisher's book was subtitled: "A banking plan designed to eliminate runs on commercial banks; largely to cure or prevent depressions; and to wipe out much of the National Debt." In a letter to FDR on June 11, 1934, Fisher stated that he had a draft of the 100 percent reserve plan ready, but wished to get critical response on it before he sent it to the president. The first edition of the book was published in April 1935.

Fisher proposed that the government, through a "Currency Commission," acquire enough of the earning assets of banks to raise the reserve requirement to 100 percent. The commission would do this by issuing currency. Hence, pocketbook money and checkbook money would be identical (Fisher [1935] 1945, 9). After the creation of enough currency to raise the reserve ratio to 100 percent, a definite policy must be decided upon to guide monetary policy in the future. Fisher suggested that the total nominal money supply remain fixed, the per capita nominal money supply remain fixed, or the real money supply remain fixed (Fisher [1935] 1945, 22–25). The backing for the money would be secure assets, as it had been since colonial times:

> The idea is traditional that all money and deposits must have a "backing" in securities to serve as a safeguard against reckless inflation ... under the 100% system there would be precisely the same backing in

securities and the same possibility of selling securities; but *in addition* there would be the credit of the United States Government. (Fisher [1935] 1945, 16)

If it was desired to return to the gold standard, Fisher observed, the 100 percent reserve system would make it work more effectively. The banks would still get funds to lend from their own capital, savings accounts, and revenue from repaid loans (Fisher [1935] 1945, 17). Fisher believed that the separation of deposit and lending functions would in the long run increase the amount available to be loaned, but that loan expansion would not necessarily involve any increase of money in circulation. The Currency Commission could always expand credit if it wished by purchasing securities with newly created money, provided it did so without creating inflation (Fisher [1935] 1945, 18). Fisher's plan would mean the nationalization of money creation, but not credit.

Fisher also proposed a price-level stabilization rule. Fisher argued that, under 100 percent reserves, the monetary authority could use variations in the money stock to correct price-level deviations from target.[6] The Chicago economists, as noted previously, while acknowledging the possibility of a price-level stabilization scheme, favored stabilization of monetary aggregates.[7]

Fisher thought that the 100 percent system would cure many, if not all, of the ills of the modern economy (Fisher [1935] 1945, 11–14). In his book and his many popular writings on the 100 percent system, Fisher argued that the proposal would eliminate the national debt, and reduce the need for branch banking—thus helping the small local bank, and ending calls for the nationalization of the banking (lending) system (Fisher 1936c; 1937a). In a speech in September 1934 to the Controllers Institute of America, Fisher also argued for the superiority of the 100 percent reserve plan over nationalization of banking:

> There is much talk today of nationalizing our entire banking system. I believe this would be a mistake. All I would do is to take over the *monetary* work of banks, leaving real banking to bankers. This is the true American way. Banking, i.e., money lending, should be left to individual enterprise just as much as railroading or insurance or farming or the grocery business. But banking should not include the manufacture of money as, practically, it does today, for the real circulating medium of this nation today is not pocketbook money but checkbook

money—the money we have—or think we have—in the banks, deposits subject to check. This "money" is really credit, a promise to furnish money and is manufactured by a bank when it extends a loan. Each commercial bank is a private mint. (address to CIA, September 18, 1934b, Fisher Papers)

Fisher felt very strongly that this reform of the banking system was crucial to the survival of the capitalist system. He noted:

I am convinced that, without stable money, the private profit system will some day go. . . . The best available safeguard against the over-throw of capitalism is the 100% system, combined with money manage-ment, to give us a stable dollar. Of all people, bankers should, therefore, favor this proposal if only in self-defense. Otherwise, by the irony of fate, they may some day be the ones to upset capitalism. (Fisher [1935] 1945, 219)

Fisher's Campaign for 100 Percent Money

In his speech to the Comptrollers, Fisher noted that support for the plan came from Chicago economists, Robert Hemphill, Lauchlin Currie, and George LeBlanc, and that Senator Cutting had introduced a bill. If the Cutting bill was not adopted, Fisher said that:

we may at least go half way and adopt the plan proposed by Frank A. Vanderlip and contained in a bill introduced by Congressman Golds-borough. But I hope we may be willing to go more than half way and adopt the entire "100 per cent" program. (Fisher 1934b, 1)

The problem with fractional reserve banking, as Fisher saw it, was that an "essential part of this depression has been the shrinkage from the 25 to the 17 billions in checking deposits." Under the 100 percent system "not a dollar of our circulating medium would have been de-stroyed" (Fisher 1934b, 2). Fisher listed these advantages of the 100 percent reserve system: an end to bank runs; fewer bank failures, a substantial reduction of the amount of outstanding government debt; a simplification of the monetary system since pocketbook and check-book money would be identical; a simplification of banking because there would be a sharp differentiation between checking deposits, which were owned by the depositor and held by banks, and savings deposits, which were an investment with no checking privileges; elimination of great inflations and deflations; and mitigation of booms and depressions (Fisher 1934b, 3). As to the objections that the transition to the 100 percent money system would be inflationary, Fisher noted that the total amount of checkbook money would not change—it would just be made equivalent to pocketbook money.

Fisher argued that the proposal was not radical, but rather was a return "to the conservative safety deposit system of the old goldsmiths, before they began lending out improperly what was entrusted to them for safekeeping" (Fisher 1934b, 4). In 1844, Fisher noted, an act was passed in England to separate the depository and lending functions of the Bank of England. This is precisely what Fisher was advocating for the United States in 1934. The address was reported in the *New York Times*, September 19, 1934, under the headline "Banks 100% Liquid, Irving Fisher's Aim."

The *Wall Street Journal* attacked Fisher on its editorial page, and left no illusions that it regarded the proposal as ludicrous:

> Could there be a more striking sign of the times we are in than the fact that a professor of economics at Yale University espouses a system of wildcat banking under Government auspices? That he thus proposes to remove all effective restraints upon the extension of bank credit and upon the volume of obligations which federal, state and local governments may issue for prompt conversion into circulating currency? ... Professor Fisher's farewell to common sense might be regarded as his own business if the air were not already full of dangerous projects for nationalizing credit, socializing bank deposits, liquidating the national debt with shinplasters and what not. In this surcharged atmosphere a veteran of the fight for soft money urges, with all professorial solemnity, that we take the governor off the engine and allow it to wreck itself. (*Wall Street Journal*, September 20, 1934, Editorial page)

Thus the editors of the *Wall Street Journal* found that the most dangerous aspect of Fisher's proposal was that it allowed government to finance its expenditures by printing money. Fisher responded to the editorial in the October 9, 1934, issue of the *Wall Street Journal*. He explained, "The writer was mistaken however in assuming that the commission would be authorized to issue unlimited money" (*Wall Street Journal*, October 9, 1934, 2).

In his reply, Fisher also noted that it would make banking and deposits safe without any need of guaranteeing or insuring deposits. Fisher acknowledged that the proposal was made by Henry Simons and economists at the University of Chicago, and advocated in a recent book by Lauchlin Currie. Further advantages of the system would be that the banks would be more profitable, and that it would "provide a way of escape from the threat of nationalization of our banking system or of a central government bank. Banking as such, i.e., money lending, would better be left to the bankers." Rather than a system of thousands of banks creating and destroying money and adding to the instability of the dollar on the foreign exchange markets, complete government control would bring greater stability. This was necessary, Fisher stated, because "either we must stabilize the dollar and prevent depression or we must risk revolution." In closing, Fisher observed that Governor Strong had begun moving in a similar direction in 1923 through his open market committee, and regrettably his policies, which might have prevented so terrible of a depression, died with him (see Cargill 1992).

In the October 18, 1934, issue of the *American Banker*, Fisher's talk was called "Professor Fisher's Funny Story." Fisher, it noted, had promised a banking utopia: no bank runs, no losses on checking accounts, elimination of U.S. government debt, and no more great inflations and deflations. If such was promised by politicians, the editors wrote, it would be discounted, however, this proposal came from a college professor who was "held worthy to make the annual address to the Controllers Institute of America." They then asked their two main questions: "What, for instance, would happen if every recipient of a check decided to turn it into a savings account for a longer or shorter time?" and "How are banks to be compensated for costs of supplying checks, bookkeeping, and statements for their business customers?" Further, they asked, what would happen if a large group of businessmen insisted on paying or defaulting on more loans than the amount of new borrowings? Would new loans be a product of political decisions by the Currency Commissioners? However, they agreed that Fisher was "close to a nubbin of truth," which was that "The only successful banking system possible, where virtually all deposit liabilities are payable on demand, is one in which all loan and investment assets are equivalent to cash on demand." The concluding remark referred to John M. "100%" Nichols, the Chicago banker (Phillips 1994a): "The problem of checking account liquidity and savings account liquidity has other angles as funny as his 100% (Nicholsian) utopia of banking" (*American Banker*, October 18, 1934, 4).

Robert Owen, one of the fathers of the Federal Reserve Act, advocated the establishment of 100 percent cash reserve on check funds and turning the twelve Federal Reserve Banks into true central banks. Owen stated that the government "will be compelled to perform its constitutional duty to furnish the country with money adequate to its needs and regulate the value thereof by regulating the supply." Owen's proposal would have the government buy up the stock of the Federal Reserve Banks. As noted in the previous chapter, Owen stated that the treasury was studying the problem of exercising control over the supply of money (*American Banker*, November 30, 1934).

Fisher responded to the *American Banker* editorial in the December 7, 1934, issue. To the point about savings accounts, Fisher stated that they are not money, and their rate of turnover was small. The only time it would be a problem would be in a depression, which would be eliminated or reduced under the 100 percent system. As to revenues, the banks would institute service charges. He also said that Governor Strong was the first great banker to favor what the 100 percent system would be adapted to do best. Though admitting that the 100 percent reserve plan was no panacea, he argued that it would strengthen a weak point in the present system—the reserves behind deposit money (*American Banker*, December 7, 1934).

Additional support for the 100 percent reserve system appeared in an article in the December 7, 1934, issue of *The Commonwealth*. The author of the article, Reverend J. Elliott Ross, noted that Roosevelt had based his recommendation of cancellation of the gold clause in contracts on the fact that there is not enough gold to pay all such debts. Ross observed that there is not enough currency to pay all bank deposits, and thus he advocated a "real honest-to-goodness 100-percent insurance of bank deposits by compelling banks to keep dollar for dollar against deposits." Widespread lack of confidence in the banks could not prevent another situation like March 1933, even with the present system of partial deposit insurance, Ross argued. Though some might be worried about government created inflation due to the complete government control of the money supply, could it be worse than the inflation and then deflation brought on by bankers, Ross asked. The article closed by reminding the reader that "the present system has not worked for the depositors in closed banks; and that it did not work for anyone in March, 1933" (Ross 1934, 167).

Conclusion

Fisher became an enthusiastic proponent of the 100 percent reserve plan, and made efforts throughout 1934 to persuade the public, Congress, and the administration on its virtues. Though Fisher became very vocal, Simons and the other Chicago economists were reevaluating the plan. The crucial difference is perhaps that the Chicago economists were more concerned about a long-term policy for reform, and Fisher was looking at a short-term expedient for getting out of the depression. Though Fisher thought that the 100 percent plan was a long-run solution, he stressed the fact that the monetary authority could directly increase checkbook money by open market operations and thereby stimulate private sector spending. Given that the administration was unhappy with bank lending, Fisher's strategy made sense.

Because Fisher had been associated with a number of schemes, it appears that his advice was "devalued." As Robert Dimand expressed it: "(Fisher's) apparently undiscriminating enthusiasm made economists wary" (Dimand 1993, 17). Jacob Viner, in a letter to Frank Taussig, wrote:

> While there is much to be said for the one-hundred-percent-reserve idea, Fisher is not the person to say these things. His book is superficial and biased and reflects the fact that he has degenerated into a crank propagandist, with the best of motives, but with little regard for accuracy or objectivity. I have in the course of my [governmental] duties had to deal with him rather brutally in order to prevent him from doing even more harm. (Viner to Taussig, October 20, 1934, Viner Papers)

While Fisher carried on his very public campaign, Currie worked within the administration to draft legislation that would move in the direction that Fisher recommended. Fisher and others provided a convenient foil for the administration as it presented its legislation. In this way, at the very least, Fisher's activities played an important part in the New Deal legislation.

——— 10 ———

The Banking Act of 1935

According to Rexford G. Tugwell, an original member of FDR's Brain Trust, the objectives for banking reform as they developed within the New Deal were (1) to make deposits safe; (2) to separate deposits from investments so that bankers could not speculate with the depositors' funds; (3) to raise and stabilize the price level; and (4) to strengthen central management so that governmental influence could be brought to bear on business activity (Tugwell 1957, 368). As already discussed, the Banking Act of 1933 addressed the first two objectives: deposit safety and separation of deposit and investment banking. The remaining goals were interconnected: centralize control of the monetary policy in Washington and undertake an expansionary policy to raise the price level. As the legislative battle unfolded, the administration found itself between the radicals and the Progressives who wanted complete centralization and government control of money and credit, and Carter Glass, one of the architects of the Federal Reserve Act, who opposed any fundamental changes in the Act.

The Banking Act of 1935:
The Administration Version

With the Eccles and Currie move to the Federal Reserve in late 1934, the impetus for banking reform shifted to the Federal Reserve. A Legislative Committee was formed composed of E. A. Goldenweiser, Chester Morrill, Walter Wyatt, and Lauchlin Currie. The plan of action was to have the committee's report sent to the Federal Reserve Board, the FDIC, the Comptroller of the Currency, Morgenthau at the Treasury, President Roosevelt, and finally presented in Congress (Eccles 1951, 193). Eccles, though respected by bankers and businessmen, had never been to college and found it difficult to formalize his ideas in writing. Currie, on the other hand, had written for both academic and nonacademic audiences (Sandilands 1990, 62). The actual writing of the Banking Act of 1935 was left largely to Currie with substantial input from Eccles on the ideas to be incorporated in the bill (Sandilands 1990, 64).

There were three titles in the Banking Act of 1935. The first established a permanent deposit guaranty program, while the third provided merely technical amendments to the Federal Reserve Act of 1913. The controversy over the Banking Act of 1935 was to be over Title II, which provided for fundamental reforms in the structure of the Federal Reserve System and the Board.

The eight major provisions of Title II of the bill were as follows: (1) The offices of governor and chairmen of the board of directors of each Federal Reserve Bank shall be combined; (2) Prior to July 1, 1937, the Federal Reserve Board may waive the capital requirements for the admission of nonmember state banks as members of the Federal Reserve System; (3) In selecting the six appointive members of the Federal Reserve Board, the president shall choose persons well qualified by education or experience or both to participate in the formulation of national economic and monetary policies; (4) Federal Open Market Committee will be created; (5) the Federal Reserve Board is empowered to change the reserve requirements of member banks as to any or all Federal Reserve districts and/or any or all classes of cities and as to time and/or demand deposits; (6) the Federal Reserve Bank may discount or make advances on any sound assets of such member banks; (7) Federal Reserve notes are to be issued by the Federal Reserve Bank and retired under such rules and requirements as the Federal Reserve Board may prescribe; and (8) National banks will be permitted to make loans, secured by first liens upon approved real estate, including farmland, business, and residential properties (*Congressional Record* 1935, 6104).

The wording with respect to reserve requirements is important, especially in light of Currie's analysis of the monetary system. In amending section 19 of the Federal Reserve Act with regard to reserve requirements, Section 209 of Title II of the bill stated:

> Notwithstanding the other provisions of this section, the Federal Reserve Board, in order to prevent injurious credit expansion or contraction, may by regulation change the requirements as to reserves to be maintained against demand or time deposits or both by member banks

in any or all Federal Reserve districts and/or any or all of the three classes of cities referred to above.

In order to assess the distance moved toward Currie's "ideal" system of 100 percent reserves, it is useful to compare his September 1934 memorandum to Morgenthau with the administration version of the Banking Act of 1935 as drafted by Eccles and Currie. It also gives an indication of what was viewed as politically possible. The reorganization of the Board, the creation of the open market committee, and the requirement that the appointees be knowledgeable about economic and monetary matters are in both the September memorandum and the draft written by Eccles and Currie. There are minor differences, though, such as the latter stating five members of the Board. With respect to reserve requirements and in line with his treasury proposal for reform, Currie intended that the board be given unlimited power to alter reserve requirements with the view of eventually raising them to 100 percent (Sandilands 1990; 66). The two major provisions that are not in Currie's memorandum are extending the discounting powers of the Board to "sound assets" and allowing national banks to make real estate loans. In his memoirs, Eccles takes credit for adding the "sound assets" provision (Hyman 1976, 157–60; Sandilands 1991, 63). Currie advocated an extension of branch banking, as did Eccles, but Roosevelt was against it with its connotation of "bigness" (Hyman 1976, 159).

The bill was clearly an administration bill, as Burns notes:

> Drafted by the president's order, the provisions welded together by his design, the contents cleared by his approval, and the law brought to fruition by his intercession, it can be considered as nothing less than a Roosevelt measure. (Burns 1974, 139)

However, when FDR sent the bill forward, he indicated that it was merely a tentative measure written by Eccles, (FDIC Chairman) Crowley, and O'Connor; and he would be happy to have any or all of these three testify before Congress in support of the bill (Burns 1974, 139).

Hemphill and Fisher met with Morgenthau in early January 1935 but did not meet with Roosevelt. In early January there was also the meeting of the National Monetary Conference, which urged the creation of a central bank and the replacement of government interest-bearing liabilities by non–interest-bearing currency (*New York Times*, January 17, 1935).

An article by W. L. Gregory, vice president and cashier of the Plaza Bank of St. Louis, appeared in the *Mid-Continent Banker* noting that "The principal fault of our system is that we promise our checking depositors that they can all have currency on demand knowing that such a thing is absolutely impossible" (Gregory 1935, 24). Of Benjamin Strong and Irving Fisher, Gregory stated, "Men like these have already written the future history of American banking. We have only to read" (Gregory 1935, 13).

In February 1935, the *Wall Street Journal* reported that "Powerful press, radio and lobby support is planned in nonadministration quarters here (Washington, D.C.) for the so-called '100% reserve plan' " (*Wall Street Journal*, February 19, 1935). However the article noted, "No support for the plan has been found in Administration circles and few banking officials are familiar with its details." This is an odd remark when it is clear now that there was considerable interest in the administration from the agriculture and treasury departments.

There was some misunderstanding in the article centering on the implications of the bills on the control over money and credit. The newspaper report stated that the administration bill would centralize monetary authority, but that the 100 percent reserve bill would abolish banks completely:

> The new banking bill would give the government unquestioned control of the Federal Reserve. The 100 per cent reserve plan would deliver the commercial banks to it as well. With such a power to generate credit, a party should be able to perpetuate its rule as long as it desired. Mr. Farley may be able to see its advantages instantly. (*Wall Street Journal*, February 25, 1935)

What the Cutting bill would in fact abolish is the ability of private banks to create credit, but they could continue to operate as 100 percent reserve banks, or convert to finance companies presumably.

The Administration bill was introduced by Senator Duncan Fletcher in the Senate (S. 1715) and Congressman Steagall in the House (H.R. 5357) on February 5, 1935. Title I of the bill made Federal Deposit

Insurance permanent, Title II contained amendments to the Federal Reserve Act, and Title III included technical amendments. The debate over the bill centered on Title II which sought to give greater powers to a revised Federal Reserve Board whose members would be appointed by the president. Senator Carter Glass denounced the Eccles bill as the most dangerous and unwarranted measure of the entire New Deal (Sandilands 1990, 64).

Senator Duncan Fletcher, in noting the importance of, and opposition to, the bill stated:

> In my opinion, the proposed Banking Act of 1935 is, in all probability, the most important piece of banking and monetary policy legislation with which this or any other Congress has dealt. This statement is based upon the importance of title II alone and, curiously enough, title II of the bill is bearing the brunt of almost all of the opposition made to the entire piece of legislation. Please be advised, however, that all of those who are offering concerted opposition to the bill on the basis of the incorporation of title II are almost spontaneous in their clamor for the enactment of titles I and III. (*Congressional Record*, 1935, 6102)

In putting forth the bill, Fletcher continued, the administration was fulfilling a promise to improve the conduct of monetary policy:

> Title II ... deals almost wholly with the creation of machinery for the effective regulation of a definite monetary policy in accordance with the campaign promises of President Roosevelt based on the Democratic platform of 1932 which advocated "a sound currency to be preserved at all hazards" and proposed to put an end to "the indefensible expansion and contraction of credit for private profit at the expense of the public." (*Congressional Record*, 1935, 6103)

Fletcher argued that the provisions of Title II did not represent a radical departure from that which had been legislated. He noted in particular that the Banking Act of 1933 created the open market committee, and the Thomas Amendment to the Agricultural Adjustment Act gave the Board, in periods of crisis, the power to "increase or decrease from time to time, in its discretion, the reserve balances required to be maintained against either demand or time deposits" (*Congressional Record*, 1935, 6104).

Carter Glass

There were two political blunders in the events surrounding the administration's proposed banking legislation. The first occurred when Roosevelt failed to consult with Carter Glass about the appointment of Eccles to the Federal Reserve. The second occurred when the Banking Act of 1935, though discussed and debated within the administration, was introduced into Congress without Carter Glass having seen it at all. Glass was a powerful senator and a Jacksonian Democrat who feared increased centralization of government. Glass held up the confirmation of Eccles and in the end was not present when the committee voted to confirm him and Glass was the lone dissenting vote when the matter was voted on by the entire Senate. The sometimes strained and confrontational relationship between Eccles and Glass undoubtedly had an impact on the ability of the administration to get its bill passed. Eccles himself recognized this in his memoirs (Eccles 1951, 177–81; Schlesinger 1960, 291–301).

Though Duncan Fletcher of Florida was the official chairman of the Banking and Currency Committee of the Senate, this was in name only. As a result of a political deal by the Democrats when they organized the Senate in 1933, it was agreed that Carter Glass, who was the acknowledged leader on banking issues, would be the actual power in committee (Hyman 1976, 162). This was perhaps a contributing factor in the failure of Roosevelt, or any of his staff, to notify Glass prior to the announcement of Eccles's nomination to the Board in November 1934. Subsequently, the administration failed to provide Glass with a copy of the administration's version of the Banking Act of 1935 prior to its introduction in the Senate in February 1935. The result was that Glass was very angry (to put it mildly) and in April 1935 wrote in a letter, "I must go to work on the Eccles Banking Bill and do my best to wreck it. I have some hope also of wrecking Eccles" (Hyman 1976, 175).

The impact of these blunders should not be underestimated in the subsequent passage of the Banking Act of 1935. As Eccles's biographer expressed it:

> It is not clear why Roosevelt failed to consult Glass, but that failure colored the senator's views toward the reforms Marriner advocated in the Federal Reserve System. Moreover, since the Senate hearings on the

confirmation of Marriner ran concurrently with the hearings on the proposed Banking Act, the two matters were fused in Glass's tactics. To avenge himself on the president, he tried to defeat the confirmation of Marriner Eccles as Governor of the Federal Reserve Board, as a means for defeating the key reforms contained in the provisions of the Banking Act. (Hyman 1976, 163)

Glass, who had introduced a proposed Banking Act of 1930, favored the following reforms: (1) restrictions on the security operations of national banks; (2) extension of branch banking; (3) regulation of securities affiliates; (4) distribution of dividends on Federal Reserve stock; and (5) removal of the secretary of the treasury from the Federal Reserve Board (Burns 1974, 8). Glass did not believe that the Federal Reserve Act needed tampering with, and the administration blunders made matters much more difficult. It should be remembered that Currie, Eccles, and Glass were in favor of branch banking, while Roosevelt and others in Congress were opposed to it.

The Legislative Battle

The House hearings went from February 21 through April 9, 1935. On March 4, Senator Fletcher asked to have a statement by Frank Vanderlip on Senate bill 1715 read into the *Congressional Record*. Vanderlip pointed out that in a country with a highly developed banking system, the volume of purchasing medium included not only currency but the volume of bank credit turned into bank deposits. He noted, "This principle is recognized in the bill, and an effective means for the control of the volume of bank credit is set up in section 209" (*Congressional Record*, 1934, 2820). Vanderlip believed that these powers were necessary in order to regulate the value of the currency, but that Congress should define its objective in exercising the power to regulate the value of currency. Further, he stated, "Congress must itself designate the price level which it desires to establish and maintain." Finally, he added:

> The regulation of the value of currency is not properly a banking function. It has, in fact, far too long remained a banking prerogative. There should be clear differentiation between the business of granting bank credits and the fundamentally important policy of regulating the value of currency. (*Congressional Record*, 1934, 2820)

Also on March 4, Senator Cutting reintroduced his bill to create a Federal Monetary Authority and require 100 percent reserve banking (S. 2204). Just a few days before, the *New York Herald Tribune* ran an article entitled "Many Withhold Opposition to Present Banking Bill Lest Legislators Put Forward Measure Requiring 100% Reserves for Demand Deposits" (*New York Herald Tribune*, February 25, 1935, 41). The article stated that many on Wall Street, though opposed to Title II of the bill, were reluctant to voice their opposition. The fear was that a "worse bill" would be put forward, which "might be a bill embodying the theories of that group advocating 100 per cent reserves for demand deposits." The article went on to note that the plan had gained wide academic support. Though no one in the administration had gone on record in support of the plan, the paper noted that "should there be a resurgence of New Dealism the 100 per cent reserve scheme might possibly get some attention in the high quarters." Though some might view the proposed bill as radical, according to the *Tribune* article, "Compared with the 100 per cent reserve plan, it will be seen, the banking act of 1935 is weak tea" (*New York Herald Tribune*, February 25, 1935, 41). The fear of bankers about bills such as Cutting's was that it would put them out of business completely; this fear was unfounded, though the bill would alter the way that they had traditionally operated. It is important to remember that many bankers had opposed deposit insurance, which was still relatively new.

As discussed earlier, Fisher's book *100% Money* was published in April 1935 in the midst of the debates over the Banking Act of 1935. Fisher mailed a copy to the president with a cover letter stressing the benefits of the plan:

> Frankly, I am terribly disappointed at the slowness of your monetary policies. Your silver policy is helping because it is creating new money but the 100% money plan could get us out of the depression *far faster* and keep us out with far greater certainty than any other plan, to say nothing of getting the government largely out of debt to boot. . . . I wish to stress with all the earnestness I can the importance of your giving this matter your personal and careful attention. I know nothing which seems to me half as important for you at this time. (Fisher to Roosevelt, April 23, 1935, Fisher Papers)

Fisher had rushed the first edition into print because of the impending legislation. He mailed copies to many individuals, including

Lauchlin Currie, Gardiner Means, and Bronson Cutting. In June, Fisher testified before the Senate Banking Committee that Title II of the Omnibus Banking Bill would enable the Federal Reserve Board to raise reserve requirements as a means of checking inflation. Fisher was quoted as saying:

> The most conservative step would be to do for our checkbook money what England did for the Bank of England money (notes) in 1844, namely, to back them with government bonds up to a certain point and beyond that point to require a cash backing, every added dollar of checking deposits being backed by an added dollar of cash. Short of this "100 per cent plan," the plan now in Title II (especially if amended as proposed by Mr. Vanderlip) would do more than any other proposal to prevent inflation and deflation alike—to mend our leaky roof and to do so before the next rain. (*New York Times*, June 2, 1935)

A revised version of the Banking Act of 1935 was introduced on April 19, 1935, by Congressman Steagall (H.R. 7617). Steagall's version included section 209 unchanged from the earlier version. Fletcher, as Chairman of the Senate Banking Committee, was deluged with letters opposing Title II of the proposed Banking Act of 1935 (H. R. 5357 and S. 1715). In a statement read into the *Congressional Record*, Fletcher asserted that the changes in the Federal Reserve System embodied in Title II did not "involve a radical change in the present powers and functions of the Federal Reserve Board and the Federal Reserve System as it is now constituted" (*Congressional Record* April 22, 1935, 6103). He explicitly stated that this applied unequivocally to section 209 granting the Board the power to change reserve requirements. Fletcher was clearly concerned that the banking system remained subject to wild fluctuations as a result of bankers' influence on the creation and destruction of credit. He stated:

> It is common knowledge, however, that there now lies within the hands of bankers the potential makings for one of the most stupendous inflations this or any other Nation has ever experienced. And experience teaches us that banker control of monetary policy will probably give us an equally devastating financial whirlwind when that bubble is pricked. (*Congressional Record*, April 22, 1935, 6104)

These comments were undoubtedly directed at the large New York banks and not the smaller banks.

An article in the *New York Times* reported that the bill would likely pass the House virtually unaltered, and that the only difficulty would be "defeating radical amendments, including those for the 'commodity dollar,' fixed-price levels, and other such proposals of the sort" (*New York Times*, April 21, 1935).

The amendments offered by Steagall and Goldsborough were met favorably by Eccles and, with virtually no exception, he readily embraced them (Hyman 1976, 173). One amendment placed the open market operations directly in the hands of the Federal Reserve Board, and the other provided a policy mandate for the Board:

> to exercise such powers as it possesses in such manner as to promote conditions conducive to business stability and to mitigate by its influence unstabilizing fluctuations in the general level of production, trade, prices, and unemployment so far as may be possible with the scope of monetary action and credit administration. (Burns 1974, 149–50)

Writing to Viner, Currie was optimistic about the banking legislation and noted that he had a hand in the wording of the policy mandate in the new version of the bill:

> The prospects for the banking bill are looking better all the time. You may have noticed that I got my objective in the bill as reported by the House Committee. I admit that the word "unstabilizing" in it is not elegant, but I couldn't think of a good synonym. I know that you will derive an enormous amount of comfort out of the assurance that we will have perfect stability in the future. (Currie to Viner, May 3, 1935, Viner Papers)

The revised bill passed easily in the House on May 9, where Alan Goldsborough had assumed responsibility for Title II, and then went to the Senate where hearings were held (Burns 1974, 169). In the House, Alan Goldsborough's proposal to create a Federal Monetary Authority along the lines presented by Cutting was defeated. Also introduced was an amendment to mandate an explicitly declared policy of the United States to restore the average purchasing power of the dollar to the level of the period 1921–29 (Leuchtenburg 1963, 159; Burns 1974, 130). After this restoration, the purchasing power of the dollar would be maintained substantially stable in relation to a suitable index of basic commodity prices (*Congressional Record*, May 8, 1935, 7163). The amendment was defeated by a vote of 128 to 122 (*Congressional Record*, May 8, 1935, 7185).

The Senate hearings were held between April 19 and June 3. On April 28, 1935, FDR made a statement about banking legislation and the need to reform the Federal Reserve. FDR told Morgenthau to testify in favor of unified examination of banks, a permanent plan of deposit insurance, the placing of the Open Market Committee under the Federal Reserve Board in Washington, and government purchase of Federal Reserve stock (Burns 1974, 163). In May, Eccles testified that the most effective way to achieve the goals of centralization, without undue political influence or banker influence, would be to have outright ownership of the Federal Reserve Banks (Schlesinger 1960, 299). Though not advocated by Currie, it was part of the Chicago plan for banking reform.

A significant blow to the Chicago plan came in May when Senator Bronson Cutting died in an airplane crash. Cutting's reelection in 1934 had turned out to be a very dirty campaign with the administration actively opposing him. After Cutting emerged as the apparent victor over Dennis Chavez by slightly over 1,000 votes, the election results were contested with Roosevelt administration approval. In was during a trip back to New Mexico to get affidavits in connection with the contested election that Cutting's plane crashed in Missouri. Schlesinger reports that some of the Progressives blamed Roosevelt for Cutting's death (Schlesinger 1960, 140–1).

The Legislative Battle Concludes

Though the banking bill had little opposition in the House, in the Senate it met with Carter Glass's determined resistance to any changes and the attacks of the Progressives who wanted more radical changes. Eccles's confirmation hearings overlapped with the debates over the banking bill. Glass had hoped to kill both, and one way to do this would be to force Eccles into the position of withdrawing his name. Glass had delayed the hearings citing pressing time constraints that prevented an earlier scheduling. The subcommittee vote on Eccles was 4 to 3, with the deciding vote cast by James Couzens, Republican of California. When the full Senate Banking and Currency Committee met to vote, it was unanimous, though Glass was conspicuously absent. The failure to stop Eccles's appointment led Glass to redirect his attention toward the Eccles bill (Hyman 1976, 176).

Glass scheduled sixty witnesses on the banking bill, the majority speaking against it—especially Title II on reforming the Federal Reserve system. There were warnings of the dangers of political control of the Federal Reserve as outlined in Title II. Eccles testified on May 10, after a final attempt by Glass to place the titles into separate bills failed. In his testimony, with respect to the intent of the bill, Eccles stated, "There is nothing in this bill that would increase the powers of a political administration over the Reserve Board. That matters of national credit and monetary policy should be under public control has been recognized since that System was first proposed" (Hyman 1976, 178–79).

What helped to turn the tide on the banking bill was bankers' realization that previous legislation had made July 1 the deadline for repaying loans from their own banks. Failure to meet the deadline would result in loss of their jobs. The bankers offered a compromise that would extend the July 1 deadline and delay the entire bill to the next session of Congress. Eccles rejected the offer but, along with Goldsborough, drafted a counter compromise. The offer was for a congressional joint resolution extending for sixty days the punitive measures in the Banking Act of 1933, but not allowing the splitting of the titles. Eccles won Roosevelt's support for this proposal, and it was accepted by Congress on June 29 (Hyman 1976, 183).

The last attempt to explicitly introduce 100 percent reserves in the Senate as part of the overhaul of the Federal Reserve System came on July 25 when Senator Nye of North Dakota introduced a substitute for Title II of H.R. 7617 (the revised Banking Act of 1935). The amendment embodied most of the Cutting bill (S. 2204) introduced in March. In addition to the 100 percent reserves and the creation of a central monetary authority, price stabilization was also included, as it had been in the original Cutting bill outlined by Simons. The amendment was defeated on a vote of 10 yes, 59 no, and 27 not voting (*Congressional Record*, July 25–26, 1935, 11842–11906).

Glass set out to rewrite H.R. 7617 to remove those elements which he thought increased unduly the government's role. As an example, the final version of the Banking Act of 1935 limited the Fed's ability to change reserve requirements with this addition to section 209:

> but the amount of the reserves required to be maintained by any such member bank as a result of any such change shall not be less than the amount of the reserves required by law to be maintained by such bank

on the date of enactment of the Banking Act of 1935 nor more than twice such amount. (Section 207 of H.R. 7617)

This effectively prohibited any move to raise reserve requirements to 100 percent.[1] Eccles had argued against any limitations on the *extent* to which reserve requirements could be changed by the Board (Hyman 1976, 186). Glass also had removed a statement that mandated the government to "promote conditions conducive to business stability" in so far as it was possible with the "scope of monetary action and credit administration" (Egbert 1967, 152).

As the debate on the bill came to a close, Senator Glass stated in remarks to the Senate:

> I may say that repeated references to the bill as an administration bill have no justification whatsoever. It is not an administration bill. The President of the United States has never read a word of it, unless he has done so very recently. The Secretary of the Treasury is on record in the printed hearings of the Appropriations Committee as saying that he had not read it. Every member, except one, of the Federal Reserve Board testified before the committee that he had not seen the bill until it was introduced and printed. ... I speak of it simply as the Eccles bill, because nobody, with a single exception, who appeared before the Banking and Currency Committee of the House or of the Senate has advocated this bill. (*Congressional Record,* July 25, 1935, 11824)

When asked if he was referring to Title II, Glass said "Yes; only to title II." Glass's strategy in declaring that the bill was not an administration bill was to defeat it, since presumably any measure with Roosevelt's strong support would pass (Hyman 1976, 174).

Despite Glass's later boast that "We did not leave enough of the Eccles bill with which to light a cigarette," the bill provided for a significant shift toward centralization of monetary policy and thus achieved what Currie believed to be a necessary reform if monetary policy was to be effective (Leuchtenburg 1963, 160). The administration had achieved its goal of enhancing the Federal Reserve's ability to manage the money supply (Schlesinger 1960, 301).

Though the House bill more closely reflected Eccles's preferences, the final bill included changes in the structure of the open market committee and allowed the Federal Reserve Board to increase or decrease reserve requirements. Though not going as far as the Cutting bill in creating absolute control of the money supply by a Federal Monetary Authority, important steps were taken in that direction. The key player for the administration appears to be Lauchlin Currie who, though an advocate of 100 percent reserves, sought to achieve measures that would be politically acceptable. In doing so, he compromised on the 100 percent reserve goal—in the end, his compromise prohibited any possibility that such reform could be achieved in the future.

There is evidence that Currie believed that Hemphill and Fisher were politically naive. In his unpublished memoirs, Currie reflected on the battle over the Banking Act of 1935, "An adviser in Washington is of limited usefulness unless he acquires some sense of what is feasible and how projects and policies should be presented to have the best chance of being adopted" (Sandilands 1991, 65). In a letter to Viner written in early 1935, Currie stated:

> You will be tickled by Hemphill's childlike naivete in suggesting that instead of his bill being introduced and then sent to the Board for comments it would save time if we drafted the bill together at the Board! I pointed out that such a procedure would make his bill in effect an administration measure, and he said very seriously he would not mind that! (Currie to Viner, January 18, 1935, Viner Papers)

Jacob Viner's Assessment of the Banking Legislation

After the passage of the Banking Act of 1935, there were academic and popular assessments of its relative merits. The most important, for the purposes of this study, are those of Jacob Viner given at the annual meeting of the American Economic Association in December 1935 and subsequently published in the *American Economic Review* in March 1936. Viner's views are important because he knew of the Chicago plan and was the director of the studies that were the background research for the administration's version of the 1935 act. He was also a close personal friend of Lauchlin Currie. Viner's article also provides an indication of why he did not support the original Chicago plan, and indicates that his views were much more in line with Currie's on the political possibilities for banking reform.

Viner pointed out that the problems of the financial system in the

United States are unique and this is because of the unique nature of the financial system structure. One of the most important features is our system of unit banking. Though Viner felt that branch banking would change the nature of the problems, he did not think that it represented a fundamental solution (Viner 1936, 107–8).

Given unit banking, we have established a complicated structure of regulation whereby numerous agencies are responsible for bank supervision and regulation. The problem is that the process of bank examination could not prevent a financial collapse in a sustained and widespread depression. The reason for this, Viner argued, is that "The process of bank examination thus tends to encourage credit expansion during the upswing of the business cycle and, more seriously, to intensify credit contraction during the downswing" (Viner 1936, 109). The solution to this problem, according to Viner, would be to require the centralization of all bank examining functions under the direction of the Federal Reserve Board.

Viner believed that the problem of bank runs had been ended with the implementation of federal deposit insurance. While recognizing the arguments that it would remove the incentive of depositors to select strong banks, he did not believe it would be a problem since deposits were only insured up to $5,000; therefore, the protection was for the small depositor (Viner 1936, 110). Though he thought that the FDIC legislation was as good as could be drafted at the time, the problem of the premiums being set as a percent of total deposits might prove inadequate. Viner advocated raising the premiums over time as a precaution against future bank system failures. Had this been implemented, it could have reduced the costs to the public of any future bailouts.

The most important part of the legislation was Title II, which dealt with the central control of credit and which generated the most controversy. The provisions had been criticized both for going too far and not going far enough. Viner remarked that originally the administration had not planned fundamental banking legislation for 1935 beyond the permanent deposit insurance program. Thus,

> The provisions in Title II of the Act of 1935, as they appeared in the original bill, were therefore somewhat of an afterthought, and do not, I hope, by any means represent the full extent of the banking reforms which the present Administration is prepared to support. (Viner 1936, 112)

Title II, Viner believed, was "good legislation in substance and form" and

> goes as far as it was wise to go in the present state of public opinion, of our monetary standard interregnum, and of imperfect knowledge and experience as to the most expedient objectives and methods of credit control. (Viner 1936, 113)

In the long run, what was needed was the centralization of credit control in the Federal Reserve, and though Title II "was moving in the right direction," it did not go far enough (Viner 1936, 114). What Viner hoped for in the future was further reform that would correct the deficiencies of Title II. He said:

> I hope that by a process of further piecemeal legislation the Federal Reserve Board will gradually acquire undivided authority over most of the other instrumentalities of credit control to which I have referred, and that in those cases where the activity cannot appropriately be lodged with the Federal Reserve Board it will on principle be so exercised as to be as neutral as possible in its bearings on the total volume of bank credit. (Viner 1936, 114)

And what of the Chicago plan for 100 percent reserve banking and the Cutting legislation? In his letter to Henry Wallace, Frank Knight had included the remark, "I think Viner really agrees but doesn't think it good politics." Though Viner believed that centralization of credit control was absolutely necessary, he did not think either the current political environment or the state of knowledge about monetary control could assure the success of the radical change in the institutional structure of banking implied by the Chicago plan. As Viner expressed it:

> We still have a long way to go before we can frame with assurance the desirable objectives and limits of credit control and a mechanical procedure to be followed in executing it. (Viner 1936, 115)

Since economists could not clearly formulate the definite objectives of credit, it would be difficult to convince others, and even if they could

> there is no evidence that they could convince Congress of its superiority to the even more confident claims of the Cutting bill, or the silverites, or the Townsendites, or the Coughlinites[;] it seems to me a matter of

rejoicing that the Board has been left free to develop, by analysis and experience, an adequate philosophy of control. Of one thing I feel sure, that if they approach a solution, its merit will be proportional to its complexity rather than its simplicity. (Viner 1936, 116)

In essence, whatever merits there were to radical monetary reform schemes such as the Chicago plan, real solutions required more than simple schemes could provide. Viner believed that by moving in a particular direction, and through the process of learning, we could gradually improve our knowledge of monetary control and thereby alleviate the problems inherent in our financial structure.

The Reserve Requirement Increase of 1936

In 1936 the Federal Reserve Board used its new tool of money supply control, reserve requirements, in a way that was misinterpreted by many to be contradictory to the goal of economic recovery. Eccles and Currie argued that the reserve requirement increase was necessary to reduce excess reserves and thus preempt an inflationary and destabilizing monetary expansion by the banks.

In late 1935 Eccles became concerned about rising bank excess reserves. Gold was continuing to flow into the United States stimulated by the treasury's gold purchases, the dollar shortage, and unstable political and economic conditions in Europe (Hyman 1976, 215). In a statement issued after the meeting of the Federal Open Market Committee on December 17 and 18, 1935, Eccles stated that the level of reserves was far beyond existing or prospective needs of business, though there was not currently evidence of overexpansion (Hyman 1976, 215). The Federal Reserve Board subsequently undertook studies, directed by Lauchlin Currie, of the excess reserve situation. In May 1936, Currie prepared a memorandum for Eccles titled "Some Monetary Aspects of the Excess Reserve Problem" (Sandilands 1990, 88). Currie argued that the large level of excess reserves frustrated the effectiveness of monetary control which, as Currie had argued previously, "depended crucially on the ability of the reserve banks to force member banks into debt" (Sandilands 1990, 88). Currie believed that there was a danger that, given a business recovery, the money supply could increase too rapidly and generate inflation.

Eccles did not wish to increase reserves without presidential approval, though the Board had been given the power to do so. Eccles did not want FDR to be held responsible for the Fed's actions. On July 9, 1936, Eccles went to the White House to explain to Roosevelt the reasons he believed a 50 percent increase in required reserves was necessary. He gave FDR a memorandum specifying that the reserve requirement increase might be interpreted as putting the brakes on the recovery. Eccles did not agree that it would do so and stated in the memorandum:

> The action contemplated (reserve requirement increase) will not satisfy those groups which have been clamoring for action in the hope that it would stiffen interest rates. If there was any serious danger of such a result, I should oppose action. I would not favor action under any circumstances unless assured of authority through the Open Market Executive Committee to counteract any recession of a point or more in the price of government securities. (Hyman 1976, 216)

As Friedman and Schwartz recognized in their review of this period, the increase in reserve requirements was not intended to affect primarily current conditions (Friedman and Schwartz 1963, 517).

With Roosevelt's behind-the-scenes agreement, the Federal Reserve Board ordered a 50 percent increase in the reserve requirements of member banks effective August 15, 1936. The increase not only provoked the public's concerns of a tightening of monetary policy, but also upset Secretary of the Treasury Morgenthau, who had not been given prior notice of the reserve requirement increase (Hyman 1976, 216–17). This contributed to further bad feelings between Morgenthau and Eccles, despite the fact that Eccles could reply that circumstances made it difficult to inform Morgenthau, and in any event, Roosevelt himself approved the increase. According to Hyman, the $1.79 billion in excess reserves merely siphoned off what was superfluous to the needs of business and therefore had no impact on credit availability (Hyman 1976, 217). This is in line with the arguments that Eccles and Currie had continually made. However Friedman and Schwartz—while recognizing the Federal Reserve Board actions were "entirely understandable," and that they were not intended to be contractionary since open market operations were to counter any dramatic disturbances in the credit markets—conclude that the increase did have important current effects (Friedman and Schwartz 1963, 525–26). However they note that, among the Federal Reserve Board members, only Governor Eccles favored large-scale purchases or a rescinding of the final rise in reserve requirements, which was announced in January 1937 to become effective in March (Friedman and Schwartz 1963, 527).

In a memorandum to Eccles on January 25, 1937, Currie warned of the long-run restrictive effects of reserve requirements against *time* deposits. In a second memorandum on the same date, he argued further that the present volume of money at a "normal" velocity of circulation was adequate to finance full economic recovery and that further expansion entailed inflationary risks (Sandilands 1990, 88). Thus in 1935–37, monetary policy was undertaken entirely in line with Eccles's and Currie's analysis of monetary control: Increasing required reserves was a precautionary measure rather than a restrictive measure and a way to enhance the effectiveness of monetary policy (Sandilands 1990, 89; Currie 1980).

Though Friedman and Schwartz attribute the recession of 1937–38 to monetary policy, Currie's analysis pointed out the importance of the decline in government expenditures in the period from September 1936 to March 1937. This is consistent with the "Keynesian" analysis of macroeconomics that Currie was developing independently of the work of John Maynard Keynes and other economists (Sandilands 1990, 89; also see Steindl 1992).

At the same time that Currie was concerned with the excess reserve problem and the recession of 1937–38, he wrote another memorandum for Eccles on the 100 percent reserve plan. This is further evidence that while he was developing a "Keynesian" analysis of economic downturns, he remained convinced that monetary reform along the lines of the 100 percent reserve plan was essential to enable the government to use all available means to combat the recession (Sandilands 1990, 385).

Conclusion

The Chicago plan for banking reform was not fully implemented in the period 1933–35, but it clearly had an influence on the ultimate legislation and provided a set of guiding principles adhered to by Lauchlin Currie, Jacob Viner, and others. *The Banking Act of 1935 went as far as was politically acceptable, given the current state of knowledge about central banking in the United States in 1935, toward the Chi-*

cago plan. Though the influence of the proposals was substantial, there are at least four reasons why the proposals to separate money and credit were not adopted: (1) administration blunders in the handling of the banking legislation; (2) an ill-informed public; (3) the death of Senator Bronson Cutting; and (4) a belief that the Banking Act of 1935 would not be the final New Deal banking legislation.

There were two political blunders in the events surrounding the administration's proposed banking legislation. The first occurred when Roosevelt failed to consult with Carter Glass about the appointment of Eccles to the Federal Reserve. The second occurred when the Banking Act of 1935, though discussed and debated within the administration, was introduced into Congress without Carter Glass having seen it at all. The impact of these blunders should not be underestimated in the subsequent passage of the Banking Act of 1935.[2]

The second reason for the failure of the plans was a misunderstanding of the implications of the 100 percent reserve plan. Despite the efforts of Irving Fisher to educate the public, there was a characterization of the plan as one to end private banking (Allen 1993). This view was fueled by articles such as that written by Bronson Cutting titled "Is Private Banking Doomed?"—which he answers with a resounding "yes" (Cutting 1934). The fear of political control of credit by the administration undermined popular support for the 100 percent reserve plan.

The third reason for the failure of the reforms proposals was the death of its leading advocate, Bronson Cutting, who was killed in an airplane crash while the debates on the Banking Act of 1935 were being held. Cutting was a rising star in the Senate, whereas Carter Glass, in his late seventies, was near the twilight of his Senate career. Had he lived, Cutting would have continued fighting for his bill.

The final reason the reforms were not adopted was a belief that the Banking Act of 1935, far from being an end to New Deal banking legislation, was the first step in reform. This view was prominently expressed by Jacob Viner and reflected a general sentiment among many economists and politicians.

The efforts of Fisher, Hemphill, and others to convince members of Congress and the administration that the 100 percent reserve plan was superior failed. Fisher and others failed to present their ideas in a way that persuaded the public or politicians (Hotson 1987). Had the proponents of the Chicago plan been able to convince the public and politicians that 100 percent reserve at demand deposit banks were superior to deposit insurance, the legislative outcome might have been different (McLane 1980, 94).

The Chicago plan represented an "ideal" system of control and, as such, represented a goal for future evolution. Evidence for this comes from the fact that the debate over the Chicago plan continued long after the New Deal legislation. In 1935 academic economists began assessing and refining the plan. At the same time, Irving Fisher increased his efforts to garner popular and political support for the 100 percent money plan.

——— 11 ———

Academic Views of the Chicago Plan

The Chicago/Currie/Fisher proposals for 100 percent reserve banking stimulated debate in the academic journals as well as the popular press. Separating the academic and nonacademic debates in one sense is an artificial division since many of the academics (Currie, Viner, and so on) were also involved in the political realm. The 1933 memorandums were disseminated to both academics and nonacademics. As already discussed, the plan was known and debated in the Roosevelt administration and Congress. The academic debates over the Chicago plan began as Simons responded to privately written comments from other economists about the original memorandums. However, in addition to the private debates, articles were published in leading economics journals as well as other academic publications. Even the passage of the Banking Act of 1935 did not end the discussion of the Chicago plan, which really began to generate widespread academic interest after 1935. Though at first reflection, one might think that the debate was for nought, as argued above, the Banking Act of 1935 was not viewed at the time as the last word on banking reform. Today we tend to think that the New Deal legislation was intended as a long-term solution, but in fact it was not. There were many who felt that more needed to be done.

Writing in 1936, Simons argued that the 100 percent reserve plan only made sense in terms of comprehensive reform:

> The so-called "100 per cent" scheme of banking reform can easily be defended only as the proper first step toward reconstruction of our whole financial organization. Standing by itself, as an isolated measure, it would promise little but evasion—small effects at the price of serious disturbance—and would deserve classification as merely another crank scheme. (Simons 1948, 331)

The comprehensive reform would include definite statements of the policy objectives of the monetary authority and rules of conduct.

Alternative "Chicago" Plans: Douglas and Whittlesey

Though Simons was the chief architect of the 1933 Chicago proposals for banking reform, others connected with the economics department at the University of Chicago presented their own views on the problems of banking and the 100 percent reserve plan. Simons's late 1934 publication of *A Positive Program for Laissez Faire*, number 15 in the University of Chicago "Public Policy Pamphlet" series, was followed by a pamphlet by Charles R. Whittlesey of Princeton University on *Banking and the New Deal*—which, according to the series editor, continued the discussion initiated by Simons's pamphlet (Whittlesey 1935, iii). Paul H. Douglas, who had signed the original memorandums and was later to become a U.S. Senator from Illinois, published a book in 1935 titled *Controlling Depressions* (Douglas 1935).

The Whittlesey pamphlet provided an assessment of the Chicago plan in light of legislation passed in 1933 and 1934, and alternative proposals for monetary reform. Whittlesey opens with a discussion of the defects of the American banking system from 1913 to 1933. He concludes that the Federal Reserve System did not operate well to prevent bank failures, there was a lack of unification in the banking structure, commercial and investment banking were entangled, and there was a perverse elasticity of bank credit. To the issue of failures, Whittlesey found it ironic that bankers were hostile to inflation given that deflation of asset values had led to massive bank failures (Whittlesey 1935, 2). The division of the banks into state and national charters had been a source of weakness often because the competition between government chartering at the state and national level was a "consequent weakening of requirements in both jurisdictions" (Whittlesey 1935, 3). Whittlesey argued that the mingling of investment and commercial banking, though not necessarily the rule, did lead to abuse. Relying on the real bills doctrine led the Federal Reserve to a "perverse elasticity" of money supply because it was precisely in times of economic downturn that the supply of commercial paper declined, thus leading the Federal Reserve to exacerbate the situation (Whittlesey 1935, 4).

Under the New Deal legislation, bank failures were dealt with through a guaranty of bank deposits. However, Whittlesey argued, "This deposit guaranty law is an admission of defeat. It acknowledges that for political rather than economic reasons it is not now feasible to give this country a genuinely strong banking system" (Whittlesey 1935, 13).

The guaranty program would lead, Whittlesey believed, to a system whereby the least cautious banks would through competition lead others to do the same, and thus what purports to be a system of strengthening the banking system is in fact "little more than a device for distributing losses, on a basis of expediency rather than equity, among the banks of the country" (Whittlesey 1935, 13).

The problem of unification of the banking system was met indirectly through the provision of incentives to join the Federal Reserve System, while the Banking Act of 1933 provided for the segregation of commercial and investment banking (Whittlesey 1935, 14–15).

Whittlesey viewed the provision of the Thomas Amendment to the Agricultural Adjustment Act, which allowed the Federal Reserve Board to increase or decrease the legal reserves of member banks, as an important tool "designed to accomplish immediately and easily what open-market operations accomplish more slowly." The amendment thus provided a means of "wiping out excess reserves that might lead to credit inflation, or of creating them with a view to encouraging expansion" (Whittlesey 1935, 15).

Whittlesey divided the proposals for further banking reform into three groups: conservative, moderate, and radical. The conservative plan favored "a refurbishing of the present banking structure with a few simple and becoming patches." The goal would be to allow a gradual process of evolution to develop a more "perfect" banking system. The conservative banking reform proponents would allow for a "trial and error" strategy for bank reform, much as evolved in England (Whittlesey 1935, 18–19).

The moderates would go as far as eliminating state banks and to promote the unification of the banking system through the development of a system of a few large banks with many branches. This proposal would meet with the resistance of the small unit banks throughout the country. The moderates would also propose further extensions of the separation of banking functions along the lines of the Banking Act of 1933. This might involve the segregation of assets held against different classes of liabilities. Whittlesey would also include nationalization of the banking system under the moderate proposals which, despite being a socialistic change, would involve "no fundamental departure from traditional banking structure or principles" (Whittlesey 1935, 21).

Whittlesey placed the 100 percent reserve plan in the "radical" category. He noted that the plan was "*radical* only in the original meaning of that term, that is, that it goes to the root of the problem" (Whittlesey 1935, 21). He was enthusiastic on the goals of the 100% reserve plan:

> Far from proposing a weakening of the present banking structure, it represents an attempt to extend to deposit credit the safeguards that have for years been attached to other forms of the circulating medium. The plan aims to take away the power of banks to expand the volume of deposit credit on the basis of fractional reserves. It is the only proposal designed to correct perverse elasticity, which was previously pointed out as one of the chief defects of the present banking system. It has as yet received little attention outside academic circles, but in spite of this fact bills embodying the essentials of the plan have already been introduced into Congress, and *it is certain to figure prominently in future discussion of banking reforms*. (Whittlesey 1935, 21, emphasis added)

Whittlesey provided a sympathetic restatement of the proposal as found in Simons's *A Positive Program for Laissez Faire*. He thought that despite the strong logical argument for the 100 percent reserve plan, "the case for the proposal is anything but strong from a tactical standpoint." It would be opposed because free services now provided by banks would no longer be available and banks, which derive benefits from creating money and then redistribute part of these benefits to individuals in society, would oppose the changes because these changes "would mean the loss of the principle source of banking profits" (Whittlesey 1935, 23). He summarized the situation pessimistically:

> In short, the strength of logic is on the side of the proposal but the strength of tradition—which is stronger than logic—is on the side of the opposition. . . . Barring unforeseen developments, the prospect for further reform, however, is not bright. The administration has announced its desire to "co-operate" with the bankers. So long as this mood continues no major banking reform is to be expected. (Whittlesey 1935, 23–24)

In his book, Paul H. Douglas devoted a chapter to the problems of the banking system and the proposals for reform. He argued that the present banking system generated instability in the economy in three ways: (1) it created a cumulative multiplication of credit at the times when it was not needed and a cumulative contraction of credit when it is needed; (2) it caused fluctuations in the demand for capital goods that tended to accentuate both the upswing and the downward collapse of business; and (3) the banking system could not redeem the claims against it if any considerable percentage of its depositors asked for cash at the same time (Douglas 1935, 165). A first step in the solution to our problems was the separation of commercial and investment banking in the Banking Act of 1933, Douglas noted (Douglas 1935, 175). Currently fashionable among businesspeople was the notion that private business could keep the profits while government would guarantee losses, but Douglas believed such a system was ultimately unworkable and certainly not a just system (Douglas 1935, 177).

Another alternative was the outright nationalization of money and credit. Though generally sympathetic toward such a proposal, Douglas was concerned with government becoming the only banker and thus subject to political pressures for loan availability (Douglas 1935, 183–84). Given the problems with other reform proposals, and that the present system was unsatisfactory, Douglas argued:

> To my mind, therefore, the way out lies in the separation of two functions, namely, (1) the creation or the manufacture of credit and (2) the retailing of credit. The former is a social function from the reasons which have been previously brought forth, and it should be in governmental hands. The latter, or determining *who* shall be given the credit, may more safely be left primarily in private hands. (Douglas 1935, 184)

The best proposal to achieve this goal, Douglas continued, was "that which a group of my colleagues at the University of Chicago under the leadership of Mr. H. C. Simons have set forth" (Douglas 1935, 184). Douglas then went on to provide the outline of the essentials of the proposal and its benefits. Under the plan, government would control the circulating medium but not the allocation of credit. Though government might make loans directly to business if it wished, Douglas thought that government should stay out of the loan making business (Douglas 1935, 187). Douglas concluded the chapter by saying:

This general proposal will, of course, be opposed by the bankers from whom it takes the lucrative privilege of creating purchasing power. It would, however, insure the safety of deposits, give large revenues to the government, provide complete social control over monetary matters and prevent abnormal fluctuations in the capital market. At the same time it would permit the allocation of productive resources as between individual concerns to remain primarily in private hands. *All in all it seems the most promising program for the reform of our monetary and credit system which has thus far been advanced.* (Douglas 1935, 187–88, emphasis added)

These were not the only the discussions of the Chicago plan by academics; in fact, in 1935, articles on the proposal appeared in the major economics journals.

The Debate in Academic Journals

In an article published in the *Quarterly Journal of Economics* in 1935, James W. Angell critically evaluated the 100 percent reserve proposal as put forward by Irving Fisher.[1] Though basically sympathetic to the proposal, Angell found it deficient in a number of respects and proposed an alternative scheme to rectify flaws in the Fisher version. Fisher argued that his plan would give complete safety to the holders of deposits subject to check and thus end bank runs, cure depressions, and wipe out much of the national debt (Angell 1935, 7). Angell had no disagreement with the merits of the plan to separate depository and lending functions of banks or, in other words, to make the money supply independent of changes in banks' loans. He noted, "These objectives seem to me not merely desirable but probably essential to achieve, if our monetary arrangements in general are ever to be put on a reasonably intelligent and equitable basis" (Angell 1935, 10).

Angell's objections were to the practical workability of the scheme. He saw no problem in the proposal to establish separate Check Banks, nor to treat deposits subject to check as merely warehouse receipts against stored currency. However the difficulties arose with Fisher's plan to create a Currency Commission, which would purchase enough of the bank's assets to raise the reserve requirements to 100 percent. The first fundamental question is which assets would be "sold" to the Currency Commission in return for the currency. Fisher proposed that the commission purchase primarily U.S. bonds. But, Angell said, "If this is done, however, the commercial banks will be made to 'sell' their most marketable (and much of their best) assets to the Commission." As a result, the savings and time deposits (noncheckable accounts) will be backed by "short-term documents, and the less good of their long-term assets" (Angell 1935, 11). The mere rumor that such a scheme was being put into place, Angell argued, would lead to a flight out of noncheckable deposits into checkable and currency. This would lead to a violent disruption of the financial markets and would greatly increase the quantity of currency in circulation and deposits for which the Currency Commission would have to provide 100 percent reserves (Angell 1935, 11).

The second problem, according to Angell, is that Fisher seriously underestimated the total size of the asset purchasing operations that his scheme would require. Angell estimated as of June 30, 1934, that net demand deposits and non-Federal reserve currency in circulation stood at about $26 billion while bank holdings of U.S. securities were about $11 billion (Angell 1935, 12–13). As a result, the Currency Commission would be forced to buy assets other than U.S. government securities, which would be of varying qualities and maturities, and perhaps many with only a local market (Angell 1935, 13).

Angell argued that continued involvement by the government inevitably will create political problems and abuse will likely occur. If the funds were used to retire government debt, then politicians "are likely to treat the resulting decline in government outlays as an excuse for further increases in other directions, rather than for diminishing tax burdens" (Angell 1935, 13–14).

Fisher's argument that the replacing of interest-bearing government liabilities with non–interest-bearing liabilities would reduce the tax burden was largely unfounded, according to Angell. In fact, banks will raise service charges in an amount equal to the return lost on the government securities. The only difference now would be that the payment of the "tax" is shifted from the general taxpayer to the holder of deposit money, and the receiver of the revenue becomes the bank instead of the government (Angell 1935, 14). The effect will be undesirable because it will encourage the creation of close substitutes for money to avoid this tax. One way to avoid this is to reimburse the banks from the general tax fund, as Currie proposed, which would render the reduction of the national debt as illusory. Angell also rejects

Currie's proposal that banks be loaned the money to raise reserves to 100 percent and then repay the "loan" over some specified period of time. Such a plan will fail, says Angell, because the banks "certainly could not make net additional payments totaling one and a half to two billions a year out of their present or their recent earnings" (Angell 1935, 15).

Perhaps the most serious problem is that if banks devise a way to evade the 100 percent reserve requirement on checkable deposits by making time deposits serve effectively as checking deposits, then the whole scheme is bound to fail since monetary control would be under-mined and fractional reserve banking would reemerge. This would require legislation to be passed by Congress to forbid near monies from developing (Angell 1935, 15).

Angell also seriously questioned whether booms and depressions would be ended under such a scheme since that hinges crucially on the actual carrying out of monetary policy. Here the problem is devising a rule for the monetary authority to follow that will assure minimum fluctuations in the money supply. Retail prices are too sluggish to be adequate guides, Angell asserted, and short-run fluctuations could still be very large (Angell 1935, 22). If the money stock is increased by some amount, then the Currency Commission must again add to its holdings of bank owned assets (Angell 1935, 23).

At one point Fisher fell back on the "real bills doctrine" by asserting that the quantity of money should expand and contract as business expands and contracts (Angell 1935, 25). According to Angell, real bills "is a doctrine, however, which I think should be expunged once (and) for all from the economic organon" (Angell 1935, 25).

Given these problems with the 100 percent proposal, does it still have merit? According to Angell,

> Of the sweeping claims made by the 100 per cent reservists for their plans, only one can be regarded as unequivocally justified. Deposits subject to check and currency would undoubtedly become "safe" from the legal point of view, since they would be exchangeable for one another without limit but legally convertible into nothing else, and since the "insolvency" of the issuer or the debtor could not itself alter their legal status. Runs on such deposits would therefore cease, and the present costly deposit insurance system could be abandoned. (Angell 1935, 28–29)

Instead of requiring the surrender of specific assets in return for additional currency as Fisher proposed, Angell recommended the government place a lien on the *total* assets of the banks equal to the value of the new currency received. The lien would carry no interest and be repaid or extinguished only slowly if at all. Banks' present demand deposit liabilities would be made liabilities of the U.S. government to be administered by the banks as the agents of the government. This proposal would put demand deposits on precisely the same level as the government's direct issue of currency. The banks would not be able to reloan the money since they are in effect holding it in trust for the demand depositors (Angell 1935, 30–31). Analogous arrangements could be made with respect to Federal Reserve and national bank notes so that there would be a homogeneous currency. Time and savings deposits (noncheckable accounts) will be converted into negotiable interest-bearing time obligations, of various denominations, maturing serially, with not more than 20 percent maturing within three months, and not more than 40 percent within a year (Angell 1935, 31). The noncheckable deposits would be backed by the full assets of the bank, subject only to a U.S. government lien that will not be exercised in the near future. Thus protection of noncheckable deposits is increased rather than *decreased* under Fisher's scheme (Angell 1935, 31).

In order to avoid service charges due to the imposition of 100 percent reserves, each commercial bank would pay into a common pool a proportion of its total earnings equal to the ratio between the original U.S. government lien on its total assets and the value of those assets at the date of the particular payment. In turn, the banks would receive from the pool a sum based on the fraction of the total demand deposits that it administers. Details would have to be worked out, of course, but the idea would be to compensate the banks for their services as administering agents while avoiding charges to depositors (Angell 1935, 32–33). Finally, actual lending and investing operations would be unaffected, gold and silver would be used only for international balances, and the monetary growth rule would be estimated using the secular growth of population and perhaps velocity (Angell 1935, 33–34).

In summary then, though Angell thought that the proposal was reasonable and workable, the fundamental objectives would be to make deposits "safe" in the legal sense and to permit a rational control of the total stock of money. Though it would not eliminate booms and depressions, it would "go far toward making economic activity reasonably stable" (Angell 1935, 35).

Angell was less worried than Simons about the problem of near monies. He wrote to Simons:

> The thing that at present makes the existence of large quantities of short debt especially dangerous (of what you call "near moneys") is the double fact that their decrease also decreases the quantity of "real money," (and conversely), that there is hence often distrust of the "real money" itself. (Angell to Simons, September 1, 1935, Simons Papers)

Frank Graham, writing in the *American Economic Review* in 1936, sought to investigate a question Angell did not address—namely, who should have the right of issue of "fiduciary circulating medium" (Graham 1936, 429). It is self-evident, Graham argued, that the right of issue of fiduciary money is the prerogative of the government since free competition would bring chaos. Further, monopoly permits seigniorage profits that are a tax on the community at large, and "the power to tax cannot with equity be granted as a privilege to any group of private citizens" (Graham 1936, 430). Over the course of two centuries, the right to the private issue of money has been recaptured by the banks, however (Graham 1936, 431). This privilege that the banks enjoy is in no way essential to the lending process and, Graham argued, "no money should be lent, by private individuals at least, which had not first been saved by someone" (Graham 1936, 431). Reserve requirements, originally intended to give liquidity, were a feeble check on indefinite currency expansion (Graham 1936, 432).

Graham found it absurd at a time (1936) when the government was pursuing an inflationary fiscal policy that it not only gave up the seigniorage profits on the new supply of money, but also paid the banks, in interest-bearing securities, for issuing bank-debt money on its behalf (Graham 1936, 434). The net result was the fractional reserve system renders banks unfit for the function they were designed to perform and "brings general ruin in its wake" (Graham 1936, 435).

Thus Graham argued that the primary goal of the 100 percent reserve system would be the disappearance of the "primary inequity of private issue of money" and "to forestall the use of time deposits, or any other private financial instruments, as money." Graham thought this would not be difficult to achieve because substitutes for cash develop only when they are of superior convenience to both the parties immediately concerned (Graham 1936, 438). Graham, as did Angell, saw no reason to fear abuse of the government's privilege on money issue, at least not any more than was already the case, and bank profits would depend upon efficiency rather than the ability to take advantage of the privilege of issue (Graham 1936, 439).[2]

If the 100 percent system were adopted, Graham believed, then the demand for socialization of the banking system would collapse, there would be no need for deposit insurance, and regulation of banking could be abandoned with the ideal of free banking safely realized (Graham 1936, 440). In summary, he said:

> What we need is not control of banking but a government monopoly of the supply of money, with commercial banks left to lend on short-term precisely as other financial institutions now take care of intermediate and long-term credit, viz., out of capital funds, debenture borrowings, and real time deposits. . . . We are certainly not likely to get stability so long as the supply of money remains even partially in the hands of those who have no responsibility for the total issue and no motive to do other than increase it as far as law, and a merely selfish prudence, will permit. (Graham 1936, 440)

According to Albert G. Hart, the extent to which the 100 percent plan allowed truly effective monetary control is the "real substance of the argument in favor of the scheme" (Hart 1951, 438). Though the plan would not do away with all influences on the money supply, "the quantity of cash plus checking deposits would certainly be completely controlled" (Hart 1951, 441).

The central problems in controlling the money supply, Hart noted, were fluctuations in the currency-demand deposit ratio, geographical factors that redistribute demand deposits and thus affect the bank reserve ratio, and the use of the rediscount window (Hart 1951, 443–44). The 100 percent reserve system would eliminate these sources of fluctuations in the money supply.

The rigidity imposed by the 100 percent system would be that the money supply would either be constant or subject to a specified rule. For Hart, the 100 percent solution is superior to such alternatives as branch banking, for which there would be political opposition from the western states. Though various programs could be implemented to achieve greater control, such as the standardization of reserve requirements to offset open market operations and the abolition of the rediscount privilege, none would eliminate the problem during economic downturns of banks holding excess reserves they would be unwilling to loan (Hart 1951, 447).

The problem that must be considered, of course, is the transition to such a 100 percent reserve system, but Hart noted such would be the case with any of the proposed reforms mentioned above. First, a sharp differentiation between cash assets and other financial assets would be necessitated by the 100 percent reserve system. But estimating the demand for money would be a problem whenever there are close substitutes. Second, as pointed out by Angell, the banks would be stripped of their best assets. Third, if substitutes arose, monetary management could be seriously undermined as it was when bank notes were outlawed and banks began issuing demand deposits (Hart 1951, 448–51). Fourth, the nature of the financial institutions would change, since the savings banks would have to have their obligations longer term or subject to very low reserve requirements that could lead to serious funding problems for such institutions. Subsidy schemes would likely have to be worked out (Hart 1951, 453–54). Hart concluded, however, that "workable methods of transition" could be found for the 100 percent scheme (Hart 1951, 454). Hart noted that there were political reasons to adopt the 100 percent reserve scheme since the average person would accept a proposal that assures that *his* money is "in the bank." It would also reduce the role of government in the lending business, and it would make it clear that the regulation of the quality of bank assets did not constitute monetary policy (Hart 1951, 455).[3]

In 1938 a study appeared by Leonard L. Watkins on banking reform proposals, with special attention to the 100 percent reserve plan (Watkins 1938). After reviewing briefly the history of banking in the United States, Watkins contrasts the popular views of banking reform as nationalization and self-regulation. For the latter, he finds that the periods of crisis that have occurred are a product of less regulation, and thus the arguments for complete self-regulation are weakened. Though England has been more successful, he notes, its banking evolution has been different from the United States where unit banking remains strong (Watkins 1938, 9). Nationalization is the other extreme and, though its proponents are able to "marshall strong arguments as to objectives," there is the fear that the cure may be worse than the disease (Watkins 1938, 11). The alternative approach, Watkins argued, which is intermediate between these two extremes is the 100 percent reserve plan.

Watkins mentions Ricardo's proposal, Soddy's early plan for 100 percent reserves, and the Chicago, Irving Fisher, and James Angell variants of the proposal (Watkins 1938, 16–23). He notes that a number of bills have been introduced in Congress—by Cutting, Patman, Goldsborough, and a closely related proposal by Congressman Martin Sweeney (H.R. 6382) (Watkins 1938, 413). Watkins recognized that the 100 percent reserve plan, with its vesting of money production solely in the hands of government, presented an opportunity for abuse. Much of Watkins's discussion is in line with previous articles reviewed and need not be repeated here. One interesting note is that Watkins, though acknowledging that John Maynard Keynes does not discuss the 100 percent reserve plan, states that "his general theory of employment, which emphasizes liquidity motives and builds a theory of interest around 'liquidity preference,' gives attention to factors implicit in the proposed reform" (Watkins 1938, 43).

Watkins cites Keynes's remarks:

> Those (monetary) reformers, who look for a remedy by creating artificial carrying-costs for money through the device of requiring legal-tender currency to be periodically stamped at a prescribed cost in order to retain its quality as money, or in analogous ways, have been on the right track. (cited in Watkins 1938, 44)

An analogous way, Watkins argues, would be through the 100 percent reserve plan, which would raise service charges (Watkins 1938, 44).

With respect to the impact on the loan market, Watkins believed that the savings banks would have to play an important new role in the distribution of short-term savings, and failures and mistakes in this area could disrupt the economic system. Thus the regulation of savings institutions would have to be enhanced under the 100 percent reserve plan, according to Watkins. This is why Henry Simons, and other advocates of the plan, recognized the need for investment trusts as new financial institutions to redistribute savings (Watkins 1938, 53–54).

The trend was toward greater government control with regard to the money and credit system; it might be possible, in Watkins's view, to achieve many of the benefits of the 100 percent reserve system by a gradual increase in the reserve requirements coupled with "increased regulation of the banking process at crucial points" (Watkins 1938, 55). Over time, with an increase in knowledge with regard to monetary control, the workings of the banking system could be greatly improved (Watkins 1938, 70).

In 1940 Harry Gunnison Brown and Rollin G. Thomas each published comments on the 100 percent reserve plan in the *American Economic Review*. Brown stressed the importance of the intermediary function of banks and their ability to avoid service charges to checking account holders as a considerable advantage of fractional reserve banking. He thus argued that the real lenders were the recipients of the checks since they are the ones who have given up tangible goods or services and are waiting for payment (Brown 1940, 309). The bank's depositors, Brown argued, were willing to place their funds at the disposal of borrowers because the lending costs them nothing (Brown 1940, 310). Further, Brown believed that a 100 percent reserve requirement, without some compensating subsidy (which Brown opposed), would make service charges necessary, and therefore the check might become "almost altogether a matter of history" (Brown 1940, 311).

Brown also repeated the objection that near monies might appear and generate instability (Brown 1940, 312). He felt that it would be likely that, even if banned initially, fractional reserve banking would be reborn rather quickly, and legislation to prevent it would interfere "greatly with the individual liberty of choice of those who have money" (Brown 1940, 313). Rather than adopt the "revolutionary changes" of 100 percent reserve banking, Brown foresaw adaption of the financial system over the centuries "through wisely planned control" (Brown 1940, 314).

A more sympathetic view of the 100 percent reserve plan is found in the article by Thomas, who argued that the "only valid claim which can be advanced for the plan is its superiority over the present fractional reserve system as a means of avoiding monetary deflation during depressions" (Thomas 1940, 315–16). The objections to the original plan with respect to the reserve holdings of the deposit banks had been met, Thomas believed, by Angell's plan to have the Federal Reserve loan cash without interest and place a lien on the total assets of the bank. The problem of near monies is met by turning time deposits into long-term debt obligations (Thomas 1940, 317). Thomas was concerned, however, that the 100 percent reserve system might lead to the total abolition of short-term lending, which would present difficulties for business borrowing over the business cycle (Thomas 1940, 318). During an economic downturn, a fall in loans would lead to increases in reserves of the lending institutions, thereby decreasing the money supply. This is why, Thomas notes, that the institutions offering savings and time deposits must be investment trusts without the privilege of making short-term loans (Thomas 1940, 319). The result, Thomas argued, would be to "drive a large volume of such borrowing into the field of trade credit." [4] Thomas concluded that the result would benefit finance companies, which he thought would not be a desirable outcome:

> It would indeed be a great day in the development of finance companies should the 100 per cent plan, implemented with a prohibition on short-term loans by the banks, be actually put into operation. But it would be intolerable to have tried to furnish the community with a controlled currency only to find the attempts failing because of an escape of short-term lending into the hands of finance companies and trade creditors. (Thomas 1940, 320)

The impact of the expansion of finance companies, Thomas argued, would be to the greatest disadvantage of small to middle-sized businesses who would face increased costs of credit, if it could be obtained at all. Had Thomas written a few decades later, after the expansion of mutual funds, his assessment might have been different.

Rather than the 100 percent reserve system, Thomas believed that branch banking offered a better way to protect the banking system without drastically affecting the availability and means of credit that existed with the current system. The problems of the banking system could best be dealt with, according to Thomas, by improvements in banking practices, better management of banks, adequate capital, appropriate amounts of secondary reserves, improved facilities for meeting emergencies by converting assets into cash through borrowing upon noneligible paper at the Federal Reserve Banks, and the introduction of federal deposit insurance with more careful supervision (Thomas 1940, 322).

Benjamin Higgins replied to Thomas and Brown that, while he recognized that the 100 percent reserve plan was not a cure-all, it offered the best means to constrain a boom in periods preceded by an increase in bank excess reserves such as existed before and after 1940. The 100 percent reserve plan, by providing an automatic check on investment in excess of voluntary savings, would mitigate dangerous (inflationary) booms, Higgins stated (Higgins 1941, 96). One other issue that should also be recognized is the question of whether demand deposits are considered by the holder to be money balances in anticipation of spending or savings. The same holds true for time deposits: They may be considered as precautionary money balances or true savings. Thus the savings and investment identity is affected by the structure of the financial system. The 100 percent reserve plan, provided it could maintain this distinction between money and credit (or holding money balances and loaning them), could aid in keeping savings and investment in line (Higgins 1940, 94–95).[5]

Conclusion

The academic debates can be summarized by noting that the discussions were for the most part sympathetic to the plan—there were some concerns about transition, but the goals of the plan were deemed desirable. The issues of transition, the nature of the reserves (interest bearing or not), service charges for checking accounts, the availability and price of credit were all clearly stated in the academic debates. The plan was seen as an effective way to enhance control of the money supply by the monetary authority and to provide a safe payments system, while also providing a means to avoid the nationalization of the money and credit system. It was clearly understood at the time that one of the chief dangers of the system established by the New Deal legislation was its susceptibility to nationalization. A system whereby the costs were socialized, but the profit remained entirely private, would lead to demands in periods of crisis that the government should control completely the allocation of credit. The proponents of the Chicago plan, and others as well, viewed this as a serious problem for the future evolution of the financial system.

It is also clear that because the issues had been clearly stated and recognized by both proponents and opponents of the plan, the only way to resolve them would be through actually implementing the plan and observing the result. The political difficulties of doing this were substantial, and this remains an important consideration in implementing monetary reform. The bankers now make profits through creating money, and they will use their position to maintain a profitable system and to resist any change that threatens the status quo, unless it can be demonstrated that the new system is more profitable.

Often underlying the academic discussions of the 100 percent reserve plan was the view that interest in the plan was largely by academics.[6] In fact, there was a lot of public interest and support for the
100 percent reserve plan. As discussed in the previous chapter, Irving
Fisher sought to rally public support while, at the same time, he sought
to influence those with the political power and influence in Washington to enact the legislation.

— 12 —

The Chicago Plan after the Passage of the Banking Act of 1935

The preceding chapters have presented the argument that the Chicago plan for banking reform had an important, and hitherto neglected role, in the banking legislation over the period 1933–35. New Deal banking legislation, as shaped by Marriner Eccles and Lauchlin Currie, clearly set the financial system on a path that moved toward the ultimate goal of greater Federal Reserve control over the money supply. With the preoccupations of world war on the horizon and the moves or departures of many of the key monetary players in the late 1930s, one would expect interest in the Chicago plan to decline. This might have occurred had it not been for the fact that Irving Fisher, who had retired from Yale, embraced the 100 percent reserve plan as his *cause célèbre* from 1935 until his death in 1947. Though the Chicago economists were the first to propose the 100 percent plan as a solution to the financial problems of the 1930s, it is Irving Fisher who is most closely associated with the proposal and certainly was its most "enthusiastic and conspicuous proponent" (Allen 1977, 582; Allen 1993, 704). Fisher's proposal was essentially the plan as it had been developed in 1933 by the Chicago economists. The only modifications in Fisher's plan were the adoption of aspects of both Currie's proposal and that of James Angell.

Fisher's Continuing Efforts

The passage of the Banking Act of 1935 did not end Fisher's campaign, and he came out with a second edition of *100% Money* in January 1936. During the same month, Fisher wrote an article on "Where Will the Bonus Money Come From?" and mailed it to Roosevelt. The issue was the payment of a bonus to veterans of World War I that was due to be paid in 1945. The march of the veterans to Washington in 1932, and their subsequent routing by Douglas MacArthur and Dwight D. Eisenhower, created such ill will toward Hoover that his reelection chances were severely damaged after the event. Fisher's proposal was connected to his monetary reform plans. Fisher proposed to:

> Let Congress amend the Federal Reserve law so as to bring back the original provision of 1913 whereby all the profits of the Federal Reserve banks beyond 6 per cent on their capital (the capital being about $140,000,000) must be turned into the Treasury. Then let the Government sell to the Federal Reserve banks enough bonds to finance the bonus. The Federal Reserve banks would buy the bonds with their credit. While the Government will have to pay interest on these bonds to the Federal Reserve banks, the banks will have to pay an equal sum to the Government in fulfillment of the above-named provision to turn into the Treasury all profits beyond the 6% limit. (Fisher 1936d, 1)

The connection with the 100 percent reserve plan is apparent because what Fisher was proposing in essence was an issue of money to pay the bonus—fiscal and monetary policy are thus merged. The government creates money and generates purchasing power, but does not have to pay interest.

Writing in the February issue of *Social Research*, Fritz Lehmann attacked the 100 percent money scheme of Fisher. Lehmann also claimed that though bills had been introduced into Congress for the scheme, they have not "influenced in any marked way recent banking legislation" (Lehmann 1936, 37). Critical, but somewhat sympathetic, Lehmann argued:

> Taken all together the single real advantage of 100% money consists in eliminating runs on demand deposits and in abolishing the destruction of demand deposits by bank failures. . . . If the banking structure had to be rebuilt the 100% principle would have to be considered seriously. In a system already made run-proof to a certain extent by deposit insurance and by wide rediscount facilities, it certainly will not pay to start such far reaching changes for so little an effect. (Lehmann 1936, 55–56)

Fisher wrote an article on "100% Money and the Public Debt" for the Spring 1936 issue of *Economic Forum* in which he presented Angell's version of the plan. Fisher suggested 100 percent reserves combined with a system of money management like Sweden's with an official index number (Fisher 1936a, 411). He stated that fear of the "money multiplier" must have been partly the cause of FDR not issuing more greenbacks (Fisher 1936a, 415).[1]

In October 1936, Fisher wrote an article on "The Bankers' Interest in 100% Money" that appeared in *Bankers' Magazine* (Fisher 1936c). The article mentions FDR's speech of July 3, 1933, and Title II of the Banking Act of 1935 where power to double reserve requirements was given. Fisher wrote FDR on November 10, 1936, congratulating him on his reelection and mentioned the 100 percent money plan. He said:

> It is, I believe, the *only* practicable plan proposed for transferring completely all control over our chief circulating medium from the banks to the Government, where it belongs. This plan has been gaining converts rapidly. Its adoption, as a part of a managed currency plan, would, I am sure, go down in history with the emancipation of the slaves. (Fisher to Roosevelt, November 10, 1936, Fisher Papers)

In early 1937, Fisher seemed very optimistic about the 100 percent money plan. He wrote to Simons:

> There seems to be no doubt that the 100% money idea has taken root in many minds in Washington, in the executive departments, the House and the Senate. It seems too good to prove true that it will win out, but it is worth fighting for. (Fisher to Simons, January 29, 1937, Fisher Papers)

He asked Simons to try to get Viner on the bandwagon. Simons replied to Fisher that he had little faith in simple legislative schemes, and that he was not the one to approach Viner. Simons said:

> To me, the scheme (whatever its potentialities during the banking crisis) is significant only for its definition of an ideal objective of gradual reform; and in such a gradual unfolding, changes outside formal banking seem even more important and indispensable than the things which we stressed in the beginning. (Simons to Fisher, February 3, 1937, Simons Papers)

In the February 1937 issue of the *Bankers' Magazine*, there was a reply by Fisher to earlier letters and a new attack on the plan from

A.V. Barber who argued that the system of currency creation would be inflationary.

On February 16, Fisher received a letter from FDR's secretary, acknowledging receipt of the pre-publication article "100% Money System." FDR requested that it be sent to Eccles at the Federal Reserve. The article, which appeared in the *Northwestern Banker*, discussed branch banking and 100 percent money. With 100 percent money making banks safe, branch banking and the need for a unified banking system would be eliminated. The problem of absentee ownership could then be avoided.

Fisher feared that monetary reform plans were falling into the background in the administration and wrote to FDR in March:

> I would like to tell you what I had in mind to discuss with you, had I had an opportunity to see you and Governor Eccles. Many now fear that money reform has been put in the background and in jeopardy. (Fisher to Roosevelt, March 6, 1937, Fisher Papers)

FDR replied that the proposal required further study, saying

> Such a proposal possesses many elements of attractiveness. As you doubtless recognize, however, it involves a number of complex considerations, in its practical applications as well as in its larger aspects. (Roosevelt to Fisher, March 23, 1937, *President's Personal File 431*)

Fisher wrote FDR in May:

> You have already laid the foundations for monetary reform. If now, following the lines previously suggested, you will start the principle going which President John Adams endorsed of taking away all money-creation from the "money changers"—the real economic royalists—so that hereafter all new money is "spent into existence by the state instead of, as at present, being lent into existence by private companies," you will have accomplished, I believe, more for posterity than by all your other cherished proposals put together. The first step is to take over the twelve Federal Reserve Banks. I believe the time is ripe. (Fisher to Roosevelt, May 14, 1937, Fisher Papers)

Fisher wrote to Currie telling him that the best version of the 100 percent plan was in the *Los Angeles Commercial and Financial Digest*, which contained a discussion of permitting government securities to be held as reserves as in the issue department of the Bank of England (Fisher to Currie, December 19, 1937, Fisher Papers).

In the February 1938 issue of *Dynamic America*, Congressman Jerry Voorhis of California restated the case for the 100 percent reserve plan in light of the recession of 1937. He also argued that the Federal Reserve Board should

> anticipate the nation's need for an average annual increase of circulating medium of about 4% by creating it in the form of Federal Reserve notes or Federal Reserve credit (on which no interest must be paid) and by putting this in circulation by paying old age pensions, and sustaining other groups of citizens such as widowed mothers, the blind and disabled, who cannot and should not be considered a part of the working population. (Voorhis 1938, 14)

In making his plea for the 100 percent reserve system, Voorhis invoked Article I, section 8 of the Constitution on Congress's right to coin money and regulate its value. His proposal to restore the price level to the 1926 level and to require 100 percent reserves in cash was essentially that introduced by Gerald Nye in July 1935, during the debates over the Banking Act of 1935.

In 1938 an attack on Fisher's 100 percent money plan came from Walter E. Spahr, a gold standard advocate. He attacked Fisher on virtually every point in the plan, but the bottom line was he objected to inconvertible paper money issued solely by the government because of its inflationary bias due to political pressures (Spahr 1938). Fisher responded to Spahr in the July 1938 issue of *Dynamic America*. Fisher stated that he believed that the creation of money was an exclusively government function and, by targeting a price level, inflation could be controlled. Fisher reiterated that he wanted the government to control money exclusively, but he would then free banks from most existing regulations (Fisher 1938b, 17).

On March 9, 1939, Fisher sent FDR a copy of a letter to the *New York Times* where Fisher, responding to an editorial, wrote that "To get a sound currency it is absolutely necessary to cut this tie between our chief currency and loans and investments" (*New York Times*, February 21, 1939). Fisher also promised to send FDR another statement on 100 percent reserves supported by Paul Douglas, Frank Graham, Earl Hamilton, Willford King, Charles Whittlesey, and, Fisher claimed, nearly 200 other economists. FDR replied to Fisher that he looked forward to receiving confidentially the program for monetary reform (Roosevelt to Fisher, March 13, 1939, *President's Personal File 431*). When he actually received the proposal, FDR merely acknowledged receipt, but made no comment (Allen 1977, 585–86). A lengthier version of "A Program for Monetary Reform" was circulated in July 1939 (Douglas, et al., 1939).

Two years later, the group, which now included John R. Commons, submitted to FDR virtually the same program with the statement that now it had the support of some 400 economists (Allen 1977, 586). The president responded that the statement "will receive careful study" (Roosevelt to Fisher, February 13, 1941, Fisher Papers). Though there is no indication of further interest in the plan from Roosevelt, a January 6, 1941, memo to Treasury Secretary Henry Morgenthau discussed "Transferring Checking Accounts of Banks to the Post Office—The 100 Percent Reserve Plan." The author of the memo wrote:

> The following is in reference to your request for a memorandum developing *your* idea that checking accounts of banks should be transferred to the Post Office, etc. Such a transfer would be one means of applying in practice the so-called 100 percent reserve plan. (Morgenthau Diary, January 6, 1941, emphasis added)

Though it may have indeed been Morgenthau's idea in 1940, as discussed earlier, Rexford Tugwell and others had suggested it to Roosevelt in 1933. The memo reviewed the pros and cons of the 100 percent reserve plan and concluded:

> Several alternative plans have been proposed for transition to the 100 percent reserve system and the details could be worked out relatively easily if the principle itself were agreed on. . . . The 100 percent reserve plan is not inherently a "radical" proposal. In the long run the balance of advantage appears strongly in its favor and it is completely compatible with a continued functioning of the competitive capitalistic order. Its great disadvantage is that it would upset a powerful vested interest. It certainly could not be adopted except after a bitter fight and should not be proposed unless such opposition is expected and prepared for. (Morgenthau Diary, January 6, 1941)

With the onset of U.S. involvement in World War II just five months later, the 100 percent reserve plan became a moot issue (along with many others) and the economy was geared up to fight a war.

The Postwar Period: Simons and Fisher

Despite his concerns, Simons continued to support and write about the 100 percent reserve plan. In an article published in December 1944 on the federal government's debt policy, Simons argued that the issuing of interest-bearing and non–interest-bearing government paper created "fiscal bedlam." He wrote pessimistically:

> There is little hope for sound monetary-fiscal policy under representa-
> tive government if our representatives persist in confusing everybody,
> including especially themselves, by issuing moneys, practically mon-
> eys, and near-moneys under other names. Trying to steer a path be-
> tween phobias about paper money and terror of high interest costs, they
> create only fiscal bedlam and intolerable monetary uncertainty. (Simons
> 1948, 221)

Simons pointed out that the federal government, under the current banking structure, attempts to control both the money supply and inter-est rates on government securities and, in doing so, creates a quandary. The guide to policy should be the stabilization of the value of money, according to Simons. He noted that "converting money into consols is an anti-inflation measure; converting consols into money is a reflation-ary or anti-deflation measure; and that is that" (Simons 1948, 223). The proper use of monetary and fiscal policy is, in Simons's view, "as simple as it is remote from our thinking or from our likely actions" (Simons 1948, 228). The solution would be that those institutions that issue money (cash or its substitute) would be required to hold 100 percent reserves and find their revenues in service charges. Those in-stitutions that issue consols would have their equity requirements in-creased to 100 percent. Thus,

> We only repeat proposals for the 100 per cent reserve scheme—for
> which I still have no great enthusiasm save as part of a gradualist
> program whose objective is recognized (and consistently pursued) as
> gradual reduction and ultimate denial of borrowing and lending powers
> to all corporations, especially as regards obligations of short term. *Mis-
> guided fiscal practice and unguided institutional evolution have placed
> us in a foolish quandary.* (Simons 1948, 229, emphasis added)

In an article published shortly before his death in 1946, Simons once again tackled the issue of "debt policy and banking policy." Though putting federal debt into either consols or currency was "obviously too radical" politically, Simons believed that "a strong case can be made for moving ahead now in the banking field" toward the 100 percent reserve plan (Simons 1948, 231). In view of the buildup of excess reserves by banks, Simons suggested:

> Instead of converting all federal issues into currency and consols, we might, as a moderate, practical policy, utilize also a third debt form, namely, a completely liquid federal "bond," continuously redeemable and callable and "on tap" but eligible only for bank ownership and required as reserve against bank deposits. . . . New reserve requirements (of, say, 60–80 per cent) as to these bonds might be superimposed upon existing reserve requirements; preferably they would take the form of requirements (of, say, 80–100 per cent) as to such bonds *and* deposits in the Reserve banks, with till-money also counted toward the requirement. (Simons 1948, 232)

Such a system could be implemented in the short run to deal with the problem of inflation. What about long-run policy? Simons argued that in the long run, he would not make an argument for a government subsidy for deposit banks. He could see "no reason why the services of warehousing and transferring private funds should not be paid for like any other economic services—by appropriate service charges" (Simons 1948, 235). The payment of interest on reserves was a government subsidy that should be explicitly admitted; however, the subsidy should only be during a transitional period to the 100 percent reserve system (Simons 1948, 236).

With regard to the financing of capital investment by the banks, Simons argued that the 100 percent reserve system would leave the banks free to provide long-term financing out of their own capital. Though the combination of providing checking facilities and investment trusts would not be precluded, this would require a "great increase in bank capital" but would "facilitate best use of existing enterprises and their established staffs" (Simons 1948, 236–37). In conclusion, he wrote:

> Over forty years . . . we might arrive at or approach an economy where all private property consisted in pure assets, pure money, and nothing

else. This, along with fiscal stabilization of the value of money, is the *financial good society*. (Simons 1948, 239, emphasis added)

In October 1942, Simons wrote to Fisher:

> I'm wondering if you are (on my standards!) properly excited about the lowering of member-bank reserve requirements. Even ardent opponents of 100% reserves can hardly look forward happily to reduction of requirements to a small fraction of their present levels—as will happen if the issue continues to be evaded. Many responsible people will now argue or concede privately that inflationary borrowing, if unavoidable by taxation, should be done by selling to the Reserve Banks, rather than to member-banks; but no one seems disposed to stick his own neck out. If the issue could be precipitated publicly, the sounder policy would find much strong support. Otherwise, Morgenthau will doubtless get whatever reductions are necessary to permit absorption of new issues in the wrong and customary way. When we reach the minima now permitted by statute, the issue will of course come before Congress; but I hate to see it go by default until that stage. (Simons to Fisher, October 19, 1942, Simons Papers)

Though the war interrupted work on the plan, Fisher continued to publish and write on 100 percent money. He wrote FDR on a variety of subjects during the period of the war (Allen 1977). Fisher and Simons also corresponded on the question of income taxation in this period.

Replying to a copy of Simons's article on debt policy and banking policy where Simons proposed a new kind of bond to back Reserve Banks, Fisher wrote:

> I see some virtue but not very much in your proposal to combine the inflationary invisible greenbacks to the twelve Federal Reserve Banks and to increase the reserve requirements of the member banks. If anything effective is done, it seems to me we should aim directly at the 100% system for the member banks and permit the Secretary of the Treasury only to do any inflating. (Fisher to Simons, November 4, 1942, Simons Papers)

In a 1944 letter to FDR regarding postwar economic policy, Fisher again lobbied for the current importance of the 100 percent reserve plan. Of his twenty-nine books on inflation and deflation, he wrote:

The most helpful at this juncture would, I think, be my "100% money." (Your advisor, Lauchlin Currie—first recommended by me, as you may remember—made this "100%" proposal earlier than I.) Four hundred other economists have endorsed the idea including Professor Angell of Columbia who has added improvements to my first version. Jerry Voorhis in the House is for it and has the following of many other Congressmen. Mr. Eccles is, I believe, at heart for it; but would, I think, not touch it politically until assured of your backing. . . . You—and I think you alone—could make it politically feasible and would thereby make good on your "bombshell" telegram to the London Economic Conference for which you have been unjustly abused ever since. (Fisher to Roosevelt, November 22, 1944, *President's Personal File 431*)[2]

In 1945 Fisher renewed his popular campaign for the proposal, this time trying to enlist larger numbers of economists in support of it. A new edition of his *100% Money* book was published that year. Jerry Voorhis, Congressman from California, introduced a bill (H.R. 3648) on July 2, 1945, to create a Monetary Authority of the United States and constitute it as the sole agent to create money. Any institution handling demand deposits must be licensed and retain the actual physical money behind demand deposits 100 percent. Service charges would be permitted on demand deposits, and time or savings deposits could only be withdrawn on appropriate notice (U.S. Congress 1945). Fisher worked closely with Voorhis in garnering support for the plan (Voorhis to Fisher, March 26, 1945, and October 10, 1945, Fisher Papers).

Albert G. Hart wrote to Fisher that "At this point in the nation's history, the possibility of going over to a system of 100% reserves *at the margin*, with a fixed 'uncovered issue' of bank credit should not be overlooked" (Hart to Fisher, cc. to Simons and others, August 17, 1945, Simons Papers). After one of his mass mailings, Fisher wrote to Simons: "I suppose you must have signed one of my cards about 100% but I haven't searched to be sure. Nearly 300 have been received and some 260 have been favorable" (Fisher to Simons, August 25, 1945, Simons Papers).

In 1946 Fisher attempted to bolster support for the 100 percent reserve plan with a mass mailing to members of the American Economics Association with a plea to endorse the plan. Of 4,662 members of the AEA in 1946, Fisher claimed to have received responses from over 1,100 who favored, in principle, the 100 percent reserve plan. In his letter of appeal to AEA members, Fisher listed among the support-ers of the plan in addition to those already mentioned the late John R. Commons, former Senator Robert L. Owen, Lester V. Chandler, Stuart Chase, John Maurice Clark, Allan G. Gruchy, C. O. Hardy, William Jaffe, Fritz Machlup, Jacob Marschak, Robert H. Montgomery, Selig Perlman, Joseph J. Spengler, George J. Stigler, Clair Wilcox, and Theo-dore Yntema. The complete list was given to Congressman Voorhis and entered into the *Congressional Record* (Fisher to Simons, May 7, 1946, Simons Papers). Fisher's plea opened with the words:

> This is the last call! If you have not already expressed approval (in principle only) of the "100% plan" for curbing future inflation and deflation, I hope you will do so now, or else read the book so titled preparatory to making up your mind. (Fisher to Simons, May 7, 1946, enclosure, Simons Papers)

For those who failed to endorse the plan, Fisher frequently wrote lengthy replies. In a long letter to Clark Warburton, Fisher reviewed the contribution of the individuals involved in monetary reform over the past three decades. Of Marriner Eccles, Fisher said:

> Incidentally, Eccles in his heart, I think, favors the 100% idea. He was educated on this idea through Currie who was his assistant. Currie left him to be the assistant of President Roosevelt. This was in consequence of a talk I had with President Roosevelt. I told him I thought Currie ought to be on the Board instead of Assistant to the Chairman and the President, who looked up Currie, appointed him his assistant. (Fisher to Warburton, July 23, 1946, Fisher Papers)

Though there were other plans for monetary stabilization, Fisher believed that "at present my influence is best exerted in favor of the 100% plan" (Fisher to Warburton, July 23, 1946, Fisher Papers).

Fisher never gave up on lobbying for the plan, which continued, according to Allen, even on his deathbed:

> [Fisher's] prodigious efforts continued almost to the moment of his death on April 29, 1947—while in a terminal stay in a hospital, he wrote a long letter to President Harry S. Truman on March 27 urging "a law which will sever the tie that now binds bank loans to the volume of checkbook money," and within a week or so of his end he corrected his

final manuscript, which called for 100 percent reserves along with "a legal requirement that money should be injected only on signs of threatened deflation and withdrawn only on signs of threatened inflation." (Allen 1993, 715)

The end of the political possibilities for the 100 percent reserve plan came in the elections of 1946 when Congressman Jerry Voorhis was defeated in his reelection bid by a young, up and coming politician, Richard M. Nixon.

Maurice Allais and the 100 Percent Reserve Plan

In 1948, Maurice Allais presented a proposal for banking reform closely related to the 100 percent reserve proposal in a book published in French and dedicated to Irving Fisher (Allais 1948). Allais's views were not published in English until 1987, though the essentials of the proposal did not change. In 1987 Allais wrote:

> The "miracles" performed by credit are fundamentally comparable to the "miracles" an association of counterfeiters could perform for its benefit by lending its forged banknotes in return for interest. In both cases, the stimulus to the economy would be the same, and the only difference is who benefits. (Allais 1987, 520)

Allais had six fundamental objections to the system of fractional reserve banking: (1) the creation and destruction of money by private banks; (2) sensitivity of the credit mechanism to short-term economic fluctuations; (3) the basic instability engendered by borrowing short and lending long; (4) the distortion of income distribution by the creation of "false claims"; (5) the impossibility of control over the credit system; and (6) nonexistence of efficient control of the aggregate money supply. The two fundamental principles guiding reform are (1) the creation of money should be the business of the state, and of nobody else; and (2) no money should be created outside the monetary base, so that no one would be entitled to the benefits that attach to the creation of bank money (Allais 1987, 525).

Allais's reform proposal is to require that deposit banks be subject to a 100 percent coverage of deposits by basic money and be forbidden to make loans. Lending institutions would be managed on the principle that all lending for a given term would be financed by borrowing of at least the same term. Whereas now banks borrow short and lend long, Allais would require that they borrow long and lend short (Allais 1987, 525).

Though Allais agreed that the Chicago plan was on the right track, it failed to fully take into consideration the development of other assets that could be used as money. The Chicago plan was an attempt to define the money supply as currency and demand deposits—the monetary base and M_1 would be identical.[3] The Chicago economists failed to realize that the money supply is, in Allais's view, properly defined as basic money and the degree to which other financial assets are viewed as money by the holder. What the Chicago plan wished to do is make the degree of substitution of money for near money equal to zero. Allais, though he might view this as ideal, recognized that it is a decision by individuals and therefore you cannot make it zero without a great deal of restriction and regulation of individuals and financial institutions. However, Allais believed that empirical work could enable an estimation of the substitution ratios, and the reserve requirements would need to be approximately equal to those ratios in order to reduce the creation of credit by the private banking system. Allais's argument is that you cannot keep near monies from developing, but you can reduce the creation of credit. Allais and Fisher not surprisingly had a similar view in this regard. Both felt the answer to the problem was empirical.

Simons viewed the 100 percent reserve plan as an attempt to apply the principles embodied in Peel's Act of 1844 which divided the Bank of England into a lending department and an issuing department. Both Simons and Fisher viewed the act as a correct guide for monetary reform if it had been applied to demand deposits as well as bank notes. However, the 100 percent reserve plan in the 1930s made the same mistake as in 1844, according to Allais. Peel's Act only applied to bank notes and demand deposits were a substitute, whereas the Chicago plan only applied to demand deposits when time deposits were a close substitute. Allais broke out of this dilemma by his redefinition of the money supply and his recognition that you cannot legislate the definition of money. It remains an open question whether reasonable estimates for the substitution ratios can be found and then legislated. Other than the political aspects of banking reform, this is perhaps the greatest difficulty in the implementation of Allais's reform.

Milton Friedman's 100 Percent Reserve Proposal

Although Maurice Allais wrote in support of the 100 percent reserve plan in the late forties, the best-known advocate of the Chicago plan for banking reform in the postwar period is probably Milton Friedman. In his article "A Monetary and Fiscal Framework for Economic Stability," Friedman included a "reform of the monetary and banking system to eliminate both the private creation or destruction of money and discretionary control of the quantity of money by central-bank authority" (Friedman 1953, 135). Friedman advocated the proposal also because it would eliminate the discount window. Under Friedman's proposal, the chief function of the monetary authorities would be to create money to meet government deficits or retirement of money when the government has a surplus (Friedman 1953, 136). Under the 100 percent reserve scheme, this mechanism would be automatic, though it could be accomplished if a rule were established that the money supply be increased only when the government has a deficit and decreased with a surplus. Hence, government expenditures would be financed either by tax revenues or the creation of money—that is, the issue of noninterest-bearing securities (Friedman 1953, 139).

With regard to payment of interest on the 100 percent reserves held against checking deposits, Friedman states that the question comes down to whether demand deposit banking should be subsidized by government, and if so, what form the subsidy should take (Friedman 1953, 140). In a later article on commodity-reserve currencies, Friedman stated his belief that the "production of *fiat* currency is, as it were, a natural monopoly ... Henry Simons ... held the view—which I share—that the creation of fiat currency should be a government monopoly" (Friedman 1953, 216–17).

Conclusion

Would we be better off today had the 100 percent reserve proposals of the New Deal been implemented? If the proposals to establish a Federal Monetary Authority and separate the depository and lending functions of banks had been adopted, what would the evolution of banking in the U.S. have looked like? The basic features of the financial system if such were the case can be summarized as follows:

1. There would have been a Federal Monetary Authority working under authorization of Congress that would be responsible for money and credit. The two functions would be kept separate: the Federal Reserve for monetary policy and a RFC-type credit allocation institution. Both would be government owned institutions. Congress would be directly accountable for money and credit, the FMA would be merely carrying out the "rules" laid down by Congress. The only policy tool available to affect the monetary base would be open market operations in government securities. There would be no discount window, though some extension of Federal Reserve liabilities would have been initially necessary to raise the reserve requirements to 100 percent on demand deposits.
2. Institutions accepting checkable deposits would have been subject to 100 percent reserves in cash or government securities. Checkable deposits could be held at private depository institutions, the Post Office, or possibly the Federal Reserve Banks. There would be no need for federal deposit insurance.
3. Savings deposits would not be subject to check and there would be a minimal reserve requirement. The most likely structure would be mutual credit associations with no federal deposit insurance for these institutions.

Whether a Federal Reserve Board directly accountable to Congress would have given us a better inflation and growth record depends on the assessment of how well one thinks that the Fed has done. There is room for great difference of opinion here. The argument for such an arrangement remains that it would make the members of Congress responsible for monetary policy, and hence neither the president nor Congress could blame anyone else for the failure of economic policies to provide the "right" rate of inflation (or unemployment). There would be no passing the buck. The job of the Federal Reserve Board would have been simplified to the extent that it merely carried out the will of Congress. The Federal Reserve would have had a high degree of control over the basic money supply (M_1), which would grow at a target rate of 4 percent per annum.

The establishment of a permanent RFC would probably have turned into a politically influenced institution. However, that danger must be weighed against the political pressure we have seen in recent years to bail out institutions favored by Congress or the Federal Reserve. It is a

toss-up whether a permanent RFC would have been worse. The elimination of the discount window would have precluded the possibility
that financial institutions would be bailed out for solvency reasons.[4] In
the debate over whether the Federal Reserve should be independent of
Congress, all of the proponents of the 100 percent reserve plan came
down firmly for congressional control of the Federal Reserve, but subject to rules established by Congress.

With regard to new deposit and lending institutions, the development of mutual funds has given us both "safe" banks and mutual credit
associations, a desirable feature of the financial system, according to
the 100 percent reserve proponents. The adoption of the 100 percent
reserve plan would presumably have stimulated these developments to
some extent. Federal deposit insurance would have been drastically cut
back, and therefore no bailout of financial institutions by either the
FDIC or FSLIC.

To the extent that credit was reduced upon implementation of the
100 percent reserve plan and the availability of credit was crucial to
economic recovery and growth, then the system might have made
things worse. Alternately, the shortage could have created an even
larger role for government allocation of credit through some structure
such as a permanent Reconstruction Finance Corporation. The bailout
of any failing institution might still be subject to political influence, as
it was in the years of the RFC.

———— 13 ————

Financial Instability and Narrow Banking: Simons Revisited

The period of unprecedented growth and prosperity in the U.S. economy in the post–World War II period, and the lack of banking panics or crises on a level experienced previously in U.S. history, contributed to the popular belief that financial system problems were a relic of bygone days. There was a widespread belief that we had in fact entered a new golden age of prosperity so that, by the end of 1965, *Time* magazine could declare:

> If the nation has economic problems, they are the problems of high employment, high growth and high hopes. As the U.S. enters what shapes up as the sixth straight year of expansion, its economic strategists confess rather cheerily that they have just about reached the outer limits of economic knowledge. (*Time*, December 31, 1965, 67b)

There were hints of looming problems, both domestic and international, and the "credit crunch" of 1966 would later be recognized as a crucial turning point in the economy. There were those who realized that the underlying institutional structure was neither unchanging nor necessarily stable, and that problems with the financial system were on the horizon.

The Financial Instability Hypothesis

In the mid-1950s, Hyman Minsky, building upon the work of Henry Simons, began to develop what he later called the "financial instability hypothesis." He began with the seemingly obvious observation concerning monetary policy carried out by the central bank:

> Essentially, the relations upon which the monetary authorities base

their operations are predicated upon the assumption that a given set of institutions and usages exists. If the operations of the authorities have side effects in that they induce changes in financial institutions and usages, then the relations "shift." As a result, the effects of monetary operations can be quite different from those desired. (Minsky 1982, 163)

What Minsky demonstrated, using the example of the federal funds market and the financing of government bond houses, was that a restrictive monetary policy during boom times could lead to "velocity-increasing and liquidity-decreasing money-market innovations" that would "result in an inherently unstable money market so that a slight reversal of prosperity can trigger a financial crisis" (Minsky 1982, 173). This increasing fragility of the economy—fragile because the debt-net wealth ratio of the private sector rises, and money market assets are more vulnerable to a fall in value—Minsky labeled the "financial instability hypothesis." As he later wrote, the fundamentals of a theory of financial instability can be derived from the writings of Simons, Fisher, and Keynes (Minsky 1986, 172).

The Minsky-Simons Connection

Though Simons remained a proponent of the 100 percent reserve plan throughout his life, the most troubling aspect of the plan for him was how to enforce the system once it had been legislated. The perennial problem for the financial system in a profit-seeking capitalist economy was the creation of what Simons referred to as "near monies." In his "Rules versus Authorities in Monetary Policy," Simons wrote:

> Banking is a pervasive phenomenon, not something to be dealt with by mere legislation directed at what we call banks. The experience with the control of note issue is likely to be repeated in the future: many expedients for controlling similar practices may prove ineffective and disappointing because of the reappearance of prohibited practices in unprohibited forms. It seems impossible to predict what forms the evasion might take or to see how particular prohibitions might be designed in order that they might be more than nominally effective. (Simons 1948 [1936], 172)

Minsky adopted Simons's view recognizing that

> Changes in financial institutions and money-market usages are the re-
> sult of either legislation or evolution. Legislated changes are typically
> the result of some real or imagined malfunctioning of the monetary-
> financial system. . . . Evolutionary changes occur typically in response
> to some profit possibilities which exist in the money market. (Minsky
> 1982, 162)

Minsky's views on the financial system, associated with post-
Keynesian economics, are very close to those of the Chicago School
of which Henry Simons was one of the acknowledged founding fathers. Though first fully developing his ideas on financial instability in
a book on Keynes (Minsky 1975), Minsky studied under Simons in the
late 1930s and has always acknowledged the importance of Simons's
contributions to his own work. This theme was analyzed by Charles
Whalen who argued that the "Minsky-Simons connection" is a neglected thread in the history of economic thought—important because
it brings together two seemingly divergent schools of economics: the
classical liberalism of the Chicago School and the interventionism of
Keynesianism. As Minsky himself has stated, Simons was much closer
to Keynes's ideas about the monetary-financial process than the Chicago School associated with monetarism (Minsky 1977, 305, note 19).

The discipline of economics does not develop in a vacuum. The postwar period of economic growth and financial stability led economists to
focus on other issues—especially growth—to the detriment of the study
of business cycles, which had preoccupied the profession during the late
nineteenth and early twentieth centuries. Whalen observes that the interpretation of Keynes and Simons as founders of opposing schools of economics coincided with the virtual abandonment of business cycle theory
in the postwar period (Whalen 1988, 541). The reemergence of the problems of unemployment, stagnation, and financial disturbances have provided an opportunity for economists to utilize the important common
insights of Keynes, Simons, and Minsky (Whalen 1988, 541).[1]

Minsky on Reform of the Financial System

Minsky does not follow the Simons's policy prescription of 100 percent reserves. Minsky takes the capitalist system as it exists with its
tendency toward financial fragility and asks what reforms will improve
the operation of the system. The Federal Reserve plays a crucial role as

a lender of last resort; however, Minsky notes, "To date the Federal Reserve System is a lender of last resort to a commercial bank in distress. It is not a lender of last resort to the money market" (Minsky 1982, 175).

In the 100 percent reserve plan, the discount window would be abolished and the Federal Reserve would affect bank reserves only through open market operations. Minsky takes the opposite view that the Federal Reserve should stop relying upon open market operations to determine reserves of the banking system and instead furnish bank reserves by discounting bank assets (Minsky 1986, 324–25). In such a system, the reserve base of banks (as well as the currency supply) would be created largely as a consequence of Federal Reserve discounting of bank loans that arise as a result of the financing of short-term business activity. The preferred asset for Federal Reserve discounting would be "to-the-asset paper that reflects commercial or manufacturing inventories" (Minsky 1986, 325). This proposal is based on the real bills doctrine; however, it avoids the dilemmas of earlier debates. In Minsky's proposal, it is central bank liabilities—the reserves of the banking system—that are subject to the real bills requirement. The Federal Reserve's discounting activities facilitate a continuing business relation between the banks and the Federal Reserve in short-term commercial loans. When loans are made, bank reserves increase; as loans fall due, bank reserves decline. Such a technique, according to Minsky, *"blunts the tendency toward fragile financing techniques"* (Minsky 1986, 325, emphasis added). This is because the discount method of creating reserves would induce favorable terms for hedge financing of short-term positions.[2] The supply of reserves would be infinitely elastic to all who hold eligible paper at some set discount rate. The interest rates on speculative and Ponzi financing will be higher than on hedge financing (Minsky 1986, 326). This discount window reform, coupled with capital requirements and reserve requirements imposed on the banks, would in Minsky's words help to "stabilize an unstable economy."

Friedman on 100 Percent Reserves

In his 1960 book *A Program for Monetary Stability*, Friedman noted that he departed from the original Chicago plan by having the Fed pay interest on the bank reserves. Friedman listed three reasons for paying interest on deposits: (1) to ensure the optimum amount of real resources utilized in the holding of cash balances (i.e., no zero opportunity cost to the individual in holding deposit money); (2) to reduce the incentive for banks to avoid the 100 percent reserve requirement; and (3) to compensate the holders of money balances and holders of government securities equally (Friedman 1960, 65).

At the time he presented his program for monetary stability, Friedman saw "no technical problem of achieving a transition from our present system to 100% reserves easily, fairly speedily, and without any serious repercussions on financial or economic markets" (Friedman 1960, 70). Interest should be paid on reserves because as structured it is effectively a tax on the banks. This would also reduce the incentive to evade the reserve requirement and create near monies (Friedman 1960, 74).

In 1967 Friedman wrote that he agreed with Simons's 100 percent reserve plan, but for the reasons that it reduces government interference with lending and borrowing, and it permits a greater degree of freedom in the variety of borrowing and lending arrangements (Friedman 1969, 83).

Testifying in 1975 before a House subcommittee, Friedman restated his 100 percent reserve proposal and the rationale for it. He said:

> I have long believed that the most effective way to reduce regulation is to separate the monetary functions of commercials banks from their credit conscience. The way to do this would be to require all institutions offering demand deposits to keep 100-percent reserves; make them depository institutions in fact and not, as now, simply in name. Free entry into this industry could be permitted. The institutions could compete for customers financed by the interest received from the Government and by service charges to customers. The lending and investing activities of today's commercial banks would be carried out by new institutions created by them which would raise their funds through time deposits or debentures or stock. These institutions would then be freed almost entirely from regulation. This is not a new proposal. It dates back over 40 years. It was supported in the 1930's by Henry Simons at the University of Chicago. It was proposed in a book by the great Yale economist, Irving Fisher. It has had a great deal of backing from the academic community. I believe it emerges naturally whenever banking reform is discussed, and I believe it deserves serious consideration as a feasible way to combine monetary security and stability with free and open competition in the capital market. (U.S. House 1975, 2156–57)

In an article published in *Challenge* in 1985 on the reform of the Federal Reserve, Friedman seemed to have abandoned his 100 percent reserve proposal. However, writing to John Hotson, Friedman stated his position on the 100 percent reserve system:

> [L]et me clear up my position on one-hundred reserves and zero percent reserves. . . . In my opinion, either extreme is acceptable. *I have not given up advocacy of one-hundred percent reserves.* I would prefer one-hundred percent reserves to the alternative I set forth. However, I believe that getting the government out of the business altogether or zero percent reserves also makes sense. The virtue of either one is that it eliminates government meddling in the lending and investing activities of the financial markets. When I wrote in 1948, we were already halfway toward one-hundred percent reserves because so large a fraction of the assets of the banks consisted of either government bonds or high-powered money. One-hundred percent reserves at that time did not look impossible of achievement. We have moved so far since then that *I am very skeptical indeed that there is any political possibility of achieving one-hundred percent reserves.* That does not mean that it is not desirable. *It does not mean that I have ever anywhere stated that I am opposed to one-hundred percent reserves,* but the sole reason why I stressed the proposal I did in the paper from which the *Challenge* piece was taken was because it seemed to me at least to be within the imaginable range of political feasibility. (letter to John Hotson, February 3, 1986, in author's possession, emphasis added)

Friedman's comments thus echo those of Lauchlin Currie and Jacob Viner, who both believed that even if the 100 percent reserves is an "ideal," political reality must be interjected.[3]

Tobin's Deposited Currency

Recently Nobel Prize winner, James Tobin, wrote that the basic dilemma for our financial system is that it has "evolved in a way that entangles competition among financial intermediary firms with the provision of transactions media" (Tobin 1985, 20). The result has been risks of default and government intervention that have created additional problems: deposit insurance, lender of last resort guarantees, and bureaucratic surveillance (Tobin 1985, 20–21). As to bank money, Tobin noted:

> Bank deposits are *inside* money, which has the macroeconomic advantage that no net national saving is tied up in its accumulation. However, the accident of history that made the principal medium of exchange inside money also made it vulnerable to events that impair the value and liquidity of the assets backing the money. (Tobin 1985, 25)

Tobin has proposed that a new type of money be issued that he calls "deposited currency." It would be payable in notes or coin on demand and offered by the Federal Reserve Banks or the commercial banks. If offered by the central bank, no deposit insurance would be needed. Private banks that offer the deposits could invest only in direct Federal Reserve obligations or government securities. Interest could be paid on the accounts. Though deposited currency would not need federal deposit insurance, it could be continued during a transition period for the commercial banks offering the deposited currency. Bank holding companies would be divided into commercial banks and investment banks and the activities of each department separated. Investment banks could issue uninsured deposits and be free to invest in whatever assets they wished.

Tobin's proposal incorporates many of the features of the 100 percent plan as put forward in the 1930s and perhaps comes closest to Angell's version of the plan. Tobin emphasizes the importance of the plan in reducing the demands on federal deposit insurance (Tobin 1985, 25; 1987, 172).

The Narrow Banking Proposal

In recent years, we have seen the emergence of "narrow banking" or "core banking" proposals, which are in the tradition of the 100 percent reserve plan.[4] A basic premise of the narrow banking proposal is that the federal government alone should have the power to create money. In the first instance, the rationale for government creation of money comes from the Constitution, which grants Congress the sole power to coin money and regulate its value (Tobin 1987, 168).

All of the narrow banking proposals seek to remedy the problems of the payments system by restricting to only "safe" assets the portfolios of financial institutions offering transactions or checkable accounts. The underlying assumption is that the primary role of banks is in the provision for a means of payment (Hart 1991). Some would make this compulsory (Tobin 1985, 1987; Lawrence and Talley 1988) while others would make it voluntary or apply it only to larger diversified institutions (Litan 1987; Spong 1991; Burnham 1991). In restricting assets, the proposal can be seen as continuing in the tradition of banking legislation—at least since the National Banking Act of 1864. Virtually all monetary legislation in the United States since that time has sought to place restrictions on the asset portfolios of banks. Further, the restrictions are always placed because of safety concerns (Pollock 1991).

All of the proposals agree that the intent of asset restriction is to reduce the private credit risk of the banks' portfolios. Narrow banking seeks to reduce five types of risks: credit (bad loans); interest rate (maturity); affiliate risk (failure and raid on narrow banking assets); activity risks (bond, foreign exchange trading); and fraud (Lawrence and Talley 1991, 346). There is some difference, however, among the narrow bank proposals on what constitutes safe assets.

John Kareken has argued that financial institutions offering transactions balances be restricted to offering only such balances and be subject to a 100 percent reserve requirement in the form of marketable treasury debt (Kareken 1986, 39–40) In essence, banks would be split into separate businesses or companies. The narrow bank would be like a mutual fund that would operate effectively to break up big pieces of government debt into little pieces (Golembe and Mingo 1985, 139; Lawrence and Talley 1988, 347).

In Kenneth Spong's version of the proposal, narrow banks would hold primarily cash, Federal Reserve balances, and short-term U.S. government securities. In order to assure an adequate supply of short-term government debt, Spong would recommend that the treasury substitute shorter term debt for longer term in its offerings. If the amount of safe government liabilities was insufficient, then the range of assets could be expanded to include other high-quality, short-term debt. Spong would also allow narrow banks to offer savings accounts, but the returns would differ little from transactions accounts (Spong 1991, 16).

Alice Haemmerli (1985, 8) would propose the creation of a "Consumer Bank," which would have 100 percent FDIC insurance coverage, no upstreaming of funds from the Consumer Bank to any other subsidiaries, close regulation of the bank, and no limitations on geographic expansion. James Burnham would allow narrow banks to hold Federal Reserve deposits, as well as deposits of other banks, both domestic and foreign; U.S. government securities of any maturity; and most government agency securities (Burnham 1991, 36–37). Stuart Greenbaum and Arnoud Boot would allow any investment grade assets, private or government (1991, 4).

Lowell Bryan's proposal is the least restrictive on assets and would allow banks to engage in traditional or "core" activities.[5] "Core banks" would be permitted to lend to individuals for mortgage loans, home equity loans, credit cards, installment loans, and auto loans. They would continue to loan to businesses for accounts receivable financing, equipment leasing, commercial mortgages, and unsecured lines of credit. In short, Bryan would allow banks to continue in those activities which they have been engaged in for more than a century and have demonstrated a competitive advantage over nonbanks (Bryan 1991, 79). It should be noted that, as one broadens the range of "safe" assets, the credit risk increases. It is for this reason that many of the core bank proposals include additional features such as increased capital requirements, interest rate ceilings, risk-based premiums, and other features found in less asset-restrictive proposals (Bryan 1991, 79–80; Hart 1991, 17).[6]

One of the important advantages of narrow banking is that banks would not need very much capital and, to the extent they incurred more credit risk, this would raise the capital requirements. However, small capital requirements could take care of any remaining risk (Lawrence and Talley 1988, 347) and then we would have a more stable payments system (Lawrence and Talley 1988, 352). Federal regulators would no longer have to worry about private sector risk factors, such as shopping mall vacancy rates, developing country creditworthiness, and oil prices (Burnham 1991, 37).

In contrast to the view that government should play a crucial role in the payments system, the narrow banking proponents would reduce government's role in private sector borrowing/lending to a largely supervisory one (Golembe and Mingo 1985, 140–1; Spong 1991, 9). Under the narrow banking proposal, savings would be channeled to investors through separate investment institutions.[7] One goal of the narrow banking proposal would be to reduce substantially the impact of government monetary policy on the private credit market. This would be a radical departure because, presently monetary policy *is* credit policy. Open market operations are intended to affect bank reserves and therefore the amount of private sector lending by banks. Narrow banking proposes to separate monetary policy and credit policy, leaving the Federal Reserve with its primary concern about the former.

Though this may seem like a radical change, it removes an asymmetry in the conduct of monetary policy. As a result of the fractional reserve system, which relies on the profit maximizing behavior of banks, it is easier for the Federal Reserve to restrain credit growth than it is to stimulate credit growth. When banks wish to accumulate excess reserves, there is little the Federal Reserve can do to cajole the banks into lending.

The difficulty with the Fed undertaking credit and monetary policy simultaneously is evident in the rhetoric of politicians today. On the one hand, as a result of the savings and loan problems, the government regulators are looking over the shoulders of banks to make sure they are not making bad loans. On the other hand, when the economy slows down, the politicians clamor for banks to loan more to get the economy moving. The problem is obvious: banks loan "too much" when times are good, and "too little" when times are bad. At the present time, after having castigated the banks for their actions in the 1980s and exhorting them to get their house in order, the same people are vehement in their attacks on the banks for paying 3 percent on deposits while charging 19 percent on credit cards. This is not a problem that can be adequately resolved under the present financial structure.

Under the narrow banking proposal, the Federal Reserve would still have its three tools of monetary policy: reserve requirements, open market operations, and the discount window. The Federal Reserve would continue to operate in pretty much the same way it does today. The main difference is that changing the money supply would not necessarily imply changing the amount of private sector credit.

Though there would not seem to be a need to restrict ownership of narrow banks, a problem would exist if the narrow bank assets were used to bail out a subsidiary owned by the holding company that also owns the narrow bank (Mingo 1987, 13). It is for this reason that, if narrow banks are to exist within a financial holding company, the narrow bank assets must be separate and unreachable (see Gilbert 1987, 13). Maintaining corporate separateness is both desirable and feasible. Carter Golembe and John Mingo present the strongest arguments that maintaining separateness is possible legally. Though they admit that there is the possibility that a bank holding company might strip the narrow bank of assets to protect another subsidiary, on balance the number of problem situations would not be great. The law is sufficiently effective, so that corporate separateness would be an appropriate regulatory vehicle (Golembe and Mingo 1985, 142; Gilbert 1987).

Robert E. Litan, one of the earliest proponents of narrow banking, would authorize the creation of new financial holding companies that would be required to separate their deposit-taking from their lending activities. In his version then, the narrow bank proposal would be an option—or enticement—for large highly diversified financial holding companies that wished to offer transactions accounts. The narrow or safe banks of such holding companies would be required to operate as mutual funds investing only in highly liquid safe securities such as treasury or other federally guaranteed instruments. The holding companies could extend loans, but only through separately incorporated lending subsidiaries wholly funded by uninsured liabilities (Litan 1987, 165).

The narrow banking proposal solves several problems with respect to the financial system: It makes the payments system safe, enhances the Fed's ability to control monetary aggregates, reduces the need for government regulation of banks, and accommodates (and perhaps accelerates) the growth of mutual funds. The narrow banking proposal would make federal deposit insurance redundant, and it is for this reason that it could logically be done away with or maintained with minimal, if any, fees. Tobin (1987, 173) states that deposit insurance would not be necessary for deposited currency, though it would be retained for commercial banks under his proposal. Burnham (1991, 36) would expand deposit coverage to all deposits in narrow banks—the $100,000 limit would be removed. Spong would extend deposit insurance to narrow banks, although it would be only to protect against fraud or macroeconomic collapse (Spong 1991, 23–24).

How politically feasible is narrow banking? William Siedman, the former FDIC head, agreed in principle with the intent of the narrow banking reforms (Siedman 1991). However, it may well be that we will await a catastrophe on the level of the Great Depression. The alternative is to move toward the less restrictive core banking, and hope that continued evolution with market forces and regulation will move us toward a more stable banking system.

The narrow banking proposal can be viewed historically as a continuation of what Peel's Act intended for bank notes in England, what the National Banking Act intended for bank notes in the United States, and what the Federal Reserve Act (through its various revisions) intended for demand deposits. To this extent, it does not solve for all time the problems of the financial system, but just raises it to the next level. Just as the use of bank notes declined and demand deposits became attractive substitutes, we now have attractive substitutes for demand deposits. The Federal Reserve controls bank notes, since it now has a monopoly, but it cannot control demand deposits. With economy-wide narrow banking, it could control M_1 but not broader definitions of the money supply.

Perhaps the strongest argument for narrow banking, however, is that it allows a way out of the federal deposit insurance mess. This is largely a political problem: Can we abolish federal deposit insurance? If we adopt narrow banking and then guarantee other financial assets, then nothing would have been accomplished.

Conclusion

The problems with the financial system that were discussed in the 1930s by Simons, Fisher, and others remain with us. Their ideas influenced others, and so continue to be of contemporary relevance for policy debates. Indeed the economics profession has moved far from 1965 when *Time* reported that we had just about reached the "outer limits of economic knowledge." What we have learned is that the financial system under capitalism does not necessarily promote economic stability. Financial institutions continue to evolve on the basis of legislative changes and as a result of the incentives in a market economy. The challenge for policy is to adjust institutions in a way that will facilitate the smooth evolution of the financial system and society.

14

Conclusion

The Chicago Plan—Would It Help Today?

Are the ideas incorporated in the Chicago plan of contemporary relevance?[1] William Allen (1993) wrote that the plan appeared to be only of historical relevance to which Friedman replied:

> You are wrong in supposing that the subject is only of historical interest. In connection with discussions of the present problems of the banking industry, stimulated in considerable measure by the course of the S & L disaster, some of the current commentators are reviving the idea of a 100 percent reserve plan as a better solution than guaranteeing bank deposits. (letter to William Allen, December 26, 1990, in author's possession)

To the question of the transition to the 100 percent reserve system, Friedman thought that technically it was not difficult. He wrote:

> All that is necessary is to pass legislation requiring that banks offering transactions deposits have as assets either cash, whether in the form of vault cash or as deposits at the Fed, or U.S. government securities equal in total amount to the volume of demand deposits outstanding. That would be 100% reserves, but 100% reserves in the form of either government securities or cash. There would also be a phase-in. The fractional reserve would be stated, let's say, 25% a year from now, 50% two years from now, and so on. The banks which offer transactions deposits, the narrow banks in Litan's phrase, would acquire the government securities by selling off their other assets, whether they are loans or investments, and purchasing government securities. (letter to author, November 7, 1991)

Is there any substantial argument that Chicago plan type reforms should be implemented today? We can answer the question by asking if the following are desirable (and require government intervention):

1. Less discretion by the Federal Reserve Board, and setting of monetary targets by Congress; a Reconstruction Finance Corporation and a Postal Savings system; and no Federal Reserve discount window.
2. "Safe" demand deposits but abolish or limit coverage of deposit insurance.
3. Greater direct intermediation between borrower and lender.

The 1930s proposals provide three policy prescriptions that remain relevant today: narrow banking, the creation of new private lending institutions with a mutual-type organization, and direct intervention by the federal government in credit markets through RFC-type institutions.

A fundamental question for financial reform today is how to enhance Federal Reserve control over the money supply and yet reduce the demand for federal government intervention in the private credit markets. As Ed Kane notes:

> The demand for credit allocation is a demand by, or on behalf of, frustrated borrowers for government intervention in their favor. It is a demand to change the rules of the economic game to assist so-called losers in credit markets (housing, small business, and nonwealthy households). Whether and how the rules are ultimately changed is determined in the political arena, with economic analysts playing only a small advisory role on both sides. The economist's role is essentially to assist participants to sort out and articulate how their sectoral self-interest would fall under alternative institutional arrangements. (Kane 1977, 56)

If Congress controlled the Federal Reserve, then no administration and no member of Congress would be able to blame the Federal Reserve Board for economic conditions. If Congress laid down definite rules, and did not change them too often, then it is conceivable that it might be superior—at least politically—to what we have now.

The pitfalls of the discount window have been recently noted by Anna Schwartz: There is a belief by some observers of bank performance that "it is impossible to know whether an institution that applies for discount window assistance faces a liquidity or a solvency problem" (Schwartz 1992, 59). Marvin Goodfriend and R. A. King (1988) and George Kaufman (1991) have argued that the lender of last resort function is not needed by the Federal Reserve to protect the money supply since liquidity difficulties may be met by open market operations.

In the words of Walker Todd, though it may inherently be a bad idea, the revival of the Reconstruction Finance Corporation is an idea "worth discussing if the only alternative permitted by the political process is central-bank funded rescues of politically designated target firms" (Todd 1992, 33). Jessup and Bochnak make the case for reviving the Postal Savings system, which currently exists in most developed economies (Jessup and Bochnak 1992).

Do we need banks to serve both a depository and lending function? Today, when we look at the current state of the financial system, banks are losing lending business to commercial paper and mutual funds, finance companies, and so on. Banks are looking more like the 100 percent reserve banks because their loans have been reduced as holdings of government securities have increased. It appears that, sixty years after the 100 percent reserve proposals, we are evolving toward a system that Henry Simons, Irving Fisher, and others would favor. The unanswerable question is whether we could have arrived at this point by taking a different path in the early New Deal years. The answer is not straightforward, because technology has been a fundamental driving force in the changes in banking. If the technology today had been available in 1933, the 100 percent reserve plan would have been imminently feasible. The policy question for today is whether government policy should continue to push the financial system along these lines of safe banks/uninsured financial institutions, or rather seek to restore the traditional role of banks in offering deposit and lending functions with federal deposit insurance.

Tobin has noted that, while the debates on monetary reform continue, we are in fact undergoing monetary reform "in a piecemeal and anarchic fashion, as a result of technological and institutional innovations, private initiatives, accidental quirks of ancient laws, administrative and judicial decisions, and actions by various states" (Tobin 1987, 167). While it is necessary to deal with immediate crises, such as the savings and loan industry, we must also reexamine the fundamental structure of our financial system and ask what reforms are necessary to avoid our present problems in the future.

The implementation of the 100 percent reserve plan is largely a political problem, just as it was in the 1930s. The technical transition to 100 percent reserves would not be difficult. It would certainly be no more difficult, and perhaps less difficult, than it would have been fifty years ago. All that is necessary is to pass legislation placing checkable deposits in financial institutions on the level with currency so they would be a direct liability of the Federal Reserve. As a first step to achieve 100 percent reserves, banks could hold present reserves (that would earn interest) and government securities against checkable deposits. The reserve ratio could then be gradually raised to 100 percent, or it could be accomplished immediately through Angell's proposal for the Fed to place a lien against the banks' assets. The important question is, once 100 percent reserves is attained, what will have been accomplished? The potential benefits of the plan would be in three areas: monetary control, stability, and safety.

Monetary Control

Though the discount window could be abolished with 100 percent reserve banking, most advocates of the 100 percent reserve plan were concerned about the availability of credit under the plan, especially during the transition period. In his version Lauchlin Currie argued that in the event that implementation of the 100 percent reserve plan created a shortage of loanable funds, then a government agency—such as the Reconstruction Finance Corporation (RFC) for the 1930s—could be empowered to subscribe to the capital of local loaning agencies, to make secured loans, or to establish loaning agencies (Currie 1968, 219). It is interesting to note that the Fed recently considered purchasing commercial loans from banks as an attempt to ease the credit crunch (*Wall Street Journal*, February 22, 1991, A2). This would undoubtedly be an expansion of the Fed's role in the economy, but it can be seen as an addition to or even an alternative to the discount window.

The question that troubled Henry Simons, but evidently not Irving Fisher, was the possibility of the development of deposit banking outside the Fed's control. Today, even more so than the 1930s, it would seem that 100 percent reserve banking would be undermined by financial innovation. Under fractional reserve banking, the Federal Reserve only controls the nonborrowed base, while M_1, M_2, and broader measures of the money supply are subject to public and bank behavior. In 100 percent reserve banking, the Federal Reserve would have eliminated the major sources of fluctuations in M_1, which are not under its control: excess reserves and the currency deposit ratio. However, public influence on the M_1 multiplier would not be totally eliminated since the public could still shift to other types of money. If the discount window is also abolished, Federal Reserve control would be improved, but it would still not be absolute.

It may be that controlling M₁ is less relevant to the macroeconomy today. This does not diminish the argument for 100 percent reserves, however (see McLane 1980). An examination of the evolution of the money supply in the United States would indicate that replacing private bank notes with government bank notes gave the government control, for a period of time, over the money supply; but with the development of checking accounts, it made currency a less relevant money supply. During the latter part of the nineteenth century and the early twentieth century, there was considerable debate over whether currency or checkable deposits were the economically relevant money supply (see Mints 1945). The government or the central bank has never had absolute control over the economically relevant money supply, and there is no reason to think that 100 percent reserves will change this completely. It is perhaps the next step in the evolution of the money supply to place checkable deposits on par with government currency.

Stability

The 100 percent reserve plan will certainly not end booms and depressions as even Irving Fisher recognized, despite the subtitle to his book that it would. The proposal may mitigate debt deflations such as occurred in the wake of the oil price collapse in the 1980s, however. The fall in oil and real estate prices may still have precipitated a downturn in the oil-based state economies, but the system of federal deposit insurance with fractional reserve banking compounded the problem.

There is little reason to believe that a 100 percent reserve system would accelerate financial innovation. In times of uncertainty, people tend to shift to safe assets, and at other times they shift to money market funds, mutual funds, and so on. The 100 percent reserve plan would not stop these shifts. There is no way to prevent this as long as financial institutions issue liabilities whose nominal values are guaranteed, while the values of the assets fluctuate. However safe demand deposits and the growth of money market mutual funds may make fractional reserve banking less competitive, especially without federal deposit insurance. People who want the nominal value guaranteed will increasingly have to hold government money. Under the 100 percent reserve system, safety would be in currency or demand deposits. The development of near monies will be a problem as long as we have a money-as-debt economy.[2]

Safety

After the implementation of 100 percent reserves, checkable deposits will then be as safe as currency, perhaps more so because there would not be the danger of losing checkable deposits in the same way currency might be lost. How would the public respond to 100 percent reserves? There is no reason to think that the public would flee from deposits, especially since safety has been enhanced. The public would pay for the high degree of safety directly through service charges or indirectly through taxation so that interest could be paid on bank reserves. Conceivably, such a system could be cheaper than the present system of federal deposit insurance.

One way of looking at the 100 percent reserve proposal is as a measure to restrict the portfolios of banks to "safe" assets. This need not require that all checkable deposits become direct liabilities of the Fed. As in Tobin's suggestion, federal deposit insurance could be continued, but it would only apply to the liabilities of these "safe" banks. The advantage of making all checkable deposits on par with currency would be to enable the complete abolition of federal deposit insurance. There would therefore be no limits on how much could be placed by individuals into these "safe" banks. Recently, Robert Litan has called for the creation of "monetary service companies." These institutions would serve strictly a payments function and would hold only safe assets such as cash, government securities, and high-grade commercial paper (Litan 1993; Pierce 1993).

Another question to be addressed is whether the safe banks could merge with nonbank corporations. There are reasons to be concerned about the merging of fractional reserve lending institutions with nonbank corporations, especially under a system of federal deposit insurance. Since safe banks cannot loan to the private sector, there is less reason to prohibit such mergers. The 100 percent reserve proposal implies raising the capital requirement ratio on lending institutions to 100 percent as well. Such a suggestion might send shudders through bankers who are presently complaining about the recent increases in capital requirements.

How would 100 percent reserves compare with branch banking in terms of safety? Though inefficient banks would be bought up if interstate banking were legalized nationally, we would then have exacerbated the "too big to fail" problem. Presently, our system of private profits and social losses places our financial system on the road to eventual nationalization. When firms become too big to fail, their losses are socialized over the populace. This is precisely the development that 100 percent reserve advocates sought to avoid by putting the safety of deposits on par with currency.

It may be that the elimination of hand-to-hand currency will be achieved much more easily if checkable deposits become a Federal Reserve liability. Just as physical commodities such as gold have disappeared as money in modern economies, paper currencies may soon follow suit. Under such circumstances, it may then make sense to have a safe government money in the form of checkable deposits.

Rebirth of the Chicago Plan

The Chicago plan has appeared in updated and revised form, but with its essentials intact. Contemporary advocates of the Simons-Fisher 100 percent plan include John Hotson (1985) and Michael Schemmann (1991) and the Committee on Monetary and Economic Reform (COMER). Others have proposed the expansion of mutual fund banking, an idea closely related to the 100 percent reserve proposal (Cowen and Kroszner 1990, 230–1). Recently Gordon Getty, an heir to the J. Paul Getty oil fortune, has proposed to replace the financial system controlled by the Federal Reserve with a parallel system based on mutual funds. There would be check clearing, and the mutual fund shares would be effectively money, but backed by the asset portfolio of the mutual fund. There would be no government insurance and no guarantee of par value clearance (Ferguson 1993). This would be a system of 100 percent reserves, but not necessarily in government securities. Still the proposal has much in common with the Chicago plan. One crucial problem is that such a system may still require government money as a unit of account. However, all this requires is that people continue to have more faith in government established fiat money than in "money" issued by a private corporation.

James R. Barth and Dan Brumbaugh, Jr. have proposed that federal deposit insurance be replaced with a federal money market mutual fund (Barth and Brumbaugh 1993, 27–28). The assets of the fund would be short-term treasury securities and liabilities would be only demand deposits. There could be electronic deposits of all government checks. The banking services provided would be large-scale electronic debit and credit mechanisms with retail outlets, perhaps at the Post

Office, much as the Postal Savings system once operated. With this proposal we have come full circle from the banking crisis of March 1933 and the proposals of the Chicago economists (Tugwell, Means, and others) to provide for a safe and efficient payments system.

Another recent concern has been the lack of effective lending institutions for communities, especially in rural or low-income areas. Proposals have been presented to establish a nationwide system of "community development banking and lending institutions" to provide basic banking services to communities who lack them (Minsky et al. 1993). Alex Pollock has proposed the revival of the mutual savings and loan association. These associations were locally organized, and the funds invested were equity or shares, and not deposits—each member was a part owner. These associations would go a long way toward creating the kinds of "proper" lending institutions that Henry Simons believed would go far toward achieving a better financial structure (Pollack 1993).

The Barth-Brumbaugh proposal for a federal mutual fund, together with the Pollock proposal to revive the mutual savings associations, and the Litan proposal, may very well deserve the label of the "Chicago plan for the twenty-first century."

Conclusion

The history of the 100 percent reserve proposal is of interest as history of economic thought. It is a fact that many of the most prominent names in economics supported the proposal at one time. One interesting question is why it continually reappears in times of financial crisis. The proposal was put forward as an "ideal" system, yet it seems to be in contradiction to the evolution toward zero reserves.

Taking into account technological innovations and the evolution of the banking system, many aspects of the 100 percent reserve proposal remain attractive. First and foremost is that 100 percent reserves (in marketable government securities) for transactions deposits is a reasonable alternative to the virtually unlimited contingent liability implied by federal deposit insurance. Future evolution of the banking system, if it follows the 100 percent proposal, will be toward mutual fund banking with high return for the risk, on the one hand; and government subsidized demand deposits, which pay little interest and have no risk, on the other. The result, if the 100 percent reserve advocates are correct, will be a system with greater stability, lower social costs, and more consistency with an economy in which private decisions play a large role in the allocation of resources.

Practically, the 100 percent reserve proposal would provide a way out of the present federal deposit insurance mess. This may be its relevance for financial reform today. To the extent there is agreement that federal deposit insurance must go, the 100 percent reserve solution—perhaps through Tobin's deposited currency—could be the easiest way out.

The policy prescriptions advocated in the 1930s for narrow banking, mutual organization of lending institutions, and RFC-type government lending institutions remain relevant today. These reforms offer the prospect of an improvement in the ability of the Federal Reserve to control the basic supply and, at the same time, reduce demands for new or expanded programs for federal credit allocation.

The problem we will continue to face in the future is whether the government would in fact let a large noninsured financial institution collapse. Presently, many people believe that the government would financially back any large financial corporation in trouble to prevent the depositors from losing financial wealth. If the government says that it will not, but people suspect that it has a strong incentive to help banks in trouble, then rational economic agents would factor that into their behavior, and the present problem of fractional reserve banking and federal deposit insurance would not have been remedied at all.

If government intends to bail out large financial institutions, then there are strong arguments that we should go ahead and make this policy explicit through nationalization of the banking system. Our present difficulties stem from the unusual mixture of government and private production of money. The real problem is how to construct financial institutions that do not impede the development of the economy, yet are flexible enough to allow for technological innovation and market discipline. The reforms of the 1930s worked reasonably well for several decades. We will be fortunate if financial reforms in the 1990s endure into the middle of the twenty-first century.

Appendix

The Chicago Plan for Banking Reform

March 16, 1933

Hon. Henry A. Wallace
Secretary of Agriculture,
Washington, D.C.

Dear Mr. Wallace:

During the past week, we have tried to formulate and agree upon a specific program which would provide, both for emergency relief, and for permanent banking reform. The results of this effort are contained in the five-page statement which we enclose. This document is strictly for your private use; and we request that every precaution be taken against mention of it in the press.

The program defined in the statement is one which we believe to be sound, even ideal, in principle. What its merits may be, in the light of political consideration, we frankly do not know. We are sensible, moreover, of an obligation not to broadcast publicly any statement which might impair confidence in Administration measures, or impair their chances of successful operation.

On the other hand, we feel that our statement may deserve thoughtful consideration, among people of interests like our own; also, that it may suggest measures which might be usefully incorporated in other, and perhaps less impractical, schemes. Moreover, most of us suspect that measures at least as drastic and "dangerous" as those described in our statement can hardly be avoided, except temporarily, in any event.

President's Official File 230, Franklin D. Roosevelt Library.

Please feel free to use the document in any manner consistent with complete avoidance of newspaper publicity. If you feel disposed to send us your comments, favorable and adverse, upon the proposals, we shall be grateful indeed for your cooperation. Communications may be addressed to any member of the group.

Sincerely yours,

G. V. Cox	F. H. Knight
Aaron Director	L. W. Mints
Paul Douglas	Henry Schultz
A. G. Hart	H. C. Simons

By Frank H. Knight (Sgd.)

P.S. We hope you are *one* of the forty odd who get this who will not think we are quite loony, I think Viner really agrees but doesn't believe it good politics. F.H.K.

*It is evident that drastic measures must soon be taken with reference to banking, currency, and federal fiscal policy. In such a situation, it seems desirable that there should be some statement of opinion by academic economists, especially by groups whose members hold substantially similar views. We therefore submit the following general recommendations.

(a) That further decline in the volume of effective circulating media be prevented, preferably by some sort of federal guarantee of bank deposits;

(b) That guarantee of bank deposits be undertaken only as part of a drastic program of banking reform which will certainly and permanently prevent any possibly recurrence of the present banking crisis;

(c) That the Administration announce and pursue a policy of bringing about, and maintaining, a moderate increase (say, of—and not to exceed—fifteen per cent) in the level of wholesale prices, pending later adoption of some explicit criterion for long-run currency-management.

It seems appropriate to translate these general recommendations into more detailed proposals. The proposals below are admittedly inade-

---

*Proposal begins here.

quate and tentative at many points; but they should serve to define what we conceive to be objectives of sound policy:

(1) That the federal government immediately take over actual ownership and management of the Federal Reserve Banks;

(2) That the Federal Reserve Banks should guarantee the deposits of all Member Banks which were open for business on March 3rd, 1933 (or on the last day preceding any moratorium then in effect), the Reserve Banks being granted full supervisory *control* over the management of these institutions;

(3) That the Federal Reserve Act be further amended, to permit issue of Federal Reserve Notes in any amounts which may be necessary to meet demands for payment by Member-Bank depositors;

(4) That Federal Reserve Notes be declared full legal tender for all debts;

(5) That numerous and generous arrangements be made for relief of non-member institutions, not included under the guarantee, including: (a) generous loans by the Reserve Banks and/or the R.F.C., such loans to be made on the basis of what bank assets are likely to be worth after the proposed increase of wholesale prices has been effected; and (b) provision for continuance of moratoria and limitations upon withdrawals if and where expedient.

Stockholders of the Federal Reserve Banks should, of course, be reimbursed by the government, preferably at par-value of their holdings. The Reserve Banks, though owned by the government, should remain separately incorporated, like the R.F.C.; and their management (The Federal Reserve Board) should be independent of the Treasury.

The precise technique of control, exercised by the Reserve Banks over the guaranteed institutions, should be left largely to the decision of the Reserve authorities. The powers, however, should be broad. The Reserve Banks should be free to take over, in return for Reserve Notes, such assets of Member Banks as they might need, as basis for note-issue, or for their open-market operations.

It is entirely improbable that the note-issue required in connection with the guarantee arrangements would be of substantial magnitude. With the guarantee, deposits would be quite as desirable as Notes; and the banks, instead of requiring currency from the Reserve Banks, would probably attract substantial amounts of currency and receive new deposits from present hoarders of currency, instead of being required to increase their issue. In any event, new issue would be fully covered by government securities (and perhaps other assets) now in the hands of the Member Banks.

(6) That the Federal Reserve Banks be instructed, over such period as may prove necessary for orderly liquidation, to dispose of all assets of the Member Banks, to pay off all deposit liabilities, and upon final settlement with the stockholders to declare the corporations dissolved;

(7) That banking legislation be enacted providing for incorporation of a new kind of institution:

    (a) which alone shall be entitled to accept funds subject to
        check or to payment on demand;
    (b) which shall be required to maintain reserves of 100% in
        lawful money and/or deposits with the Reserve Banks;
    (c) which shall serve exclusively as institutions for deposits and
        transfer of funds;

(8) That additional legislation be enacted, providing for incorporation of a distinct class of institutions, in the general form of investment trusts, and subject to government regulation and examination, which institutions shall perform the functions of existing banks with respect to savings deposits;

(9) That losses incurred by the Reserve Banks in liquidating particular Member Banks be collected, so far as legally possible, from stockholders of those banks.

(9a) That the Member Banks, under Reserve Bank supervision (and the non-member institutions), should continue to make loans and accept deposits, pending the development of reasonably adequate facilities by other institutions, and in general to make such renewals of loans as seem consistent with most successful ultimate liquidation.

The primary objective of these proposals for permanent reform is that of effecting a complete separation, between different classes of corporations, of the Deposit and Lending functions of existing commercial banks. The now typical commercial bank would, in effect, be broken up into at least two distinct corporations, say, a Deposit-Bank and a Lending Company. The Deposit-Bank would serve exclusively as a depository and agency for transfer of funds (checking); it would derive earnings solely from service-charges. The Lending Company, on the other hand, would engage in the business of short-term lending, discounting, and acceptance; it would be prohibited from accepting demand-deposits, and even from providing their short-term creditors, if any, with any effective substitute for checking facilities; thus, it, like other corporations, would be in position to lend and invest only the funds invested by its stockholders (and, perhaps, bondholders). Considerable specialization might develop among these Lending Companies. For investors preferring the savings-deposit form, the facilities of the Postal Savings System would still be available. [Incidentally], the liquidation of existing commercial banks, during the transition period, would probably be effected in part by sale of their assets to newly incorporated Lending Companies.

It is contemplated that the loss of circulating media consequent upon the gradual liquidation of existing Member Banks would be offset by corresponding increase in the Deposits and Notes of the Reserve Banks. Here likewise, however, no substantial increase in the issue of Federal Reserve Notes is likely to occur. During final liquidation of a particular institution, the holders of Demand Deposits would be paid off, in Notes or in drafts upon the Reserve Banks; and these, in turn, would promptly be deposited in the New Deposit-Banks, which in turn would deposit them with the Reserve Banks. Savings-depositors might be induced to accept direct transfer to the Postal Savings System, or to take government bonds in exchange; but no restrictions need be placed upon payment in currency or drafts. At the end of the transition period, the total of reserve Notes in circulation would probably be much smaller than at present. Our circulating media, as heretofore, would consist largely of demand deposits of private institutions; and these deposits would be backed dollar for dollar, by currency and, predominantly, deposits of the Reserve Banks. The liabilities of the Reserve Banks, in turn, would be supported by assets, largely or exclusively government bonds, acquired through liquidation of the member institutions.

(10) That the administration announce and pursue a policy of bringing about, by fiscal and currency measures, an increase of fifteen (15) per cent in Wholesale Prices.

(11) That adequate and detailed preparations be made for preventing any further increase of prices than that originally determined upon and announced.

Adoption of the proposed guarantee arrangements, far from being inflationary, would actually involve, by comparison with conditions of the recent past, a marked reduction in the quantity of circulating media. Expansion of Reserve-Note circulation, if it occurred, could not exceed the contraction of Member-Bank deposits. The inevitable reduction in the "deposit-circulation" of the non-member institutions would represent a net reduction for the whole banking system. Thus, measures of the kind contemplated in (10) above would probably be necessary, if only to prevent contraction of the country's supply of media of exchange.

The proposal for increasing the price level contemplates additional issue of Federal Reserve Notes against federal securities, for the purpose of covering the fiscal deficit and of meeting forthcoming maturities. It is not unlikely, given the stimulus of the guarantee arrangement, that quite moderate measures might suffice to bring about the specified price-level change. Substantial increase of federal, emergency expenditures might, however, prove necessary.

In order to stop the increase of prices at the point determined upon, it is only necessary to prepare for impounding of currency—by sale of Reserve-Bank assets and/or new federal issues in the open-market, by reduction of emergency expenditures of the government, and, as a drastic move unlikely to prove necessary, by the levy of some form of sales tax. Balancing of the federal budget should prove continuously less difficult, as revenues rise from improvement of business, and as demands for unemployment relief abate.

We wish to emphasize especially the importance of proclamation by the President as to the precise objective of Administration measures with reference to the price-level. Such proclamation will enormously facilitate the tasks, both of bringing about the increase and of stopping it at the proper time.

It is worth noting, that the measures required for raising the price-level may be rather drastic, if there occurs a large immediate loss of circulating media in the form of demand-deposits. If policies adopted toward the non-member banks result in the "freezing" of a large part of their deposits, substantial increase of federal emergency expenditures (for unemployment-relief and for public works) might be required even to maintain the present level of prices. These considerations would seem to argue for prompt and generous assistance to the non-member institutions.

(12) That the following measures be taken with respect to gold:

    (a) Suspension of the free-coinage of gold and a lowering of the price obtainable for gold at the Mint;

    (b) Absolute embargo upon the import of gold;

    (c) Prohibition of the export of gold by *private* individuals or institutions;

    (d) Commandeering of all gold coin and gold certificates by the government, in exchange for Federal Reserve Notes;

    (e) Suspension by Presidential Proclamation of enforcement of all gold-clauses in debt-contracts;

    (f) Substantial sale and export of gold abroad by the government and/or the Reserve Banks;

The measures outlined above would, we feel, meet the immediate emergency, provide a permanent solution of the banking problem, and bring about marked improvement in production and employment. Their adoption, however, would leave one major problem still to be faced, namely, that of long-run currency management. Within our group, there are slight differences of opinion as to what constitutes the most desirable policy. Some of us favor a stabilizing of the total quantity of circulating media; some, a stabilizing of total "circulation" ("MV") per period; some favor more complex formulas (e.g., stabilizing per-capita "circulation"). The criterion of price-stabilization seems to us quite satisfactory, however, as a short-run expedient.

At all events, the problem of long-run currency management is one which need not, and probably should not, be settled for some time. Ultimately, it may even prove expedient to return to gold, especially if it appears that popular movements for "cheap money" cannot be checked without recourse to the old symbols.*

DEPARTMENT OF AGRICULTURE
WASHINGTON

March 23, 1933

The President,

The White House.

Dear Mr. President:

The memorandum from the Chicago economists which I gave you at the Cabinet meeting Tuesday, is really awfully good and I hope that you or Secretary Woodin will have the time and energy to study it. Of course the plan outlined is quite a complete break with our present banking history. It would be an even more decisive break than the founding of the Federal Reserve System. Personally, I think the banking policy should be in the direction of increasing prices by twenty to twenty-five per cent rather than the fifteen per cent suggested by Professor Knight. However, I have no doubt that Professor Knight has an adequate statistical basis for this suggestion.

At first thought it might seem inadvisable to make any statement about a banking policy as related to prices. If you think over the matter further, however, I think the idea might intrigue you.

I still have the feeling that practically no one in the Government

---

*End of proposal.

realizes how tremendously important is the centralized control of the open market policy of the Federal Reserve System. When Benjamin Strong was Governor of the Federal Reserve Bank some rather constructive things were done with this open market policy, but in recent times this tremendous power has been exercised in a rather hap-hazard fashion by men from the twelve regional banks who did not have the training to fit them to deal with the matter of a central banking policy. I hope these open market operations can be taken completely out of the hands of these representatives from the regional banks and placed in the hands of men who have the viewpoint that central bankers must have. This philosophy is the same as that of Bagehot, the English banking historian. The all important thing is to place the powers that have to do with central banking, with international exchanges, and with general price levels in the hands of those who are concerned with the broad national interest and the stability of price levels rather than, as has been the case in the past, with the selfish concern of local bank profits.

Frankly, I question whether the members of the Federal Reserve Board have ever fully caught the vision of what might be done in the way of enlightened central bank control. I know that Governor Frank Lowden has this vision, and I regret that he is not young enough to serve.

Respectfully yours,

H. A. Wallace (signed)

Secretary

——————— Notes ———————

Notes to Chapter 1

1. A government issued currency that is *not* convertible into specie, or anything else, is referred to as *fiat* currency. Inconvertible government currencies that are issued in the purchase of assets, and therefore form the liabilities side of a "balanced" balance sheet, are referred to as *fiduciary* currency (Russell 1991, 39). Bank created money, whether bank notes or demand deposits, is *fiduciary* money.

2. The question of whether or not the free banking era was marked by greater instability than later periods will not be directly discussed, though it merits scholarly attention. There has been a great deal of literature in recent years that seeks to reassess the free banking experience in the United States and elsewhere. The conclusion of this line of research has been that the views of unstable, wildcat banking are a misrepresentation of the real experience. This reexamination of the period has led many to call for monetary reform along the lines of allowing free entry and competition to prevail in the production of money, as in other industries (see White 1984; Selgin 1988; and a contrary view by Rothbard 1988).

3. The importance of "war news" in the determination of the value of greenbacks in the United States during the Civil War was discussed extensively by Wesley C. Mitchell (1903, pp. 210–38) in his study of the greenback era and later by Friedman and Schwartz (1963, pp. 74–76). For a contemporary application, see Phillips (1988b).

4. As James Grant notes, "the government undertook to socialize the money supply, or an important part of it. It was a measure that anticipated many of the financial expedients of the twentieth century. If the Civil War was the first modern war, the National Currency Act was the first modern financial legislation" (Grant 1992, 48).

5. The Federal Reserve issues liabilities and acquires assets in doing so. Theoretically, it could issue its bank notes and acquire in assets what others are willing to give up for Federal Reserve notes. In other words, the Federal Reserve could buy and sell television sets if it wished and in the process create new liabilities. Using television sets (or private sector debt for that matter) sounds odd but buying and selling gold, other bank notes, or securities does not because of convention.

Notes to Chapter 2

1. On April 5, 1918, Congress created the War Finance Corporation to "augment capital investment markets and make loans to war industries." The WFC made loans to banks, public utilities, railroads, and building and loan associations. Worried about the postwar adjustment of the economy, Congress authorized the WFC to make export loans. The WFC continued after the end of the war. The Agricultural Credits Act of 1921 gave the WFC $300 million to loan to farmers needing intermediate credit, and in 1924 the Federal Intermediate Credit Bank system assumed those responsibilities. The government began liquidating the WFC in 1924, a process that took six years. By 1931 prominent private bankers as well as Eugene Meyer, chairman of the Federal Reserve Board and a former member of the WFC board of directors, were urging Hoover to revive the WFC (Olson 1988, 13–14).

2. World War I veterans had been promised a bonus payment from Congress to be paid in 1945. Because of the dire economic situation many of them faced in the thirties, they wanted the bonus paid early. Federal troops, led by Douglas MacArthur with Dwight Eisenhower in second command, routed the Bonus Army from their encampment on the Mall in Washington in July 1932.

3. Say's Law stems from the observation that since every purchase is simultaneously a sale, supply creates its own demand, and there can never be a general insufficiency of aggregate demand. As long as markets adjust price and output freely, then unemployment is not possible in the long run. However this conception of Say's Law, popularized by John Maynard Keynes, is probably a "straw man," and the analysis of the role of Say's Law in classical economics would undoubtedly present a more complicated picture.

4. Irving Fisher's role in the 1930s debate on monetary reform is discussed in chapter 9.

Notes to Chapter 4

1. Though this is not the place for a debate on the meaning of that phrase, nor on the membership of such a school, there is little doubt that the influence of all three, and particularly Knight and Simons, was profound in the subsequent development of economics in the United States. For more on this, see *The New Palgrave* entry "The Chicago School" and the recent article by Laidler (1993). On Mints see Peterson and Phillips (1991)

2. For more on the economic thought of Frederick Soddy and Knight's assessment of Soddy see Daly (1980). I am grateful to Ross B. Emmett for bringing to my attention this reference to Knight's early views on banking.

3. A complete history of the 100 percent reserve idea prior to Soddy, though extremely interesting and useful, will not be attempted. It is clear that Soddy's ideas had an immediate impact on the Chicago economists, and it is for this reason discussion begins with Soddy. Lloyd Mints (1945) discusses the 100 percent reserve idea in the history of banking theory in the United States and Great Britain until 1913. Ludwig von Mises (1912) was an advocate of 100 percent reserves in gold. For others who advocated 100 percent reserves, see Bromberg (1939).

4. Soddy published a second edition of his 1926 book in 1933 (Soddy 1933b), and a second book emphasizing his proposal (Soddy 1934). Soddy cites the work of Arthur Kitson as an important influence on his own work (Kitson 1895, 1917a, 1917b, 1933). Also see Lindenthal (1935).

5. All of the signers were members of the faculty at Chicago, though A. G. Hart was a doctoral candidate. Paul Douglas later became Senator Douglas, Democrat of Illinois. In economics, one of his claims to fame was the Cobb-Douglas production function.

6. In her book, Susan Kennedy says "the plan submitted by economists of University of Chicago to Secretary of Agriculture Henry A. Wallace is typical of the recommendations offered at this time." She lists only about half of the provisions of the plan and does not mention at all the 100 percent reserve proposal (Kennedy 1973, 166).

7. Fisher concurred with Wallace's view (Cargill 1992) as did Friedman and Schwartz, 1963, chapter 6.

Notes to Chapter 5

1. The permanent plan was postponed until the passage of the Banking Act of 1935.

2. In his detailed accounting of the debates over deposit insurance in 1933, Mark Flood concludes that the legislators both understood the difficulties with deposit insurance and incorporated in the legislation numerous provisions designed to mitigate the problems associated with it (Flood 1992, 52).

3. It should be noted that the deposit guarantee did not put the "full faith and credit" of the federal government behind the guarantee. This did not occur until the enactment of the Competitive Equality in Banking Act of 1987.

Notes to Chapter 6

1. In a letter to Paul Douglas, Simons wrote:

> Actually I did write the thing alone; but it would never have been written except for my conversations with other people, Mr. Director especially; and it never would have been circulated without favorable critical reports from yourself and the other members of the group. So, what is uniquely my own is merely the phrasing. (Simons to Paul Douglas, October 2, 1934, Simons Papers)

2. Means wrote seven memorandums during 1933–34 that are in the Means Papers at the Franklin Roosevelt Library. Though not all of the memos are dated, the order in which they were written is evident from the text (Means 1933a–e, 1934a–b).

3. Means presented his proposal in print in a coauthored book (Ware and Means 1936).

Notes to Chapter 7

1. In November 1934, the Census Bureau released the results of a survey on *The Credit Requirements of Small Industry for Recovery*. The author of the survey, Theodore N. Bechman of Ohio State University, recommended liberalization of examination policies of supervisory agencies as well as increased Federal Reserve bank and RFC lending to the private sector. This was to be coupled with the creation of a system of intermediate credit banks to lend directly to industry and to discount bank loans to industry (Reeve 1943, 86).

2. Writing in 1934, Simons stated that a primary intent of the Chicago plan was to counter the demands for the socialization of banking. He stated:

> The so-called 100 per cent scheme was suggested, at least by its Chicago proponents, largely, if not primarily, with the notion that reform along such lines would serve to minimize the danger of increasing political control over the direction of investment, i.e., the danger, both of socialization of banking in its present form and of "financial planning" administration by organizations of private banks. . . . If a rigid separation could be achieved between the business of warehousing and transferring funds and that of mobilizing funds for lending and investment, the state might properly limit its regulation of the latter type of business to the provision of ordinary safeguards against fraud and the maintenance of competitive conditions in the investment markets.
>
> The 100 per cent banking scheme has been characterized as socialistic and advocates of quantitative control have been charged with the intention of turning the banking business over to politicians. While both observations are intellectually beneath notice, they might be countered, for purposes of vulgar debate, with the remark that most defenders of qualitative control are impliedly espousing syndicalist ideas and, for their own purposes, a corporative state. (Simons 1948, 332–33)

3. Simons wrote to Irving Fisher regarding his efforts on the Cutting bill:

> While in Washington, I prepared for Senators Cutting and LaFollette a rough outline of some features of a possible bill. I am enclosing a copy of this outline–although it is too crude for critical examination. (Simons to Fisher, March 29, 1934, Simons Papers)

In a later letter to Fisher, Simons wrote: "The Cutting Bill, for present purposes at least, is much better than I had anticipated. It was written by Robert Hemphill, of the Hearst staff and formerly with the Richmond (?) Reserve Bank" (Simons to Fisher, July 4, 1934, Simons Papers). Simons's reluctance to become more involved in the legislative battle apparently reflected his growing reservations about "crucial details of the scheme as I had outlined it" (Simons to Frank Taussig, November 12, 1934, Simons Papers).

Notes to Chapter 8

1. Albert G. Hart, in a letter to Henry Simons encouraging wide distribution in government of the Chicago proposal, noted that "Viner complained to us this summer that before he went there (Treasury) he was deluged with circulars on policy, but that there seemed to be a taboo among economists against writing on policy to people who might conceivably be in positions of some power" (Hart to Simons, December 9, 1934, Simons Papers).

2. The reports were as follows: Edward C. Simmons, "The Currency System"; Benjamin Caplan, "Branch Banking"; A. G. Hart, "Federal Credit Institutions"; Lauchlin Currie, "Monetary Control in the United States," and "Deposit Insurance"; Alan R. Sweezy, "Objectives and Criteria of Monetary Policy"; H. D. White, "Selection of a Monetary Standard for the United States"; and H. W. Riley, "Bank Examinations and Bank Reports" (Mrs. Belsley to Mr. Viner, December 20, 1934, Morgenthau Papers, Viner File 1933–34).

3. Currie became known as an early "Keynesian" economist. Though his thinking on the role of fiscal policy was evolving at the same time he was working on monetary problems, the focus of this section is on his monetary theory and policy. For a detailed presentation of his early "Keynesian" views, see Sandilands (1991).

4. Henry Simons greatly admired Currie's book on the supply of money and reviewed it in the *Journal of Political Economy*. In a letter to Fisher, Simons says: "I'm interested in your mentioning the Currie book. It's the only book on banking, and almost the only decent book in American economics, which makes me genuinely envious of the author for having written it" (Simons to Fisher, November 9, 1934, Simons Papers).

5. In a footnote in his book, Currie stated that Albert G. Hart had brought the Chicago proposal to his attention after the book had gone to press (Currie 1934, 156).

6. The story of John M. "100%" Nichols deserves mention. He was a banker in Chicago who put theory into practice and operated on the 100 percent reserve principle for over a decade (see Phillips 1994a).

Notes to Chapter 9

1. Fisher was known for changing his mind with regard to financial reform. In 1932 he had testified to Congress in favor of the deposit guarantee program, especially the fact that it was to be a permanent feature of the system (Fisher 1932a, 145). The 100 percent reserve plan makes deposit insurance redundant, a fact that Fisher later, of course, acknowledged. He wrote subsequently: "As a temporary expedient, deposit insurance was a helpful measure designed to get us out of the depression. But, in the case of State banks, experience shows that insuring deposits has usually increased the risk insured against, by encouraging careless banking" (Fisher [1935] 1945, 161).

2. The book *Booms and Depressions* first stated the debt-deflation theory. The *Econometrica* article is a summary of the book. Chapter 7 of *100% Money* contains a summary of the article and is used in the discussion that follows.

3. Though Fisher believed he was making an original contribution to the theory of business cycles, in his *Econometrica* article, he stated that Wesley Mitchell had pointed out the similarities of Fisher's debt-deflation theory to that of Thorstein Veblen in *The Theory of Business Enterprise*, chapter 7. For a comparison of Veblen and Simons, see Phillips (1988a).

4. John Hotson laments: "How much better off society as a whole would have been if Fisher and Simons had led us out of the Great Depression instead of Keynes" (Hotson 1987, 189).

5. Frederick Soddy, whose work was discussed previously, continued to expound on his version of the 100 percent reserve plan throughout the depression years. Dimand notes that one of the curious aspects associated with the publication of the first edition of *100% Money* was an exchange of several letters between Fisher and Soddy in the *Economic Forum* concerning the former's recognition of the original contribution of the latter. Dimand writes: "Soddy repeatedly upbraided Fisher for failing to mention that 100% reserves were discussed in Soddy (1926), and Fisher repeatedly provided references to the discussion and full citation of Soddy (1926) in *100% Money* and to proponents of 100% reserves before Soddy, going back to Thomas Joplin a century before. The final issue of the *Economic Forum* in 1937 promised further letters from Fisher and Soddy in the next issue. The correspondence closed without Soddy admitting either that Fisher had cited him in *100% Money* or "even that Fisher was stating that he had done so" (Dimand 1993).

6. For a recent discussion of Fisher's price-level stabilization scheme, see (Humphrey 1992).

7. Though both Fisher and the Chicago economists would be classified as adherents to the Quantity Theory of Money (QTM), they had differences of interpretation. A careful analysis of the respective interpretations would undoubtedly provide insight into their differences over stabilization schemes. Because it goes beyond the intent of the present study, comparisons of their views will be restricted to correspondence between Fisher and Simons (see below), and no attempt to compare and contrast their somewhat different versions of the QTM will be attempted.

Notes to Chapter 10

1. As an historical note, on August 16, 1948, in a Joint Resolution of Congress (S.J. Res. No. 157, 80th Cong., 2nd sess.), the Banking Act of 1935 was temporarily amended (1) in order to prevent injurious credit expansion; and (2) to raise the limit on time deposit reserves to a maximum of 7–1/2 percent, and the maximum reserves against demand deposits in central reserve cities to 30 percent (Krooss 1969, 2999–3000). The increased reserve requirements of the resolution expired on June 30, 1949.

2. The late Lauchlin Currie concurred in this view of the importance of the Eccles-Glass confrontation. In response to a direct question about the provision in the House version of the Banking Act of 1935 that would allow the Federal Reserve to raise reserve requirements to 100 percent, if it wished, Currie stated, "I agree with you that Eccles' difficulties with Sen. Glass resulted in changes in the

bill as planned. Not only was the proposed change in reserve requirements affected but also the control of open market operations. The consequences of a lack of flattery!" (Letter to author, July 29, 1993).

Notes to Chapter 11

1. Burnham P. Beckwith, who received his Ph.D. from the University of Southern California in 1932, advocated 100 percent reserve banking in a privately published book. With regard to the Chicago plan for 100 percent reserve banking he wrote: "By pure coincidence, in 1934 I had written an article advocating the elimination of commercial banking and had sent it to the *Journal of Political Economy*, edited by the Department of Economics at the University of Chicago. The idea must have been in the air, due to the 1929–33 collapse of the commercial banking system" (Beckwith n.d., 82).

2. An article and a note by Lin examined the issue of time deposits (Lin 1937a, 1937b).

3. For an application of the Chicago plan to England, that was published as an appendix to Hart's article, see Walker (1935).

4. Though not recognized at the time Thomas was writing, the existence of mutual fund institutions would eliminate this problem completely since the value of shares or their return would fluctuate with changes in the asset portfolio of the institutions.

5. This issue plays a prominent role in the monetary reform proposal of Maurice Allais (1948) to be discussed in chapter 12. This distinction also led Lauchlin Currie to propose a study on who owned the money supply when he was working at the Federal Reserve.

6. The extensive treatment of the 100 percent reserve plan in the 1930s by Ned Chapin (1959) discusses only the academic debates over the Chicago, Fisher, and Angell plans.

Notes to Chapter 12

1. Though the Thomas Amendment to the Agricultural Adjustment Act in 1933 had authorized the issue of "greenbacks," Roosevelt did not use this power.

2. Roosevelt's telegram stated that henceforth, domestic economic recovery in the United States would take precedence over international exchange relations.

3. As previously discussed, Irving Fisher thought that the 100 percent reserves should be in cash—non–interest-bearing government liabilities. Later Chicago economists, such as Friedman (1960) who is discussed below, proposed that government securities be counted as reserves. If one considered government securities as nonmoney, then there could be a difference between the monetary base and M_1. Allais avoids this problem by his definition of the money supply that takes into account the substitutability of assets for basic money.

4. The treasury would not have been restricted in its borrowings, especially since federal debt backed the basic money supply, but the degree of crowding out would have been readily apparent.

Notes to Chapter 13

1. For the Minsky-Simons connection to Thorstein Veblen, see Phillips (1989) and Whalen (1989). As mentioned earlier, Fisher acknowledged a similarity between his debt deflation theory and Veblen's theory of the business cycle. Phillips (1988a) draws upon the work of Fernandez (1984, 1985) and Khan (1986) who provide formalizations of the Simons model of instability and reform.

2. It should be noted that Minsky's use of the term "hedge financing" is not the same as the way "hedge" is used today.

3. Minsky and Friedman were both influenced by Simons, yet their respective views on monetary theory and policy are quite different. Minsky, on the one hand, emphasizes financial instability yet rejects the policy conclusion of 100 percent reserves and a monetary growth rule. Friedman, on the other hand, does not develop a theory of financial instability, yet advocates the policy prescriptions of Simons. Minsky has recently stated the view that the 100 percent reserve principle, with government securities backing the transactions money supply, would be a means of providing a safe payments system. Though not recanting his discount window reform, he has found merits in the 100 percent reserve proposal (Minsky 1994). The differences center on the issue of the endogeneity of money as discussed in the post-Keynesian literature (see Wray 1990, chapter 3). For a discussion of endogenous money and the Chicago plan, see Kregel (1990).

4. In a letter to Robert E. Litan, who coined the term "narrow banking," Milton Friedman pointed out the connection between Litan's proposal and the Chicago plan. Friedman wrote: "(Y)our proposal, which I find very appealing, has a very direct antecedent in the proposals going back to the 1930s for 100 percent reserve banking that were made by Henry Simons, Irving Fisher, and others. . . . In subsequent work that was done, it was suggested and recommended by various people who wrote on the subject that the proposal be altered by having the government pay interest on the 100 percent reserves. It is in that form that your proposal is almost identical to the earlier ones" (letter to Robert E. Litan, October 28, 1986, in author's possession).

5. For a similar proposal that banks be allowed to hold marketable assets, see the report by the Brookings Task Force (1989).

6. Because of an expansion of the assets eligible for core banks, there is some question about whether such proposals should in fact be placed in the same category as the narrow, or safe, banking proposals. Gardiner Means proposed allowing commercial paper as backing for 100 percent reserve banks.

7. The narrow bank proposals all agree that it is crucial that only narrow banks have access to the payments system, and that the asset portfolios of narrow banks be legally separate from any affiliate lending institutions.

Notes to Chapter 14

1. The discussion in this chapter will focus on the relevance for the United States. An extensive literature has emerged in recent years on Islamic banking,

which is a 100 percent reserve system. On the issue of Islamic banking and its connection to the Chicago plan see Khan (1986, 1989), Khan and Mirakhor (1985), and Doak (1989).

2. If we established a commodity reserve system, such as a 100 percent gold standard, we would no longer have the near monies problem, because there only would be one kind of money—gold. For a contemporary version, see Murray Rothbard's essay in Yeager (1962).

References

Abramson, S. H. 1934. "A Proposal for Banking Reform." *The Canadian Forum* (October): 15–16.

Allais, Maurice. 1947. *Économie and Intérêt: Présentation nouvelle des problèmes fondamentaux relatifs au rôle é'conomique du taux de l'intérêt et de leurs solutions*. 2 vols. Paris: Librairie des Publications Officielles.

———. 1968. "Irving Fisher," in *International Encyclopedia of the Social Sciences*, vol. 5, D. L. Sills, ed.

———. 1987. "The Credit Mechanism and Its Implications," in George Feiwel, ed., *Arrow and the Foundations of the Theory of Economic Policy*. Washington Square, New York: New York University Press.

Allen, William. 1977. "Irving Fisher, F.D.R., and the Great Depression." *History of Political Economy* 9: 560–587.

———. 1993. "Irving Fisher and the 100% Reserve Proposal." *Journal of Law and Economics* (October): 703–17.

American Banker: October 18, 1934; November 30, 1934; December 7, 1934; May 6, 1991; August 23, 1991.

Angell, James W. 1935. "The 100 Per Cent Reserve Plan." *Quarterly Journal of Economics* 50: 1–35.

Barber, G. Russell. 1973. "The One Hundred Percent Reserve System." *The American Economist* 17 (Spring): 115–27.

Barber, William J. 1985. *From New Era to New Deal*. Cambridge: Cambridge University Press.

Barth, James R. 1991. *The Great Savings and Loan Debacle*. Washington, DC: American Enterprise Institute.

Barth, James R. and Brumbaugh, R. Dan, Jr. 1993. *The Changing World of Banking: Setting the Regulatory Agenda, Financing Prosperity in the Next Century, Policy Brief No. 8*. The Jerome Levy Economics Institute, Annandale-on-Hudson, NY.

Beckwith, Burnham P. n.d. *The Future of Money and Banking: A United National Non-Bank Payment System*. Palo Alto, CA.

Berle, Adolf. Papers. Franklin D. Roosevelt Library, Hyde Park, NY.

———. 1933a. "The Future of American Banking." Speech at the annual meeting of the American Bankers Association, Adolf Berle Papers, Franklin D. Roosevelt Library, Hyde Park, NY.

———. 1933b. "Memorandum Re: Proposed Speech at Chicago." Adolf Berle Papers, Franklin D. Roosevelt Library, Hyde Park, NY.

————. 1933c. "Speech at Swarthmore College, December 10, 1933." Adolf Berle Papers, Box 139, Franklin D. Roosevelt Library, Hyde Park, NY.

Bernanke, Ben S. and Alan S. Blinder. 1988. "Credit, Money, and Aggregate Demand." *American Economic Review* (May): 435–39.

Bromberg, Benjamin. 1939. "Two Neglected Twentieth Century 100 Per Cent Reserve Economists." *American Economic Review* 29: 553.

Brookings Task Force on Depository Institutions Reform. 1989. *Blueprint for Restructuring America's Financial Institutions*. Washington, DC: The Brookings Institution.

Brown, Harry Gunnison. 1940. "Objections to the 100 Per Cent Reserve Plan." *American Economic Review*, (June): 309–14.

Bryan, Lowell L. 1988. *Breaking Up the Bank*. Homewood, IL: Business One Irwin.

————. 1991a. "A Blueprint for Financial Reconstruction." *Harvard Business Review* (May–June): 73–86.

————. 1991b. *Bankrupt: Restoring the Health and Profitability of Our Banking System*. New York: Harper Collins.

Burnham, James B. 1991. "Deposit Insurance: The Case for the Narrow Bank." *Regulation* 14 (Spring): 35–43.

Burns, Helen. 1974. *The American Banking Community and New Deal Banking Reforms: 1933–1935*, Westport, CT: Greenwood Press.

Business Week: May 12, 1934; June 2, 1934.

Calomiris, Charles. 1988. "Institutional Failure, Monetary Scarcity, and the Depreciation of the Continental." *Journal of Economic History* 48: 47–68.

Cargill, Thomas F. 1992. "Irving Fisher Comments on Benjamin Strong and the Federal Reserve in the 1930s." *Journal of Political Economy* 100: 1273–77.

Chandler, Lester V. 1971. *American Monetary Policy, 1928–41*. New York: Harper and Row.

Chapin, Ned. 1959. "An Appraisal of the One Hundred Per Cent Money Plan." Ph.D. Dissertation. Illinois Institute of Technology.

Congressional Record. 1935. Washington, DC.

Cowen, Tyler and Kroszner, Randall. 1990. "Mutual Fund Banking: A Market Approach." *Cato Journal* 10: 223–38.

Currie, Lauchlin. 1934. *A Proposed Revision of the Monetary System of the United States*. Submitted to the Secretary of the Treasury Henry Morgenthau, September. Reprinted in Currie (1968).

————. 1968. *The Supply and Control of Money in the United States*. New York: Russell and Russell. (Originally published by Harvard University Press, 1934.)

————. 1980. "Causes of the Recession." *History of Political Economy* (Fall): 316–35.

————. 1993. Letter to author, July 27.

Cutting, Bronson. Papers. Library of Congress.

————. 1934. "Is Private Banking Doomed?" *Liberty* (May): 7–10.

Daly, Herman. 1980. "The Economic Thought of Frederick Soddy." *History of Political Economy* 12: 469–88.

Dimand, Robert W. 1993. "100 Percent Money: Irving Fisher and Banking Reform in the 1930s." Paper presented at the annual meeting of the History of Economics Society, Philadelphia, June 27.

Doak, Ervin J. 1988. "Islamic Interest-Free Banking and 100 Percent Money: Comment." *International Monetary Fund Staff Papers* 35 (September): 534–36.

Dorfman, Joseph. 1959. *The Economic Mind in American Civilization*, vol. 5. New York: The Viking Press.

Douglas, Paul H. 1935. *Controlling Depressions*. New York: W.W. Norton and Co. Inc.

Douglas, Paul H., Fisher, Irving, Graham, Frank D., Hamilton, Earl J., King, Willford I., and Whittlesey, Charles R. 1939. "A Program for Monetary Reform." Unpublished paper, July.

Eccles, Marriner. 1951. *Beckoning Frontiers*. New York: Knopf.

Egbert, Arch O. 1967. *Marriner S. Eccles and the Banking Act of 1935*. Ph.D. Dissertation, Brigham Young University.

Emerson, Guy. 1934. "Guaranty of Deposits under the Banking Act of 1933." *Quarterly Journal of Economics* (February): 229–344.

Everest, Allan Seymour. 1950. *Morgenthau, the New Deal and Silver*. New York: King's Crown Press, Columbia University.

Federal Reserve System. 1959. *All Bank Statistics, United States, 1896–1955*. Washington, DC: Board of Governors.

Feinman, Ronald L. 1981. *Twilight of Progressivism: The Western Republican Senators and the New Deal*. Baltimore: The Johns Hopkins University Press.

Ferguson, Tim W. 1993. "Business World: Getty Thinks There's a Buck in Mutual Funds." *Wall Street Journal* (March 2): A17.

Fernandez, Roque B., 1984. "Implicancias dinámicas de la propuesta de Simons para reforma del sistema financiero." *Ensayso Económicos*, Banco Central de la República Argentina (Buenos Aires), (March):1–30.

———. 1985. "The Expectations Management Approach to Stabilization in Argentina during 1976–82." *World Development* 13 (August): 871–92.

Fisher, I. N. 1956. *My Father Irving Fisher*. New York: Comet Press.

Fisher, Irving. Papers. Yale University Library.

———. 1932a. Statement to the Subcommittee of the Committee on Banking and Currency, House of Representatives, March–April.

———. 1932b. *Booms and Depressions*. New York: Adelphi Company.

———. 1933. "The Debt-Deflation Theory of Great Depressions." *Econometrica* 1: 337–57.

———. 1934a. *Stable Money: A History of the Movement*. New York: Adelphi Company.

———. 1934b. "Monetary Cure for Depression." *The Controller* (published by Controllers Institute of America) 2 (October): 155–59.

———. 1934c. "The 100% System and Bank Credit." *American Banker* (December 7): 2.

———. 1936a. "100% Money and the Public Debt." *Economic Forum* (Spring): 406–20.

———. 1936b. "100% Money Again." *Social Research* (May): 236–44.

———. 1936c. "The Bankers' Interest in 100% Money." *The Bankers Magazine* (October): 285–88.

———. 1936d. "Where Will the Bonus Money Come From?" Irving Fisher Papers, Yale University Library.

―――――. 1937a. "100% Money—and Branch Banking." *The Northwestern Banker* (March): 9, 29–30.

―――――. 1937b. "Note Suggested by Review of '100 Per Cent Money.'" *Journal of the Royal Statistical Society* 100: 296–98.

―――――. 1937c. "Reply to Letter in December 1936 Issue." *The Banker* (May): 115–18.

―――――. 1937d. "When Our 'Check Book Money' Disappeared; A Warning Note Looking toward Tomorrow." *Personal Finance News* (August): 6–7, 16.

―――――. 1937e. "Reply to Letter in June 1937 Issue." *The Banker* (October): 26–27.

―――――. 1938a. "The Principle of 100% Reserves." *Dynamic America* (July): 13–17.

―――――. 1938b. "Reply to Dr. Spahr." *Dynamic America* (September): 2.

―――――. 1945. *100% Money*. 3rd edition. New Haven: The City Printing Company, 1945.

Flood, Mark. 1992. "The Great Deposit Insurance Debate." *Review*, Federal Reserve Bank of St. Louis, 74 (July/August): 51–77.

Friedman, Milton. 1960. *A Program for Monetary Stability*. New York: Fordham University Press.

―――――. 1969. *The Optimum Quantity of Money and other Essays*. Chicago: Aldine.

―――――. 1985. "The Case for Overhauling the Federal Reserve." *Challenge* (July–August): 4–12.

Friedman, Milton and Schwartz, Anna J. 1963. *A Monetary History of the United States, 1863–1960*. Princeton University Press.

Fusfeld, Daniel. 1956. *The Economic Thought of Franklin D. Roosevelt*. New York: Columbia University Press.

Gale, William G. 1991. "Economic Effects of Federal Credit Programs." *American Economic Review* 81 (March): 133–52.

Gayer, A. D. 1935. "The Banking Act of 1935." *Quarterly Journal of Economics* 50: 97–116.

Gilbert, R. Alton. 1987. "Banks Owned by Nonbanks: What Is the Problem and What Can Be Done about It." *Business and Society* (Spring): 9–17.

Girton, Lance. 1974. "SDR Creation and the Real-bills Doctrine." *Southern Economic Journal* (July): 57–61.

Golembe, Carter. 1960. "The Deposit Insurance Legislation of 1933." *Political Science Quarterly* 76: 181–200.

Golembe, Carter and Mingo, John J. 1985. "Can Supervision and Regulation Ensure Financial Stability?" *The Search for Financial Stability: The Past Fifty Years*. San Francisco, pp. 125–46.

Goodfriend, Marvin, and King, R. A. 1988. "Financial Deregulation, Monetary Policy, and Central Banking," in W. S. Haraf and R. M. Kushmeider (eds.), *Restructuring Banking and Financial Services in America*. Washington, D.C.: American Enterprise Institute.

Goodhart, Charles. 1988. *The Evolution of Central Banks*. Cambridge: MIT Press.

Graham, Frank. 1936. "Partial Reserve Money and the 100 Per Cent Proposal." *American Economic Review* (September): 428–40.

Grant, James. 1992. *Money of the Mind: Borrowing and Lending in America from the Civil War to Michael Milkin*. New York: Farrar Straus Giroux.

Greenbaum, Stuart I., and Boot, Arnoud W. A. 1991. "Modified 'Narrow Bank' Is Best Reform Plan." *American Banker* (August 23): 4.

Gregory, W. L. 1935. "Pay Your Debt Mr. Banker." *The Mid-continent Banker*. (February): 12–13, 24.

Haemmerli, Alice. 1985. "Quarantine: An Approach to the Deposit Insurance Dilemma." *Banking Expansion Reporter* 4 (September): 7–10.

Hamilton, David E. 1991. *From New Day to New Deal: American Farm Policy from Hoover to Roosevelt, 1928–1933*. Chapel Hill: The University of North Carolina Press.

Hart, Albert G. 1938. *Debts and Recovery, 1929 to 1937*. New York: The Twentieth Century Fund.

———. 1951. "The 'Chicago Plan' for Banking Reform," in F. A. Lutz and E. W. Mints (eds.), *Readings in Monetary Theory*. Homewood, IL: Irwin, Inc. First published in *Review of Economic Studies*. 1935. (February): 104–16.

———. 1991. "How to Reform Banks—and How Not to." *Challenge* (March–April): 16–24.

Hayek, F. A. 1989. *Monetary Nationalism and International Stability*. Fairfield, NJ: Augustus M. Kelley, Publishers.

Hemphill, Robert H. 1934. "Coming Changes in Money and Banking." *Magazine of Wall Street* (November): 66–69.

Higgins, Benjamin. 1941. "Comments on 100% Money." *American Economic Review* (March): 91–96.

Hixson, William. 1991. *A Matter of Interest*. New York: Praeger.

Hoag, W. Gifford. 1976. *The Farm Credit System: A History of Financial Self-help*. Danville, IL: The Interstate Printers & Publishers, Inc.

Hotson, John H. 1985. "Ending the Debt-Money System." *Challenge* (March–April): 48–50.

———. 1987."The Keynesian Revolution and the Aborted Fisher-Simons Revolution or the Road Not Taken." *Economies et Societes*, Serie "Monnaie et Production," 9: 185–219.

Humphrey, Thomas M. 1992. "A Simple Model of Irving Fisher's Price-Level Stabilization Rule." *Economic Review*, Federal Reserve Bank of Richmond, 78: 12–18.

Hurst, James Willard. 1973. *A Legal History of Money in the United States, 1774–1970*. Lincoln: University of Nebraska Press.

Hyman, Sidney. 1976. *Marriner S. Eccles: Private Entrepreneur and Public Servant*. Stanford: Graduate School of Business.

Jessup, Paul and Bochnak, Mary. 1992. "A Case for a U.S. Postal Savings System." *Challenge* 35 (November/December): 57 (3).

Kareken, John H. 1986. "Federal Bank Regulatory Policy: A Description and Some Observations." *Journal of Business* 59 (January): 3–48.

Kahn, George A. 1991. "Does More Money Mean More Bank Loans?" *Economic Review*, Federal Reserve Bank of Kansas City, 76 (July/August): 21–31.

Kane, Edward J. 1977. "Good Intentions and Unintended Evil: The Case against Selective Credit Allocation." *Journal of Money, Credit, and Banking* 9 (February): 55–69.

Kaufman, George G. 1991. "Lender of Last Resort: A Contemporary Perspective." *Journal of Financial Services Research* 5: 95–110.

Kennedy, Susan 1973. *The Banking Crisis of 1933.* Louisville: University of Kentucky Press.

Khan, Mohsin S. 1986. "Islamic Interest Free Banking." *International Monetary Fund Staff Papers* (March): 1–27.

———. 1988. "Islamic Interest-Free Banking: Reply," *International Monetary Fund Staff Papers* 35 (3) (September): 537.

Khan, Mohsin S. and Mirakhor, Abbas. 1985. "The Financial System and Monetary Policy in an Islamic Economy." *International Monetary Fund*, Departmental Memoranda Series (November 18).

Kitson, Arthur. 1895. *A Scientific Solution of the Money Question.* Boston: Arena Publishing Company.

———. 1917a. *Trade Fallacies: A Criticism of Existing Methods and Suggestions for a Reform towards National Prosperity.* London: P.S. King and Son Ltd.

———. 1917b. *A Fraudulent Standard.* London: P.S. King and Son Ltd.

———. 1933. *The Bankers' Conspiracy! Which Started the World Crisis.* London: Elliot Stock.

Knight, Frank. 1926. "Comments on Interest Theory and Price Movements." *American Economic Review* Supplement (May): 120–21.

———. 1927. "Review of Frederick Soddy's *Wealth, Virtual Wealth, and Debt*," *The Saturday Review of Literature* (April 16): 732.

———. 1933a. "Memorandum on Banking Reform," March. Franklin D. Roosevelt Presidential Library, *President's Personal File 431.* (Reproduced in Appendix.)

———. 1933b. "Review of Alvin Hansen's *Economic Stabilization in an Unbalanced World*." *Journal of Political Economy* 41 (April): 242–45.

Kregel, J. A. 1990. "The Policy Implications of the Current Bank Crisis or 'Is Free Market Capitalism Compatible with Endogenous Money?' " Paper presented at the Jerome Levy Economics Institute, November 1–3.

Krooss, Herman E., ed. 1969. *Documentary History of Banking and Currency in the United States* (4 volumes). New York: McGraw-Hill.

Laidler, David. 1993. "Hawtrey, Harvard, and the Origins of the Chicago Tradition." *Journal of Political Economy* 101 (December): 1068–1103.

Lash, Joseph P. 1988. *Dealers and Dreamers: A New Look at the New Deal.* New York: Doubleday.

Lawrence, Robert J. 1985. "Minimizing Regulation of the Financial Services Industry." *Issues in Bank Regulation* (Summer): 21–31.

Lawrence, Robert J., and Talley, Samuel H. 1988. "Implementing a Fail-Proof Banking System." *Proceedings of a Conference on Bank Structure and Competition.* Federal Reserve Bank of Chicago.

Lehmann, Fritz. 1936. "100% Money." *Social Research* (February):37–56.

Lester, Richard A. 1934. "Are Small Depositors Over-Charged?" *Bankers Magazine* 129 (August): 161–163.

———. 1935. "Check-Book Inflation." *American Scholar* 4 (Winter): 30–40.

Leuchtenburg, William E. 1963. *Franklin D. Roosevelt and the New Deal.* New York: Harper and Row.

Lin, Lin. 1937a. "Are Time Deposits Money?" *American Economic Review* (March): 76–86.

———. 1937b. "Professor Graham on Reserve Money and the 100 Per Cent Proposal." *American Economic Review* (March): 112–13.

Lindenthal, Gustav. 1935. "A Scientific Money System." *The American Engineer* 1 (August and September): 6–25.

Litan, Robert E. 1987. *What Should Banks Do?* Washington, DC: The Brookings Institution.

———. 1993. "Deposit Insurance, Gas on S & L Fire." *Wall Street Journal* (July 29): A12.

McCallum, Bennett T. 1989. *Monetary Economics: Theory and Policy.* New York: Macmillan.

McLane, Stephen Eric. 1980. *Improving Monetary Control: The Abolition of Fractional Reserve Banking.* New Brunswick, NJ: The Stonier Graduate School of Banking.

Means, Gardiner C. 1933a. "The Present Crisis and a Proposal for Banking Action." Box 1, File: Banking and Currency Reform, The Papers of Gardiner C. Means, Franklin Roosevelt Library, Hyde Park, NY.

———. 1933b. "Comment on the Chicago Plan for Banking and Currency Reform." Box 1, File: Banking and Currency Reform, The Papers of Gardiner C. Means, Franklin Roosevelt Library, Hyde Park, NY.

———. 1933c. "Proposals for Banking and Currency Reform." Box 1, File: Banking and Currency Reform, The Papers of Gardiner C. Means, Franklin Roosevelt Library, Hyde Park, NY.

———. 1933d. "Reorganization of the Banking System." Box 1, File: Banking Policy, The Papers of Gardiner C. Means, Franklin Roosevelt Library, Hyde Park, NY.

———. 1933e. "Memorandum RE: The Credit of the Federal Government (November 21, 1933)." Box 3, File: Federal Credit, The Papers of Gardiner C. Means, Franklin Roosevelt Library, Hyde Park, NY.

———. 1934a. "Currency Issue (September 8, 1934)." Box 2, File: Currency Issue, The Papers of Gardiner C. Means, Franklin Roosevelt Library, Hyde Park, NY.

———. 1934b. "Monetary Policy and the New Function of the Banking System (October 1934)." Box 3, File: Monetary Policy, The Papers of Gardiner C. Means, Franklin Roosevelt Library, Hyde Park, NY.

Miller, Harry E. 1927. *Banking Theories in the United States before 1860.* Cambridge: Harvard University Press.

Mingo, John H. 1987. "Narrow Banks Part of Plan for Restructuring Regulatory System." *American Banker* (September 15): 5–13.

Minsky, Hyman P. 1975. *John Maynard Keynes.* New York: Columbia University Press.

——— 1982. *Can "It" Happen Again?: Essays on Instability and Finance,* Armonk, NY: M. E. Sharpe.

———. 1986. *Stabilizing an Unstable Economy.* New Haven: Yale University Press.

———. 1994. "Financial Instability and the Decline (?) of Banking: Public Policy Implications," Conference on Bank Structure and Competition, Federal Reserve Bank of Chicago.

Minsky, Hyman P., Papadimitriou, Dimitri B., Phillips, Ronnie J. and Wray, L. Randall. 1993. *"A Proposal to Establish a Nationwide System of Community Development Banks." Community Development Banking:* Public Policy Brief No. 3. The Jerome Levy Economics Institute of Bard College.

Mints, Lloyd W. 1945. *A History of Banking Theory*. Chicago: University of Chicago Press.

Mitchell, Wesley C. 1903. *A History of the Greenbacks*. Chicago: University of Chicago Press.

Moley, Raymond C. 1939. *After Seven Years*. New York: Harper and Brothers.

Morgenthau, Henry. Papers. Franklin D. Roosevelt Library. Hyde Park, NY.

———. Diary. Franklin D. Roosevelt Library. Hyde Park, NY.

Neuman, A. M. 1937. "100 Per Cent Money." *The Manchester School of Economics and Social Studies* 8: 57–62.

New York Herald Tribune: February 25, 1935.

New York Times: January 7, 1934; January 28, 1934; April 21, 1934; May 6, 1934; May 20, 1934, 32:1; June 20, 1934; September 19, 1934; September 21, 1934; October 10, 1934; November 10, 1934; December 28, 1934; December 29, 1934; January 17, 1935; January 19, 1935; June 2, 1935; September 15, 1935; October 6, 1935; November 16, 1935; April 10, 1939; August 21, 1941; December 18, 1988; February 9, 1989.

Newsweek: September 21, 1935.

O'Hara, Maureen and Easley, David. 1979. "The Postal Savings System in the Depression." *Journal of Economic History* 39 (September): 741–53.

Olson, James Stuart. 1988. *Saving Capitalism: The Reconstruction Finance Corporation and the New Deal, 1933–1940*. Princeton, NJ: Princeton University Press.

Patrick, Sue C. 1993. *Reform of the Federal Reserve System in the Early 1930s: The Politics of Money and Banking*. New York: Garland Publishing, Inc.

Pesek, Boris and Saving, Thomas R. 1968. *The Foundations of Money and Banking*. New York: Macmillan.

Peterson, Rodney and Phillips, Ronnie J. 1991. "Lloyd W. Mints, 1888–1989: Pioneer Monetary Economist." *The American Economist* 35 (Spring): 79–81.

Phillips, Ronnie J. 1988a. "Veblen and Simons on Credit and Monetary Reform." *Southern Economic Journal* 55 (July): 171–181.

———. 1988. "*War News* and Black Market Exchange Rate Deviations from Purchasing Power Parity: Wartime South Vietnam." *Journal of International Economics* 25: 373–78.

———. 1989. "The Minsky–Simons–*Veblen* Connection: Comment." *Journal of Economic Issues* 23, 3 (September): 889–91.

———. 1991."Safe and Stable Banking: The 100% Reserve Proposal." Presented at the Roundtable on Monetary Policy, Federal Reserve Bank of Kansas City, April 25.

———. 1994a. "Safe Banking During the Great Depression: John M. Nichols, the FDIC and 100% Reserves." *Consumer Finance Law Quarterly Report*, 48 (1) (Winter).

———. 1994b. "An End to Private Banking: Early New Deal Proposals to Alter the Role of the Federal Government in Credit Allocation." *Journal of Money, Credit, and Banking* 26 (2) (August): 552–568.

Pierce, James L. 1993. "The Functional Approach to Deposit Insurance Regulation." Paper presented at a symposium on "Safeguarding the Banking System in an Environment of Financial Cycles," Federal Reserve Bank of Boston, November 18.

Pollock, Alex. 1991. "The Same Old Banking Question." *American Banker*, May 6.

————. 1992. "Collateralized Money: An Idea Whose Time Has Come Again." *Challenge* (September/October): 62–64.

————. 1993. "No Need to Reinvent the Wheel for a Community Reinvestment Bank." *American Banker*, July 8.

Reeve, Joseph E. 1943. *Monetary Reform Movements: A Survey of Recent Plans and Panaceas*. Washington, DC: American Council on Public Affairs.

Ricardo, David. 1951. *The Works and Correspondence of David Ricardo*. Volume 4: Pamphlets and Papers 1815–1823. Cambridge: Cambridge University Press.

Robinson, George Buchan. 1937. "100% Bank Reserves." *Harvard Business Review* (Summer): 438–47.

Roosevelt, Franklin D. *President's Official File 230*, Franklin D. Roosevelt Library, Hyde Park, NY.

————. *President's Personal File 431*, Franklin D. Roosevelt Library, Hyde Park, NY.

————. *The Public Papers and Addresses of Franklin D. Roosevelt*. Volume 2. New York: Random House, 1938.

————. 1950. *Franklin D. Roosevelt: His Personal Letters*. New York: Duell, Sloan and Pearce.

Rosen, Eliot A. 1977. *Hoover, Roosevelt and the Brains Trust: From Depression to New Deal*. New York: Columbia University Press.

Ross, J. Elliot. 1934. "Deposit Insurance 100 Percent." *The Commonweal* (December 7): 167–69.

Rothbard, Murray N. 1988. "The Myth of Free Banking in Scotland." *Review of Austrian Economics* 2: 229–45.

Russell, Steven. 1991. "The U.S. Currency System: A Historical Perspective." *Review*, Federal Reserve Bank of St. Louis, 73: 34–61.

Sandilands, Roger J. 1990. *The Life and Political Economy of Lauchlin Currie*. Durham: Duke University Press.

Schemmann, Michael. 1991. *Money in Crisis*. Vancouver: Schemmann.

Schlesinger, Arthur M. 1956. *The Crisis of the Old Order*. New York: Houghton Mifflin.

————. 1958. *The Coming of the New Deal*. New York: Houghton Mifflin.

————. 1960. *The Politics of Upheaval*. New York: Houghton Mifflin.

Schwartz, Anna J. 1992. "The Misuses of the Fed's Discount Window." *Review*, Federal Reserve Bank of St. Louis, 74 (September/October): 58–69.

Seidman, L. William. 1991. "Testimony on Proposals to Establish a Core or Narrow Bank." Committee on Banking, Finance and Urban Affairs, U.S. House of Representatives, June 18.

Selgin, George. 1988. *The Theory of Free Banking*. Totowa, NJ: Rowman & Littlefield.

Simons, Henry. Papers. D'Angelo Law Library, University of Chicago.

————. 1933a. "Banking and Currency Reform—Revised April 1933." Henry Simons Papers, The University of Chicago.

———— et al., 1933b. "Banking and Currency Reform," manuscript. Printed in Warren Samuels (ed.), *Research in the History of Economic Thought and Methodology*. Archival Supplement, Volume 4. Greenwich, CT: JAI Press, forthcoming.

————. 1935. "Review: Lauchlin Currie, *The Supply and Control of Money in the United States.*" *Journal of Political Economy* 63 (August): 555–58.

————. 1948. *Economic Policy for a Free Society.* Chicago: The University of Chicago Press.

Soddy, Frederick. 1933a. "Wealth, Capital and Money, A Résumé of My Theories." *Economic Forum* (Summer): 291–301.

————. 1933b. *Wealth, Virtual Wealth and Debt.* 2nd American edition. New York: E.P. Dutton.

————. 1934. *The Role of Money.* London: G. Rutledge & Son.

Spahr, Walter. 1938. *The Fallacies of Professor Irving Fisher's 100 Per cent Money Proposal.* New York: Farrar and Rinehart.

Spong, Kenneth. 1991. "Narrow Banks: A Better Alternative." Federal Reserve Bank of Kansas City.

————. 1994. "Narrow Banks: An Alternative Approach to Banking Reform," in Dimitri Papadimitriou (ed.), *The Stability of the Financial System*, New York: Macmillan, 1995.

Stein, Herbert. 1969. *The Fiscal Revolution in America.* Chicago: University of Chicago Press.

Steindl, Frank G. 1991. "The Monetary Economics of Lauchlin Currie." *Journal of Monetary Economics* 27: 445–61.

Sternsher, Bernard. 1964. *Rexford Tugwell and the New Deal.* New Brunswick, NJ: Rutgers University Press.

Thomas, Rollin G. 1940. "100 Per Cent Money: The Present Status of the 100 Per Cent Plan." *American Economic Review* (June): 315–23.

Timberlake, Richard H. Jr. 1965. *Money, Banking, and Central Banking.* New York: Harper & Row.

Time: July 1, 1934; October 19, 1936; December 31, 1965.

Tobin, James. 1985. "Financial Innovation and Deregulation in Perspective." *Bank of Japan Monetary and Economic Studies* 3: 19–29.

————. 1987. "The Case for Preserving Regulatory Distinctions," in *Restructuring the Financial System*, Federal Reserve Bank of Kansas City, pp. 167–83.

Todd, Walker. 1990. "Conservatorship: Repairing the Statutory Damage." Federal Reserve Bank of Cleveland, October 10.

————. 1992. "The History of and Rationales for the Reconstruction Finance Corporation." *Economic Review*, Federal Reserve Bank of Cleveland, 28 (Quarter 4): 22–35.

Tugwell, Rexford G. Papers. Franklin D. Roosevelt Library. Hyde Park, NY.

————. 1957. *The Democratic Roosevelt.* New York: Doubleday and Son.

U.S. Congress. House. 1932. Hearings before the Subcommittee of the Committee on Banking and Currency. U.S. House of Representatives. *To Provide a Guaranty Fund for Depositors in Banks.* Washington DC.

————. House. 1935a. *Radio Address by Congressman Steagall regarding H.R. 5357.* 74th Congress, 1st session, January 24.

————. House. 1935b. *A Bill to Provide for the Sound, Effective, and Uninterrupted Operation of the Banking System.* H.R. 5357, 74th Congress, 1st session., February 5.

————. House. 1935c. *A Bill to Provide for the Sound, Effective, and Uninter-*

rupted Operation of the Banking System (Banking Act of 1935). H.R. 7617, 74th Congress, 1st session., February 5.

————. House. 1935d. Amendment by Senator Goldsborough to H.R. 7617 (Banking Act of 1935). 74th Congress, 1st session, May 8.

————. House. 1938. Dollars and Sense: Remarks of the Honorable Jerry Voorhis of California in the House of Representatives. Washington, DC, June 6.

————. House. 1976. "Financial Institutions and the Nation's Economy, Discussion Principles." Hearings before the Subcommittee on Financial Institutions Supervision, Regulation and Insurance, December 18, 1975; January 20, 21, 22, 27, 28, and 29, 1976. 94th Congress, 1st and 2nd sessions.

————. House. 1991. Committee on Banking, Finance, and Urban Affairs, *Core Banks Proposal.* 102nd Congress, 1st session, June 18.

U. S. Congress. Senate. 1934. *A Bill to Regulate the Value of Money.* S.3744, 73rd Congress, 2nd session, June 6.

————. Senate. 1935a. *A Bill to Provide for the Sound, Effective, and Uninterrupted Operation of the Banking System.* S. 1715, 74th Congress, 1st session., February 5.

————. Senate. 1935b. Text of Senate bill 1715. 74th Congress, 1st session, *Congressional Record,* February 6.

————. Senate. 1935c. *A Bill to Regulate the Value of Money.* S. 2204, 74th Congress, 1st session, March 4.

————. Senate. 1935d. Statement by F. A. Vanderlip on S. 1715. 74th Congress, 1st session, March 4.

————. Senate. 1935e. Statement by Senator Fletcher on S. 1715. 74th Congress, 1st session, *Congressional Record,* April 22.

————. Senate. 1935f. Text of article "Fletcher Attacks Bankers," *New York Times,* April 21, 1935. 74th Congress, 1st session, *Congressional Record,* April 22.

————. Senate. 1935g. Text of article by Senator Cutting. "Is Private Banking Doomed?" 73rd Congress, 1st session, *Congressional Record,* May 4.

————. Senate. 1935h. Amendment by Senator Nye to H.R. 7617 (Banking Act of 1935). 74th Congress, 1st session, *Congressional Record,* July 25.

————. Senate. 1935i. Statement by Senator Glass on H.R. 7617 (Banking Act of 1935). 74th Congress, 1st session, *Congressional Record,* July 25.

U. S. Department of the Treasury. 1934. *Press Release, June 27.* National Archives. Washington, DC.

————. 1991. *Modernizing the Financial System,* Washington, DC.

Veblen, Thorstein. 1904. *The Theory of Business Enterprise.* New York: Charles Scribner's Sons.

Viner, Jacob. The Jacob Viner Papers. Mudd Library, Princeton, NJ.

————. 1936."Recent Legislation and the Banking Situation." *American Economic Review,* Supplement 26 (March): 106–119.

Von Mises, Ludwig. 1912. *Theorie des Geldes und der Umlaufsmittel.* Munich: Dunker & Humbolt.

Voorhis, Jerry. 1938. "The Power of the Money Monopoly." *Dynamic America* (February): 11–14, 38.

Walker, Charles H. 1935. "The Chicago Plan of Banking Reform: Application of the Proposals in England." *Review of Economic Studies* (February): 117–21.

Wall Street Journal: September 20, 1934; October 9, 1934; February 19, 1935; March 4, 1935; May 5, 1989; May 8, 1989; August 29, 1990; February 22, 1991; May 29, 1991; October 3, 1991.

Ware, Caroline, and Means, Gardiner C. 1936. *The Modern Economy in Action.* New York: Harcourt, Brace & Company.

Watkins, Leonard L. 1938. *Commercial Banking Reform in the United States.* Ann Arbor: University of Michigan.

Whalen, Charles J. 1988. "The Minsky-Simons Connection: A Neglected Thread in the History of Economic Thought." *Journal of Economic Issues* 22 (June): 533–44.

————. 1989. "The Minsky–Simons–*Veblen* Connection: Reply." *Journal of Economic Issues*, vol. 23, no. 3 (September): 891–95.

White, Eugene. 1983. *The Regulation and Reform of the American Banking System, 1900–1929.* Princeton: Princeton University Press.

White, Lawrence H. 1984. *Free Banking in Britain: Theory, Experience, and Debate, 1800–45.* Cambridge: Cambridge University Press.

Whittlesey, Charles R. 1935. *Banking and the New Deal.* Chicago: Public Policy Pamphlet No. 16, University of Chicago Press.

Wilson, Thomas. 1991. *The Power "to Coin" Money.* Armonk, NY: M.E. Sharpe.

Wray, L. Randall. *Money and Credit in Capitalist Economies.* Brookfield, VT: Edward Elgar, 1990.

Yeager, Leland B. *In Search of a Monetary Constitution.* Cambridge: Harvard University Press, 1962.

Index

About the Author

Ronnie J. Phillips is Professor of Economics at Colorado State University in Fort Collins and a Research Associate of The Jerome Levy Economics Institute of Bard College, Annandale-on-Hudson, New York. He received his B.A. degree from the University of Oklahoma in 1973, and a Ph.D. in economics from The University of Texas at Austin in 1980. He previously taught at Texas A&M University in College Station and has been a visiting scholar in the Bank Research Division of the Office of the Comptroller of the Currency. His current research interests are banking regulation, financial institutions, and financial history of the United States. His articles have appeared in numerous journals including *The Journal of Post-Keynesian Economics*, *The Journal of International Economics*, *Southern Economic Journal*, and the *Journal of Money, Credit, and Banking*.